Library of
Davidson College

POLITICAL THEORY AND POLITICAL PHILOSOPHY

Seventeen Volumes of Previously Unavailable British Theses

Edited by
MAURICE CRANSTON
London School of Economics and Political Science

A Garland Series

THE PROBLEM OF POLITICAL OBLIGATION

Noel O'Sullivan

Garland Publishing, Inc., New York & London
1987

Copyright © 1987 by Noel O'Sullivan
All rights reserved

Library of Congress Cataloging-in-Publication Data

O'Sullivan, Noel.
The problem of political obligation.
(Political theory and political philosophy)
Originally presented as the author's thesis
(University of London, 1969) under title: The problem
of political obligation in the writings of T.H. Green,
B. Bosanquet, and M. Oakeshott.
Bibliography: p.
1. Political obligation.   2. Green, Thomas Hill,
1836-1882—Contributions in political science.
3. Bosanquet, Bernard, 1848–1923—Contributions in
political science.   4. Oakeshott, Michael Joseph,
1901–   —Contributions in political science.
I. Title.   II. Series.
JC329.5.086   320'.01'1   86-27010
ISBN 0-8240-0828-6

All volumes in this series are printed
on acid-free, 250-year-life paper.

Printed in the United States of America

THE PROBLEM OF POLITICAL OBLIGATION IN THE WRITINGS OF
T. H. GREEN, B. BOSANQUET AND M. OAKESHOTT

THESIS TO BE SUBMITTED FOR THE DEGREE OF
Ph.D. IN THE UNIVERSITY OF LONDON

by

NOEL KERRY O'SULLIVAN

- 1969 -

Abstract

Chap. 1   The thesis commences with an attempt to distinguish the problem of political obligation as it was formulated in the ancient world from the problem as it has presented itself in the modern world. Some modern solutions are then considered and found to be unsatisfactory. Their breakdown leads naturally to a consideration of the idealist treatment of the problem. Having tried to establish in Chapter 1 the significance of the idealist treatment in relation to other

Chap. 2 solutions, in Chapter 2 we delve down more deeply into the assumptions underlying the problem of political obligation; they are examined in such a way as to bring into focus the issues against which the doctrine of the concrete universal – the central concept of idealism – emerged. Because the emphasis at this stage is on what all three idealists were concerned to deny, and not on what they wished to assert, this chapter provides a <u>negative</u> specification of the general

Chap. 3 nature of idealist metaphysics. In Chapter 3 a <u>positive</u> specification is attempted, although there is no attempt to minimize the differences between the idealists in order to

Chaps. 4-6 present a monolithic doctrine. In Chapters 4-6 the positive specification is pursued in detail in relation to the philosophy of each thinker, with a particular view to highlighting those metaphysical limitations within each system which reproduce themselves in idealist political thought. In

Chaps. 7-9 Chapters 7-9 attention is concentrated more closely upon the specifically political side of idealist thought. Limitations appear in each of the three theories of politics and

Chap. 10 political obligation examined. The Conclusion assesses the idealist achievement in the philosophical treatment of the problem of political obligation.

TABLE OF CONTENTS

PART A: THE PROBLEM — Page 6

Chapter 1   The Problem of Political Obligation 7
- Its formulation in ancient philosophy   8
- Its formulation in modern philosophy   11

Chapter 2   The Underlying Philosophical Assumptions 27

PART B: THE CONCRETE UNIVERSAL   46

Chapter 3   The Issues 47

Chapter 4   T. H. Green...50

Chapter 5   Bosanquet..69

Chapter 6   Oakeshott..88
- The Practical Mode: the presuppositions of action, including political activity   99
- Oakeshott's conception of political philosophy   124

PART C: POLITICAL OBLIGATION   132

Chapter 7   T. H. Green..133
- Sin   133
- The sinner's robe: Utilitarianism   143
- The sinner's inspiration: Kant   150
- The sinner's guide: T. H. Green's theory of the common good   158
- The instrument of salvation: the state   169
- Conclusion   188

Chapter 8	Bosanquet...	191
	– The vision	191
	– The problem	194
	– The first look	210
	– The vision again: the general will	215
	– A heavenly freedom	225
	– Conclusion	230
Chapter 9	Oakeshott...	233
	– Comparison of his treatment of the problem of political obligation with that of Green and Bosanquet	233
	– The four themes further developed	245
	– The logical foundations of traditionalism	269
	– Political reasoning	278
	– Conclusion	281
Chapter 10	Conclusion...	285
Appendices	....	287
Appendix A	A brief comparison of Oakeshott and Bosanquet in the light of Chapters 5 and 6.	288
Appendix B	A note on Dr. Milne's discussion of the concrete universal.	294
Bibliography	....	296

Principal Abbreviations [1]

T. H. Green

Pro.	Prolegomena to Ethics
Lectures	Lectures on the Principles of Political Obligation

B. Bosanquet

Essays	Essays and Addresses
Civilization	The Civilization of Christendom and Other Studies
Essentials	The Essentials of Logic
Aspects	Aspects of the Social Problem
P.T.S.	The Philosophical Theory of the State
Principle	The Principle of Individuality and Value
Value	The Value and Destiny of the Individual
Ideals	Social and International Ideals
Suggestions	Some Suggestions in Ethics
Meeting	The Meeting of Extremes in Contemporary Philosophy
Science	Science and Philosophy

M. Oakeshott

Experience	Experience and Its Modes
Rationalism	The volume of essays Rationalism in Politics
C.J.	The Cambridge Journal, in which a number of Oakeshott's most important essays appeared.

Other

Lev.	Hobbes' Leviathan
Essay	Locke's Essay Concerning Human Understanding

(( )) indicates words inserted in quotations to clarify a reference therein, or else to give continuity of meaning where some of the original passage has been omitted

---

1. For details of editions used, see Bibliography.

Professor Maurice Cranston supervised my graduate work. My gratitude for his encouragement and supervision cannot, of course, relieve me of sole responsibility for the conception and execution of this thesis.

PART A.

THE PROBLEM

Chapter 1

The Problem of Political Obligation

The problem of political obligation in the modern world is inseparably bound up with the more general assumptions and intellectual attitudes of the thinkers who have written upon it. These general assumptions and intellectual attitudes will be explored in the next chapter: they involve questions in metaphysics, logic and epistemology. In this chapter we wish only to formulate the problem and to show how an endeavour to solve it forces one to move from relatively narrow and specific considerations to broad and general philosophical questions.

For some political philosophers the problem of political obligation is coextensive with political philosophy itself: it is something which emerged with Plato and then continued to preoccupy men who turned their attention to political theory. T. D. Weldon, for example, writes that "The aim of political philosophy is to discover the grounds on which the state claims to exercise authority over its members".[1] Amongst those who would follow Weldon are "realist" philosophers such as H. A. Prichard[2] and E. F. Carritt,[3] both of whom maintain that all ethical theories can be divided into theories of interest and theories of duty.[4] On this view, Plato's enterprise does not differ greatly from J. S. Mill's. Other philosophers would wish to remove it from the concern of philosophy altogether. Thus T. McPherson concludes his analysis by remarking that "...we may well feel justified in dispensing with the concept of political obligation".[5]

---

1. States and Morals, published by J. Murray, 1946, p.1.
2. See Moral Obligation, and Duty and Interest; first issued together by O.U.P., 1968.
3. Morals and Politics, O.U.P. 1935.
4. For a criticism of the attitude of "realism" towards political and moral philosophy, see R. G. Collingwood, Autobiography, O.U.P., 1967, especially pp 61-65; first published 1939.
5. Political Obligation, Routledge and Kegan Paul, 1967, p 84.

In the present essay the problem of political obligation is taken to be the problem posed by the question, Why ought the individual to obey the state? By accepting that it is a problem we differ from McPherson. By accepting (for reasons to be given shortly) that it is basically a modern problem, and not the concern of every philosopher who has reflected upon politics since Plato we differ from Weldon, Prichard, and Carritt. If we set McPherson's view aside until later in the chapter and begin by indicating briefly that the problem of political obligation originates in an ethical experience unknown, for example, to the ancient world, we will be doing something to delimit the range of the problem and to clarify the issues confronting the idealist philosophers. Our concern with the ancient rather than the medieval world, it may be remarked in passing, is explained by the similar concern of Green and Bosanquet, who found in the dictum of Plato, that the state is the individual writ large, and that of Aristotle, that man is a political animal, the key to the treatment of the problem of political obligation.

1. **Its Formulation in Ancient Philosophy**

If individualism had been known in the ancient world, then indeed the problem of political obligation might plausibly be said to be the fundamental problem of all political philosophy. But the first philosopher who put the individual in the forefront of his analysis was Hobbes. The group, in one or another of its manifold forms, and not the individual, was the concern of previous political philosophers. Both Plato and Aristotle, for example, concern themselves almost overwhelmingly with the objective side of moral action, with (that is) the good or happiness, and the beautiful or virtuous.[1] The subjective side of these conceptions - the relation of the "me", of the will and consciousness of the individual, to the good in life and action - is scarcely touched upon.[2] The nearest approach to it is to be found when

---

1. On the interpretation of Socrates' *to daimonion*, see A. Grant, *Aristotle's Ethics*, Longmans, 2nd ed., 1866, Vol. I, p.113.
2. *Ibid*, Vol. I, Essay VII, *On the Relation of Aristotle's Ethics to Modern Systems*.

Aristotle, in discussing the voluntary, notes the gap between our desires and their lawful objects, and writes that "There are some things at which we _ought_ to feel angry, and others which we _ought_ to desire, health, for instance, and the acquisition of knowledge".[1] It is the subjective side which, in modern times, has assumed a paramount importance in moral and political experience and characterizes the problem of political obligation in the sense with which we are concerned. As Bosanquet remarks, in antiquity "the individual was, for an onlooker, magnificently developed. His limitations were in him, and did not oppress him; but for all that, free choice and the career open to talents were not for him."[2]

Turning now from the difference between ancient and modern thought, we may endeavour to bring out the general similarity in their treatment of the problem of political obligation. To do so we must first recall that the Sophists had argued that the social whole, the polis, is not really a whole at all but collapses into two separate and opposed sides, those of the weak and the strong. Rulers and ruled, according to this doxa, are not merely distinguishable aspects of the unified entity, they are the exploiters and the exploited. When Thrasymachus claimed that "Justice is the interest of the stronger",[3] he first of all illustrated his meaning by claiming that each ruling class makes laws that are in its own interest, a democracy making democratic laws, a tyranny tyrannical ones and so one, and that "in making these laws they define as 'right' for their subjects what is in the interest of themselves, the rulers, and if anyone breaks their laws he is punished as a 'wrong-doer'."[4] But he proceeded to generalize his position, applying it not only to the political relationship but to all relationships. Thus shepherds and herdsmen work not for the good of their employers but for personal gain only. Hence "Justice or right is really what is good for some-

---

1. _Ethics_, III, i, 23-27, emphasis added.
2. _P.T.S._, p 255.
3. _Republic_ 338c.
4. _Ibid_, 338c.

one else".[1] Justice is simply "supreme simplicity" and "well-considered shrewdness".[2]

If we now compare Thrasymachus' formulation of the problem of political obligation with that of (for example) Bosanquet, a modern philosopher, the similarity between ancient and modern thought upon that subject becomes apparent. Bosanquet writes that:

"The paradox of political obligation starts from what is accepted as authority or social coercion, and asks in what way the term 'self', derived from the 'individual' mind, can be applicable at once to the agent and patient in such coercion, exercised prima facie by some persons over others. Both relations and their connection have been pointed out by Plato".[3] Bosanquet's statement of the problem and his reference to Plato make clear that the problem of political obligation is, for him, a problem which is not necessarily tied to the modern concept of the individual. It arises, rather, whenever there is a failure to perceive that acts done by the government can be ascribed to the community as a whole as opposed to the group of individuals who actually initiate them. The problem of political obligation, to put it crudely, arises whenever the state is conceived as absolutely divisible into "them" and "us". And this division is the one which we saw occur in the thought of Thrasymachus. In other words, while it is true that the Sophistic argument did not involve making the individual will the sole principle of rightness and obligation, it is also true that Bosanquet's formulation of the problem does not entail the more specifically modern assumption that the individual will is the ultimate source of right. The similarity of the views of Thrasymachus and Bosanquet at one level is even more clearly brought out by a remark which Bosanquet makes when summarizing the main characteristic of the "theories of the first look" which generate the problem of political obligation. Their main implication is that "government, in fact and in principle, reveals itself as coercion exercised by 'the others' over 'the one'".[4]

---

1. Ibid, 343b.
2. Ibid, 348c-d.
3. P.T.S. p 52.
4. P.T.S. p 71.

Thrasymachus merely specified more closely the meaning of the two opposed terms; the logical similarity of his problem is not thereby altered. For him "the others" are the strong, and for "the one" he substitutes the weak.

The widest significance which may be given to the phrase "the problem of political obligation" arises, then, when the state is assumed to be merely 'other" or "them", and if this is what is meant by the problem of political obligation, it is indeed a problem shared by ancient and modern political philosophy. It was generated in the ancient world by the Sophists' distinction between nomos and physis,[1] and in the modern world by the acceptance of the given individual (i.e. the individual as he presents himself, here and now, to the senses) as unconditionally real. On the other hand, when we place the emphasis on the words "individual" and "ought" as they occur in the question, Why ought the individual to obey the state? there are present ideas about the state and individual sovereignty which were not found in Greece, and the fact to which we wish to draw attention is that such ideas are always present in the minds of modern thinkers who have addressed themselves to the problem, colouring the whole of their ethical vocabulary and constituting an important element in the background to the problem of political obligation.

2. Its Formulation in Modern Philosophy

In order to examine more closely the difficulties presented by the problem of political obligation as it occurs in the modern world we will attempt to construct a scale of theorizing upon the subject. At the lowest level in the scale we will place the theory which appears to make the most assumptions, or to leave the greatest number of questions unresolved. As we said at the beginning, we will not stop at this stage to examine those assumptions in detail; the point of the scale is rather to show that we are forced by the impetus of the inquiry to go beyond the initial, common-sense position to a higher level, if we wish to progress in the resolution of the problem of political obligation.

---

1. For Bosanquet's discussion of the nomos-physis dichotomy see The Philosophical Theory of the State, p 119 et seq; and for Green's, see Works Vol. II, Lectures on the Principles of Political Obligation, Third Edition published by Longmans, 1894; sections 8-11.

We will refer to a theory as being at a higher level on the scale when it not only answers all the questions which the theory below it answered, but also answers questions which the antecedent theory had not faced at all or to which it provided only an implicit answer. The conclusion which will emerge from this enterprise may be anticipated: it is that a level of approach to the problem below that which relates it to experience as a whole leaves the offered solution ultimately incoherent and arbitrary. The idealist theory is placed at the top of the scale because it goes furthest in unravelling and confronting the difficulties presented by the problem of political obligation. The justification for placing the different theories at particular points on the scale will be given as the analysis proceeds.

We may begin with Locke. That his theory is placed at the bottom of the scale implies no disrespect but reflects rather the fact that it was as much a response to a particular situation as a statement of universal principle.[1] Laslett has argued convincingly that the important part of the work of composition of the Two Treatises belongs to the years 1679-80,[2] and that it is "a demand for a revolution to be brought about, not ((as is often thought)) the rationalization of a revolution in need of defence".[3] More precisely, Two Treatises is an Exclusion Tract, designed to refute Filmer's Patriarcha,[4] and to provide a general theoretical argument for Shaftesbury's revolutionary schemes, in which Locke himself was implicated.[5] For Locke, then, the issue of political obligation was more than an academic and theoretical one: it was, at the stage of his career when the Two Treatises was conceived, an urgent practical problem, and it is the overwhelmingly practical dimension of his treatment of the problem which warrants its being placed at the bottom of the scale.

---

1. See Locke's Two Treatises of Government, edited by P.Laslett, C.U.P., 1960; Introduction, p77-78.
2. Ibid.,p35.
3. Ibid.,p61.
4. Ibid.,p61.
5. Ibid.,p31.

Locke's Second Treatise was the work in which he endeavoured to provide an alternative to the divine right theory of government advocated by Filmer. After summarizing his argument against Filmer, Locke states his purpose thus:

"...he that will not give just occasion to think that all government in the world is the product only of force and violence, and that men live together by no other rules but that of beasts, where the strongest carries it, and so lay a foundation for perpetual disorder and mischief, tumult, sedition, and rebellion (things that the followers of that hypothesis so loudly cry out against), must of necessity find out another rise of government, another origin of political power, and another way of designing and knowing the persons that have it than what Sir Robert Filmer hath taught us".[1]

In pursuit of this aim he begins by considering the condition of man in the state of nature. This is a state of perfect freedom, in so far as there is no dependence whatsoever on the will of any other man: each has complete right to order his actions and dispose of his possessions and person as he thinks fit. However, this freedom is not licence. Caprice is excluded by the law of nature. The law of nature is a concept to which Locke devotes very little space within the essay, in spite of its crucial role in his theory, but he says enough to indicate that the law of nature is part of the divine law.[2] Locke does, it is true, speak of the law of nature as the law of reason,[3] but nature and reason are not for him "peculiar metaphysical entities with law-giving and privilege-bestowing powers of their own."[4] Cranston is one of the few commentators who emphasises the fundamentally religious premise on which Locke's argument turns. This is that man is God's creature and God's property; therefore he has not free disposal of himself; and therefore, a fortiori, no other man can have free disposal of him. As Locke expresses it, "...for men being all the workmanship of one omnipotent

---

1. Second Treatise, I, section 1.
2. Ibid., XI, section 135.
3. E.g. II, section 6.
4. M. Cranston, John Locke, A Biography, Longmans 1957, p 210.

and infinitely wise Maker; all the servants of one sovereign Master, sent into the world by His order and about His business; they are His property, whose workmanship they are made to last during His, not one another's pleasure."[1]

The state of nature, besides being a condition of perfect freedom, is a state of perfect equality, in which each is "equal to the greatest and subject to nobody",[2] for there can be "nothing more evident" than that "creatures of the same species and rank, promiscuously born to all the same advantages of Nature, and the use of the same faculties, should also be equal one amongst another, without subordination or subjection".[3]

In the state of nature every man has two duties, to preserve his own life and to do as much as he can to preserve the rest of mankind, when his own preservation is not thereby jeopardized. Each also has the right to execute the law of nature, although the criminal must be treated "as calm reason and conscience dictate" (Ibid., II, 7). The state of nature is not, as for Hobbes, a state of war. It only becomes so when a man endeavours to get another into his absolute power.[4]

The problem of political obligation arises from the conception of individuals as, by nature, "all free, equal and independent";[5] for "no one can be put out of this estate and subjected to the political power of another without his own consent".[6] Civil society is formed by each "agreeing with other men to join and unite into a community for their comfortable, safe, and peacable living, one amongst another, in a secure enjoyment of their properties, and a greater security against any that are not of it".[7] Locke

---

1. Second Treatise, II, 6.
2. Ibid., IX, 123.
3. Ibid., II, 4.
4. Ibid., III, 17.
5. Ibid., VIII, 95.
6. Ibid., VIII, 95.
7. Ibid., VIII, 95.

sees that the retention of sovereignty by individuals would make political society impossible, and endeavours to lift the state beyond the sphere of the voluntary by arguing that "when any number of men have, by the consent of every individual, made a community, they have thereby made that community one body, with a power to act as one body, which is only by the will and determination of the majority".[1] This is not a very satisfactory way of closing the gap between the two sides of a society. We are simply told that "the act of the majority passes for the act of the whole",[2] but the sense in which "the whole" might have a genuine unity is not made clear. Even if Locke's insistence on majority rule as a term of the contract is accepted, he is still left with the task of explaining how the successors to the contracting parties come to have an obligation to the state, for they cannot be said to have entered it by an act of explicit consent. He deals with this problem by introducing the idea of tacit consent, and writes that "The difficulty is, what ought to be looked upon as a tacit consent, and how far it binds i.e. how far any one shall be looked on to have consented, and thereby submitted to any government, where he has made no expressions of it at all." The answer he gives is that "every man that hath any possession or enjoyment of any part of the dominions of any government doth hereby give his tacit consent".[3] It follows that all are equally obliged to obey the government, since "barely travelling freely on the highway" is as much enjoyment of property as possession of land by a man and his heirs for ever.[4] In short, obligation arises from "the very being of anyone within the territories of that government", for this is enough to indicate tacit consent. With this extension of the idea of consent, we observe (what was commented on by Bosanquet in connection with Mill),[5] the danger of the defence of individuality turning round into its annihilation, for the definition of tacit consent

---

1. Ibid., VIII, 95.
2. Ibid., VIII, 96.
3. Ibid., VIII, 119.
4. Ibid., VIII, 119.
5. P.T.S., p 59.

given by Locke is so wide that any act of government could be said to have the consent of a subject who is not prepared to abandon his property. The liberty which Locke rescues for the subject is merely that of selling his property and incorporating himself into any other commonwealth, or of agreeing with others to begin a new one in any part of the world they can find free and unpossessed.[1] This, at least, would be the impression left were it not for the final right of an "appeal to heaven" which Locke attributes to the people, in the event of the government violating the trust in accordance with which it exercises power.[2]

Bosanquet pin-points the origin of Locke's difficulties. He commends Locke for bringing to bear "a truer political experience" than Hobbes, by which he means that Locke goes beyond the world of juridical fictions. Locke "feels that actual government is a trust, and that the ultimate supreme power remains in the community as a whole. The difficulty in his case is to understand how the will or interest of the community as such obtains determinate expression." Locke, that is, moves away from the conception of the individual as the fundamental reality, and hence from seeing the reality of the community as fictitious. But Locke does not have the philosophical equipment to determine the precise sense in which the community is real, so that when he locates the ultimate sovereignty in the community at large, the right which was to be displayed as <u>social</u> remains a latent right in <u>individuals</u> to assent or to dissent. Hence, in the end, society is not represented by Locke as a genuine unity.[3]

Thus Locke is brought to an impasse. The requirements of individuality and of order breed a tension which he fails to resolve, without sacrificing one or other of the terms. The modern problem of political obligation presents the philosopher with the task of finding a conception of the state such that its reality is established without the sacrifice of the claims of individuality; or, to put it the other way, a conception of individuality must be

---

1. <u>Ibid</u>., VIII, 121.
2. <u>Ibid</u>., XIX, 222.
3. Bosanquet, P.T.S., p 98.

found which does not exclude its realization in the state. The demand for such a view is best represented by Rousseau who, starting from the contention that "when a man renounces his liberty he renounces his essential manhood, his rights, and even his duty as a human being",[1] concluded that "Some form of association must be found as a result of which the whole strength of the community will be enlisted for the protection of the person and property of each constituent member, in such a way that each, when united to his fellows, renders obedience to his own will, and remains as free as he was before."[2]

We will consider next some of the more recent attempts to deal with the problem of political obligation. The four philosophers we have selected are chosen, not because they are great philosophers (the question whether they are or not may be left open), but because their approaches to the problem reflect the predominant styles and levels of inquiry which have held sway since Locke. At a philosophical level slightly above that of Locke there is the analysis of T. McPherson,[3] who may be taken as representative of that school of philosophy which contents itself with determining the possible meanings of any given concept, aspiring no higher than to convict some usages of the concept of absurdity or "logical oddness".[4] Conceptual analysis and clarification is the limited aim upon which this school prides itself, and the criterion of absurdity or logical oddness is conformity or non-conformity with ordinary patterns of thought. If this criterion is relaxed and legitimate departures from ordinary usage recognized, it nonetheless remains the case that system and necessity are not the goals to which this philosophy aspires. Turning to McPherson's book, we see the sentiments of this school reflected:

"My concern is...with the question what, if anything, could be meant at the present time by anyone who used the expression 'political obligation' or who offered as his own one of the standard theories about the grounds of political obligation that have come down to us from the past".[5] McPherson

---

1. <u>Social Contract</u>, Bk 1, chap. IV.
2. <u>Ibid.</u>, Bk I, chap VI.
3. <u>Political Obligation</u>, Routledge & Kegan Paul, London 1967.
4. P.H.Nowell-Smith, <u>Ethics</u>, Penguin ed., 1961, p.83; first published 1954.
5. <u>Political Obligation</u>, op.cit., p.1.

eventually arrives at an important conclusion about the problem which he presented to himself, and it is because his conclusion displays an awareness above that attained within Locke's own thought that we have placed his theory at a higher level. (A further, more general, reason for doing so would be that the philosophic school represented by McPherson is not concerned (as Locke was) with a genetic approach towards thought: its appeal is to the public conventions governing the meaning of concepts). It is that "political obligation is an important concept for certain theorists only - in general liberals, individualists, believers in the artificiality of society. For theorists of what we may broadly call the Lockean type the concept of political obligation, and questions about the grounds of political obligation, have seemed central".[1] However, the positive side of his work, in which he endeavours to establish whether or not the Lockean type of theorist has a stronger case than other varieties, brings only disappointment. His solution occurs in chapter 7, entitled "Justifying Obligation", and his first approximation is the suggestion that the question, Why ought we to obey the government? is "pointless".[2] It is pointless because it rests upon a confusion about the ordinary meaning and usage of words. Thus to refer to something as "the government" is to imply that that thing has authority; and to hold that some person or some body has authority is to hold that he or it ought to be obeyed.[3] Pursuing this line of thought, McPherson illustrates its implications by taking the instance of a person who is prepared to choose order rather than anarchy, and then (within order) liberal democracy as it exists in Britain rather than some form of totalitarian democracy. He concludes that "If anyone who has so chosen should ask, 'But why ought we to obey the government?' he would only be showing himself up as insufficiently clear-headed".[4] This does not tell us whether or not a policeman is really

---

1. <u>Ibid.</u>, p 63.
2. <u>Ibid.</u>, p 59.
3. <u>Ibid.</u>, p 59.
4. <u>Ibid.</u>, p 61.

only a man in a blue suit; it merely assumes that those who use the word "policeman" to mean something more than that, have arbitrarily been assigned the status of arbiters in questions of current philosophical usage. In short, to acknowledge that a group of men are "the government" is immediately (if that word is understood by the user) "to acknowledge that the government has in general a right to be obeyed, that it ought to be obeyed"[1]. McPherson recognizes that this view comes in the end to the trivial proposition that we ought to do what we ought to do, and admits that it may be too formal to afford much satisfaction,[2] but insists that he has not won a merely verbal victory.[3] However, his reason for maintaining this seems to amount to only another verbal victory. We are simply told that "The question whether society is natural or artificial is an unreal one. The point is that we do live in society....",[4] and no attempt is made to rebut the possible charge that what is called society is a mere collection of individuals, organized according to strength or wealth. This "fact" is the ground of McPherson's assertion that to live in society <u>entails</u> obligation to government, which therefore needs no further justification or explanation once the meaning of the word "society" has been fully understood. His argument culminates in the following thesis: "That social man has obligations is an analytic, not a synthetic, proposition. Thus any general question of the form 'Why should I (a member) accept the rules of the club?' is an absurd question. Accepting the rules is part of what it <u>means</u> to be a member".[5] Unless men could be shown to have an obligation to settle their ethical problems by settling on the ordinary usage of terms (without resting upon a circular appeal to ordinary usage), which McPherson does not attempt to show, such an approach would not take us very far. And even if that were shown, what makes a policeman more than an aggressive man in a blue suit, or a society more than a collection of individuals, would remain unexplained.

---

1. <u>Ibid</u>., p.62.
2. <u>Ibid</u>., p.62.
3. <u>Ibid</u>., p.63.
4. <u>Ibid</u>., p.64.
5. <u>Ibid</u>., p.64, his emphasis .

The criticism levelled by Hobhouse against the idealist theory of the state[1] rests upon an equally uncritical attitude towards experience, but may be classed as a higher level of philosophizing because it does not seek to establish its conclusions by appeals to "what is ordinarily meant" by a particular concept. Its uncritical character lies rather in the implicit acceptance of every day conceptions of individuality and identity.[2] In particular, Hobhouse's essay contains three assumptions, which he takes to be so evidently true that they scarcely require justification. They are that (1) we know exactly what the terms "state" and "individual" denote; that (2) we know that these terms are antithetic and mutually exclusive concepts; and that (3) when a conflict arises between them, we are in no doubt that the individual must be put above the state. The unsatisfactory character of this position becomes apparent when we seek a definition of individuality, rather than a mere designation of its nature. More will be said about the problem of individuality at a later stage, but we may note here that Hobhouse seeks to find the essence of individuality in some unity existing apart from relations. It is "the reallife" which lies behind "institutions, laws and forms";[3] and the difficulty is that when we strip off all the institutions, laws and forms we are left, not with the true individual, but with nothing, for all content has been removed. When Hobhouse attempts to recognise the reality of institutions,[4] without thereby losing the individual in the determinacy acquired in the process, he necessarily ends by turning them into the very suprapersonal entities which he attributes to Bosanquet's theory of the state. For unless his relations stand outside the individual, he loses his

---

1. In his book *The Metaphysical Theory of the State*, Allen & Unwin, 1960; first published 1918.
2. Which is not to say, of course, that these notions are necessarily incorrect: it is to claim that they are not obviously satisfactory. The idealists, indeed, have been as fond of the ordinary man as McPherson, being quite prepared to assert - with justification - that they were only helping him along.
3. *Ibid.*, p.26.
4. E.g. p. 27, "In any human association it is true, in a sense, that the whole is something more than the sum of its parts".

individuality. The nature of the social bond is conveyed in psychological terms: individuals modify, condition or influence one another in a semi-mechanical and essentially external way.[1] Any relationship which is thereby established is of no ethical significance, and hence cannot explain the nature of political obligation. His claim that in society "...there are many wills and in obedience to law we conform, as we suppose, to the will of another"[2] reveals the extent of his failure. That the "ought" in all ethical relationships cannot be reduced to the "is" of psychological relationships or to the "here and now" given in perception, is too elementary a point to require further emphasis. Nonetheless, Hobhouse does recognize that there is a problem to be solved, and that his tools are inadequate for solving it should not prevent us from recognizing that his possession of them and his effort to use them distinguish him from McPherson.

Messrs. Benn and Peters occupy a still higher place on the philosophical ladder. They do not rest upon the appeal to "what concepts *mean*", explicitly criticising Quinton's use of this technique in dealing with punishment.[3] Nor do they fall foul of psychologism. They begin by accepting the universality of reason, and base their argument on the nature of rationality. It is an impressive beginning, but once again uncriticised values and assumptions break through and force their way into a central position in the argument. That this is so will become clear if we accept their view that political obligation is a species of moral obligation[4] and consider the fundamental structure of their treatment of moral obligation; for their treatment of the problem of political obligation stands or falls with this. Their contention is that being moral is involved in being rational. The first step in the argument by which they seek to establish this is the contention that "...if a person like Socrates, asks *seriously* whether a particular rule is right, whatever

---

1. E.g. pp.28-29.
2. Ibid., p.39.
3. See A.Quinton, in vol. I of Philosophy, Politics and Society, ed. P.Laslett, Blackwell, 1956; referred to by Benn and Peters in Social Principles and the Democratic State, Allen & Unwin, 1959, p.182.
4. Social Principles and the Democratic State, p.318.

the traditional authority for it, or attempts <u>seriously</u> to decide between the demands of different authorities, then he must, as a rational critical individual, accept certain normative standards of procedure. He must respect truth at all costs."[1] What might constitute "truth" in moral or political contexts is never made very clear. We are told that "The very idea of searching for truth takes for granted...a norm of <u>impartiality</u> which holds that issues should be decided according to the <u>relevant</u> criteria and that exceptions should not be made on irrelevant grounds."[2] But the difficulty, of course, lies in recognizing what is relevant. And when it is said, for example, that a man's social position has nothing to do with the truth or falsity of what he says,[3] there seems to be no reason why we cannot (in the sphere of moral and political utterances) reject the assertion, as an arbitrary attempt to derive a definite content from a bare formula. The second step in the argument is extremely suspect. We are told that the pursuit of truth commits one not merely to being impartial and relevant, but to respect for persons;[4] for one's interest in truth is assumed to require respect for those who are the sources of the arguments by which it is attained.[5] The major assumption underlying their position is brought in when the notion of rational and relevant discussion is narrowed until it becomes identified with utilitarian reasoning. This identification of reason with utility is facilitated by nothing more than a "surely":

"Surely, the only sorts of reasons that count when a demand ((for the justification of a rule)) is made are those that refer to the effects of the rule on someone or other's interests", and again: "Notions like 'harm', 'injury', 'advantage', 'benefit', and so on are surely not accidentally associated with the discussion of the rightness of rules. For what other sorts of reasons could there be that would count?".[6] The last quotation is eventually

---

1. <u>Ibid</u>., p.31, their emphasis .
2. <u>Ibid</u>., p.31, their emphasis .
3. <u>Ibid</u>., p.31.
4. <u>Ibid</u>., p.32.
5. <u>Ibid</u>., p.32.
6. <u>Ibid</u>., p.32.

transformed into a criterion for deciding upon what legislation is just; only those measures are just and obligatory which can be justified "in terms of more general rules and ultimately of a balance of advantage to all concerned".[1] The word "seriously", which (along with "surely") plays an important part in the formulation of this position, is in itself highly ambiguous. If it is taken in its objective meaning it is otiose, since it is then the logical coerciveness of what Socrates says, and not his seriousness in saying it, which interests the philosopher; whilst in its subjective meaning it serves only to applaud the position being favoured and to rule the opponents of the writers out of court as frivolous and irrational.

Our main criticisms are that, under the guise of purely procedural criteria, we are being committed to the identification of morality with a specific moral and political practice, and that no moral obligation to pursue truth is demonstrated. There may well be such an obligation, but what is required from a philosopher is a demonstration of its existence and reality, and not the simple assumption of these. So long as it is merely assumed, it remains no more than the authors' personal moral sentiment. The implications of the writers' position for the problem of political obligation is clear from their observation that "The crucial distinction is between those who are prepared to discuss rules rationally and those who are content to rely on the external authority of custom, leader, Pope or book".[2] Only a state which reasons with its subjects, and not (for example) a traditionalist order as such, can morally obligate its citizens. The difficulty once again, is that the authors' rejection of traditionalism (as such) as irrational rests upon a restriction of the word reason to a content which is given by their caprice alone. They have indeed been severely criticised for this by M. Cowling, who observes that "...the authority which asks for 'reasons' and claims to be the guardian of 'rational justification' is no freer than any other of the tendency to make arbitrary assumptions. From these assumptions a structure of argument and justification does, it is true, develop: but so it does when the assumptions are the truths of Christianity

---

1. *Ibid.*, p.112.
2. *Ibid.*, pp.33-34.

((a quotation from R.S.Peters)]."[1]

Underlying the treatment of the problem of political obligation by Benn and Peters there is also the same uncritical acceptance of the everyday notion of individuality which we observed in McPherson and Hobhouse. They endeavour to avoid the problem of potential anarchism (displayed in Locke's thought) which would follow from their assertion that "every man...must decide for himself whether he has a duty to accept a given authority"[2] and that a moral obligation to accept anything must always be conditional,[3] by qualifying their thesis so that "the point is not that a man must have consented before a government can properly consider him under an obligation to obey, but that he must see the point of the obligation before he can consider himself bound".[4] This in no way modifies the underlying assumption, that individuals are mutually exclusive centres or points. It does not take us beyond Locke's difficulties but merely restates them in a different form: we are still left with the problem of explaining the obligation of the individual to obey the state on occasions when he has failed to see the point of his obligation.

Benn and Peters' usage of the term "reason" (the ultimate ground for their whole argument) provides us with the opportunity of setting down a passage from Bosanquet which offers an almost direct comment upon it, as if Bosanquet were familiar with the work itself. The interest of the passage lies in the fact that it makes clear that the next step on the philosophical ladder must lead into the level of the doctrine of the concrete universal, with its conception of rationality in terms of system and completeness. It therefore makes a suitable conclusion to our attempt to delineate an ascending scale of theorizing upon the problem of political obligation. Bosanquet writes that "It is most difficult to understand in many cases what is the meaning of the term Reason or practical Reason as appealed to in ethical treatises. It seems to be something which gives necessary judgments on self-evident principles affecting practice. But self-evidence is of one kind only, and depends on the relation of propositions to experience as a whole. There is

---

1. *The Nature and Limits of Political Science*, Cambridge University Press, 1963, p.103.
2. *Social Principles and the Democratic State*, op.cit., p.327.
3. *Ibid.*, p.329.
4. *Ibid.*, p.329.

no special kind of intuition which refers to propositions affecting conduct. <u>The only true and comprehensive meaning of reason is the tendency of mind to construction, wholeness, completeness...</u>"[1] (Benn and Peters, of course, do not appeal explicitly to self-evidence; they are not overt intuitionists. But their use of the words "surely" and "seriously", commented upon already, is clearly one form of the appeal to self-evidence).

The break-down of the solutions to the problem of political obligation which have been considered makes clear that a more radical treatment is required. The highest level of theorizing, found in Benn and Peters, can only be replaced by a deeper theory of rationality, individuality and value. It is only in idealist literature that such a theory is to be found, a theory which seeks not to overthrow the positions we have examined, but to assign them their due place in the circle of necessity which alone can provide a satisfactory solution to the problem of political obligation.[2]

When we have laid the necessary foundations by developing the doctrine of the concrete universal, we will turn to the more purely political aspect of the problem of political obligation. We saw at an earlier stage that the problem of political obligation in the modern world contains two elements, viz. (A) the presupposition that the community falls into two parts, individuals and their government and law, with the consequence that it becomes possible to ask, Why ought the individual to obey the state? It is when we turn to examine this view that the typical idealist concepts (of the general will, the actual and the real will, of positive and negative freedom) appear - but it cannot be emphasised too much that the meaning of these terms is completely lost if their consideration is not preceded by an examination of the fundamental metaphysical principles from which they emerge. We also saw that the conception of the state as something alien to individuals was common to

---

1. <u>Some Suggestions in Ethics</u>, p. 157; emphasis added.

2. "Philosophy forms a circle. It has a beginning, an immediate factor (for it must somehow make a start), something unproved which is not a result. But the terminus a quo of philosophy is simply relative, since it must appear in another terminus as a terminus ad quem. Philosophy is a sequence which does not hang in the air; it is not something which begins from nothing at all; on the contrary it circles back into itself" (Hegel, <u>Philosophy of Right</u>, trans. J. M. Knox, Oxford University Press, p.225).

the ancient world, but that (and this is the second element in the modern problem of political obligation) modern ethical ideas have been coloured by (B) the belief that the individual's will is the only final source of obligation. It follows that a completely adequate treatment of the problem of political obligation must include a demonstration of (a) the sense in which acts done by the government may be ascribed to the whole community, and not simply to the particular individual or group of individuals who hold office, and (b) a demonstration of the sort of social organization which will be capable of accommodating the individual's demand to recognize for himself the rightness (or compatibility with his conscience) of the way of life and form of rule to which he is subject.

Chapter 2

The Underlying Philosophical Assumptions

We said at the beginning of the last chapter that the problem of policial obligation is bound up with the more general assumptions and intellectual attitudes of the thinkers by whom it has been theorized. When we discussed several different treatments of the problem in the last chapter their underlying assumptions about the nature of epistemology, logic and metaphysics were not made explicit. In this chapter we will endeavour to detect these assumptions.[1] We will refer to them collectively as the philosophy of classical empiricism, understanding by that name the philosophical school which emerged in England in the seventeenth century and which flourished, with relatively minor modifications, until the time of John Stuart Mill, or even later. What we refer to as classical empiricism might equally well be called the classical theory of individuality, which we wish to contrast with the idealist theory of individuality, otherwise termed the concrete universal.

Since the present argument is analytical rather than historical, it is not essential to do more than single out the foundations on which classical empiricism rests. It is not vital for our purpose to establish whose doctrines in particular were being criticized by the idealists on any given occasion. To lay bare the foundations of empiricism, it is as appropriate to turn to Hobbes, Locke or Hume as to John Stuart Mill. That an argument becomes more subtle or elaborate in Mill's hands does not necessarily alter its basic presuppositions - in fact it may well be a disadvantage from our point of view since it distracts from those presuppositions. The aim, in short

---

1. It will be evident that the ensuing discussion of classical empiricism is most directly applicable to determining the philosophic assumptions upon which the treatment of political obligation by philosophers such as Locke and Hobhouse has rested. McPherson and Benn and Peters have been influenced by important subsequent developments in philosophy which we do not discuss. However, our analysis of these latter philosophers in the last chapter would indicate that the new philosophy has not really changed the underlying assumptions very drastically, for the problems which emerged in their handling of the problem of political obligation were noticeably similar to those encountered by thinkers standing squarely within the unmodified tradition of classical empiricism.

is to construct a model rather than to do justice to the complexity of the thought of individual empiricist philosophers.

Our concern, however, is not simply with classical empiricism. We bring it in only as a vehicle for a further end, which is an understanding of the idealist doctrine of the concrete universal. By digging down to the philosophic foundations of the problem of political obligation we will be able to recognise more easily the large questions which the idealists considered to be in need of settlement (and which they believed would be settled by the concrete universal) before a satisfactory moral and political philosophy could be created. Most writers on idealism have in fact agreed that the moral and political philosophy of the English idealists cannot be satisfactorily considered apart from the metaphysical system in which it is located, and since it is always pleasant to find authority supporting what philosophy alone would suggest, we venture to cite a few of their conclusions. The Abbé Paul Montagné remarks that "la pensée politique de T. H. Green est organiquement liée à ses conceptions épistémologiques et morales".[1] B. Pfannenstill writes that "Bosanquet's political philosophy is not to be regarded as an isolated part of his philosophy in general. Its position can perhaps be described best by saying that it is the focal point to which his fundamental philosophical ideas have been brought".[2] W.H.Greenleaf finds that "Oakeshott's political ideas are...very definitely the reflection of a philosophical standpoint, the outcome of a coherent attitude to the world of knowledge and experience as a whole".[3] Similar views about the unity of idealist thought have been expressed in connection with the work of F.H.Bradley and R.G.Collingwood by W.F.Lofthouse and A. Donagan respectively.[4]

---

1. <u>Un Radical Religieux</u>: T. H. Green, Toulouse, 1927, p.99.
2. <u>Bernard Bosanquet's Philosophy of the State</u>, Lund, H. Ohlsson, 1936, Preface p.III.
3. <u>Oakeshott's Philosophical Politics</u>, Longmans, 1966, p.2.
4. <u>F. H. Bradley</u>, The Epworth Press, 1949, Preface p. V; <u>The Later Philosophy of R.G.Collingwood</u>, O.U.P. 1962, pp.18-19.

Before considering the doctrines of classical empiricism, a little more must be said about the method by which we think the meaning of the doctrine of the concrete universal is best approached. The difficulty is in knowing where to begin with a philosophy which holds that everything is related to everything else. However, a sound methodological rule when seeking to determine the meaning of any concept is to begin by finding out what that concept denies. Adopting this rule, we were led to conclude that the term "concrete universal" is best approached by first exhibiting the main features of the philosophical tradition in opposition to which it emerged, the emphasis being upon the problems for understanding moral and political life posed by the basic philosophical tenets of that tradition. Having given this negative specification of the concrete universal - negative because emphasising what all idealists would deny, rather than what they would assert - we will distinguish at the beginning of the next chapter the issues around which the philosophic debate amongst idealists themselves has revolved. First, then, the negative specification of the concrete universal.

We take as our point of departure a pregnant sentence from J. H. Muirhead's The Platonic Tradition in Anglo-Saxon Philosophy:[1] "What was central to nineteenth century idealism in England and America, was its determination to have done with the dualism of a here and a beyond, whether this took the form of the two worlds in religion, the 'ought' and the 'is' in ethics, the individual and the community in politics, or the relative and the absolute in metaphysics.... 'here or nowhere'...((is)) the keynote of all sound idealism."[2]

The doctrine of the concrete universal, in short, was nothing less than an endeavour to provide the western mind with a new, integrated world-view which would restore the intelligibility which the universe had lost for it with the decline of religion and the rise of science. To do so it had to heal the various dualisms to which Muirhead refers. These dualisms received theoretical expression in the epistemological, logical and metaphysical doctrines of classical empiricism. Each of these doctrines had consequences for

---

1. Muirhead Library of Philosophy, Allen & Unwin, 1931.
2. Ibid., p.414.

the treatment of moral and political obligation. We may consider them in turn.
a) The epistemological problem as it confronted Hobbes, Locke and Hume took the form of the question, how do ideas get into our minds? The answer they gave was that objects outside our minds work upon the senses in such a way as to produce ideas. We may give Locke's definition of an idea because it is characteristic of empiricism in general, in that the idea is not taken to be constitutive of the mind itself but is that upon which the mind works. Locke defines an idea thus:

"It being that term which, I think, serves best to stand for whatsoever is the object of the understanding when a man thinks, I have used it to express whatever is meant by phantasm, notion, species, or whatever it is which the mind can be employed about in thinking."[1] In the resulting tripartite division of the epistemological process into mind - idea - object, the precise location of ideas is difficult to establish. On the one hand they are not in the mind, since they are its object. But they are not outside it, in the sense in which external objects are taken to be outside it. On the other hand while they are supposed to represent the non-mental objects which generate them, to find objects which are not ideas involves the empiricist in arguments whose mere statement thwarts the intended conclusion, for whatever he turns to ipso facto becomes an idea.

The action by which objects were held to create ideas was causal, often being conceived mechanically. Things act upon our nerves (or "press" upon them, as Hobbes puts it), which are thought of as strings attached to the brain, transmitting ideas to it.[2] Locke thought that objects worked upon us by transmitting "insensible particles" which set our nervous system in motion. Why certain motions should create the ideas that they do was explained by Locke only by invoking the deity: God attaches certain ideas to certain motions, affixing the idea of pain to the motion of steel entering our flesh, for example.[3]

---

1. *Essay*, Book 1, chap. I, 8.
2. Hobbes, *Lev.* chap. I.
3. *Essay*, Bk II, chap. VIII, 11-14.

The assumption which lies behind this account of cognition is important, and a number of commentators have drawn attention to its relevance for social theory. It is that the mind is an essentially passive[1] recipient of the sensations upon which it later proceeds to work.[2] It is a white paper void of all character, without any ideas."[3] It follows that the mind is ultimately at the mercy of its environment: alter the environment and you alter the man. The mind then, on this view, is not free in cognition.

We will see at a later stage that Green felt that the salvation of more speculative men depended upon overthrowing this theory of mind, and that he was perhaps even more worried about a further aspect of it, which we will consider now. Classical empiricism rested upon the so-called "faculty psychology", according to which the mind is composed of a number of different faculties. Thought is only one of its faculties, others being sensation, perception, imagination, desire, volition.[4] The important thing to notice is that these faculties were thought to involve separate intellectual processes. This was what idealists were to criticise: they did not mind "faculties" being distinguished for purposes of analysis, but they considered that separating them created mysterious entities which led to pseudo-problems. For Locke faculties were disclosed to the mind by reflection, which is the power the mind has to work inside itself and perceive its own operations.[5] Because faculty psychology involved the assumption that willing is determined by external and internal (but involuntary) stimuli, it reinforced the destruction of mind's freedom by removing freedom not only from the cognitive situation but also from the volitional one. This is what worried Green (and other philosophers, of course).

---

1. See R.I.Aaron, John Locke, O.U.P., 1st. ed. 1937; 2nd ed. 1955, p.133, for a discussion of the precise sense in which the mind is passive. It remains true that sensation is completely non-ideational for Locke.
2. E.g. A. Cobban, Edmund Burke, Allen & Unwin, 1929, p.24: "No more revolutionary doctrine has ever been put forward, for by it most obviously education and environment become lord and master of men, and it is possible to change the whole face of society in a single generation."
3. Ibid., Bk II, chap. I.
4. Cf. The Logic of Hegel, trans. Wallace, O.U.P., 2nd ed. 1892, p.35.
5. Essay, Bk II, chap I. 4.

We may now indicate some of the difficulties (other than the broad question of mental freedom and responsibility already mentioned) which the empiricist epistemology posed for moral and political philosophy. In the first place, how is it possible to explain our experience of ethical entities, such as the family and the state, when our senses reveal only particular, material things? The empiricists always found it very hard to find a criterion by which the identity and reality of such ethical entities could be established. We may observe Locke's difficulties in this connection by referring to his treatment of what he termed "collective ideas of substances". He writes that

"by putting together several particular substances,((the mind)) makes collective ideas of substances, as a troop, an army, a swarm, a city, a fleet; each of which everyone finds that he represents to his own mind by one idea, in one view, and so under that notion considers those several things as perfectly one, as one ship, one atom. Nor is it harder to conceive how an army of ten thousand men should make one idea: it being as easy to the mind to unite into one particular all the distinct ideas that make up the composition of a man and consider them all together as one".[1]

Locke is worth quoting at this length because the limitations of his analysis of the unity of a community are the limitations of all empiricist philosophy in so far as it starts from sensation.[2] Only a paragraph before Locke had emphasized that the contents of a complex idea retain their identity as distinct substances, so the veneer of unity which (say) an army possesses is superficial: the reality is a collection of men. But if we cannot put things the other way round and say that "the army" is the reality and "the group of men" is the abstract description of it, it becomes very difficult to explain the phenomenon of obligation. If a state, for example, is really just a group of ordinary, private men; or if a policeman is really just a man in a blue suit; then it becomes impossible to distinguish convincingly between power and authority, might and right, violence and force,

---

1. *Essay*, Bk II, chap XXIV, 2.
2. Cf. our analysis of Hobhouse, chap I.

aggression and punishment, and so on. Hobbes' political theory raises the difficulty in a rather acute form. It is essential for his argument that we should distinguish between natural and artificial persons, for it is through representation by an artificial person that a multitude attains its unity.[1] The leviathan is an artificial person, but on Hobbes' epistemological premises it cannot be real: it is a mere fiction.[2]

In the second place, there is the problem of personal identity. All the treatments of the problem of political obligation mentioned in chapter 1 assumed that we knew what an individual person was, and of course in one sense we do; but are we able to specify the precise principle upon which we individuate the self? We would surely expect a comprehensive moral and political philosophy to give a satisfactory answer: a solution to the problem of political obligation which failed to do so would not be intellectually satisfying. The empiricists, however, found it very hard to explain wherein lies the unity of the self. Locke wrestled with the problem but could only deal with it by introducing the notion of "substance", a mysterious entity which only served to push the question onto new ground. He wrote that "self is that conscious thinking thing (whatever substances made up of, whether spiritual or material, it matters not) which is sensible or conscious of pleasure and pain, capable of happiness or misery, and so is concerned for itself, as far as that consciousness extends".[3] David Hume was more candid and consistent when he gave up and contented himself with saying that when he tried to find his self he only stumbled upon some particular perception.[4]

In the third place, it was very difficult for the empiricists to give a satisfactory account of the general nature of value. Value is not something given to sensation and its appearance therefore remains inexplicable, for there seem to be no simple ideas out of which it could be constructed. We get, then,

---

1. *Lev.* chap. XVII.
2. *Lev*, chap. XVII.
3. *Essay*, Book II, chap xxvii, 17.
4. *Treatise of Human Nature*, Book I, Part IV, section vi.

the gap between "is" and "ought". Attempts were made to explain the "ought" of course, but they always reduced it to a feeling of one kind or another, and it was difficult to avoid the conclusion that might and right were dangerously close together. It will be sufficient for our purpose to illustrate by setting down Hume's account of the way the ideas of duty and political authority are to be analyzed: he uses the language of causality:

"We may...remark, not only that two objects are connected by the relation of cause and effect, when the one produces a motion or any action in the other, but also when it has a power of producing it. And this we may observe to be the source of all the relations of interest and duty, by which men influence each other in society, and are placed in the ties of government and subordination. A master is such a one as, by his situation, arising either from force or agreement, has a power of directing in certain particulars the actions of another, whom we call servant. A judge is one, who, in all disputed cases, can fix by his opinion the possession or property of anything betwixt any members of the society. When a person is possessed of any power, there is no more required to convert it into action, but the exertion of the will; and _that_ in every case is considered as possible, and in many as probable; especially in the case of authority, when the obedience of the subject is a pleasure and advantage to the superior."[1]

These, then, are some of the difficulties which followed from the classical epistemology. The doctrine of the concrete universal aimed to get around them (we shall see) by rejecting the theory of cognition from which they arose. It jettisoned the faculty-psychology and rejected the notion that ideas must derive from a non-ideational source, together with the notion that ideas could be merely the private property of an individual knower. It substituted the notion that we begin from meaning and that there is only meaning, which is in some sense bigger than us (or "transcends" us).

b) We may consider next the difficulties presented by the empiricist theory of logic. We use that term somewhat loosely, to cover not only its theory of

---

1. Hume, _Treatise_, Book I, Part I, section iv.

inference but also its theory of meaning, i.e. of how words are related to things. Our main interest is in seeing how difficulties deriving from classical empiricism's conception of truth and rationality carried through into the theory of moral and political reasoning and reinforced the gap between fact and value.

The basic unit in empiricist logical theory was the proposition: this was the bearer of truth or falsity. When propositions were linked in certain ways, they yielded the syllogism. The principle which determined what propositions might appropriately be combined was termed by Hume "the association of ideas." Constant association gave probability of truth to one's inferences.

The idealists were to find much to criticize in this account of the thinking process. Their main attack was upon the significance assigned by empiricists to the proposition. Empiricists held that the proposition was made up of words, and thereby implied that isolated words could be meaningful, although not true or false - for this they had first to be joined to other words. In essence the idealist objection was that the empiricist theory thereby confused grammar and logic, and by failing to grasp the true nature of words created pseudo-problems such as the question, How do words refer to things? Empiricist logical theory was really confused grammatical analysis because in its treatment of the proposition "it tends to confuse the heard or written sentence in its separate words with the proposition as apprehended and intellectually affirmed. And these two things have quite different characteristics".[1] The consequences of this unfortunate confusion was that much time was spent in asking which predicates could fittingly be attached to which subjects. Bosanquet put the matter rather well when he said that the empiricists tended to treat the proposition like two railway carriages which had to be linked together:

"We have it impressed upon our minds, ((viz. by the logic of Jevons and Mill)) that there is one 'thing' corresponding to the Subject-word (or clause)

---

1. Bosanquet, Essentials of Logic, p105.

and that these are somehow separate, like two railway carriages, till we bring them together by the coupling-link of the copula."[1] The idealists, instead of making truth a predicate of the isolated proposition, made it a predicate of a world or system of ideas. They did not worry about words and their reference to things because "words" are grammatical abstractions: all meaning refers to, or is identical with, reality; the only difficulty is in making sure that reality has been qualified at the appropriate point, not in making sure that it has been qualified at all.

We have touched on large and difficult matters, but fortunately we can bring out the difficulties which empiricism experienced in dealing with moral and political reasoning without pursuing them to a depth where we might founder. Empiricism's theory of language and of inference made moral and political argument (in the strict sense of that word, which implies the possibility of contradicting one's opponent on logical grounds) impossible. Moral and political opinions for this philosophy are, in the end, mere opinions, and as such are neither rational nor irrational. We may give some examples.

Moral speech, for Hobbes, is speech which refers to the appetites, aversions and passions of men, and is subject to this difficulty, that "the names of such things as affect us, that is, which please and displease us, because all men be not alike affected with the same thing, nor the same man at all times, are in the common discourses of men, of <u>inconstant</u> significance."[2] Thus, since "one man calls wisdom, what another calls fear; and one cruelty, what another justice," it follows that "such names can never be true grounds of any ratiocinations."[3] This state of affairs obtains in the state of nature and objectivity is created when the sovereign is recognized to have authority by the contracting parties, but even in civil society it is will rather than reason which is the ultimate ground of agreement.

---

1. <u>Ibid.</u>, p 105. See also Collingwood, <u>Autobiography</u>, op.cit., chap V, on the logic of the proposition and "the logic of question and answer". Also T.H.Green, <u>The Logic of J.S.Mill</u>, Works Vol.II.
2. <u>Lev.</u> chap IV.
3. <u>Ibid.</u>, chap IV.

Locke failed to work out a coherent theory of moral reasoning, favouring at one time hedonism and at another an appeal to divine law (he does not make clear whether its obligatoriness derives from its rationality or from its positive character). In fact, by concentrating on the possibility of creating a moral science and by likening moral thinking to mathematical thinking he fails altogether to consider the basis of obligation. Moral ideas are complex ones, and are of a "mixed" variety since they are composed of more than one kind of simple idea. As complex ideas they are their own archetypes and are not intended to be copies of real things. But they will not necessarily be without reference to reality; if the agreement between the moral ideas happens to coincide with an agreement between acts in the world, there will then be correspondence with reality, but such correspondence is not the ground of the truth of moral science.[1] On this view, moral ideas must be, in the end, merely personal ideas, for complex ideas (other than those of substance) are "combinations of ideas which the mind, by its free choice, puts together, without considering any connexion they have in nature."[2] What aims to be a moral science renders moral argument an impossibility.

Neither Hobbes nor Locke, however, achieved a presentation of the implications of its theory of logic and meaning for empiricism's moral and political theory as systematic as that of Hume. They both brought in extraneous elements to correct the movement towards subjectivism. Hume directs his attack against the view that the morality of our actions is to be discovered through a rational faculty which operates in independence of sense-perception and reveals to us eternal and invariable moral laws or principles. Hume's contention is that reason or understanding cannot operate in this way. He assigns to reason two specific modes of operation, and neither of them involves the possibility of discovering natural laws of right and wrong. In the first place, reason can reveal "true abstract relations of our ideas", and here Hume has in mind the kind of deductive reasoning displayed in mathematics. But such deductive reasoning, he insists, has no relevance for action:

---

1. <u>Essay</u>, Bk IV chap IV 7, 8.
2. <u>Ibid.</u>, Bk IV chap IV 5, emphasis added.

Reason in this sense is not something which could "move the will", or constitute a "cause" of action. Hence our moral judgements cannot be said to be rational in this deductive sense. The second function of reason is to infer or discover "matters of fact". The passage in which Hume dismisses the relevance of this sense of rationality for moral judgement and concludes that "our moral perceptions are as subjective as our perceptions of the qualities of objects" justifies quotation in full:

"Can there be any difficulty in proving that vice and virtue are not matters of fact whose existence we can infer by reason? Take any action allowed to be vicious - wilful murder, for instance. Examine it in all lights, and see if you can find that matter of fact or real existence which you call <u>vice</u>. In whichever way you take it, you find only certain passions, motives, volitions, and thoughts. There is no other matter of fact in the case. The vice entirely escapes you, as long as you consider the object. You never can find it till you turn your reflection into your own breast and find a sentiment of disapprobation which arises in you towards this action. Here is a matter of fact; but it is the object of "feeling", not of reason. It lies in yourself, not in the object. So that when you pronounce any action or character to be vicious, you mean nothing but that from the constitution of your nature you have a feeling or sentiment of blame from the contemplation of it. Vice and virtue, therefore, may be compared to sounds, colours, heat, and cold, which, according to modern philosophy, are not qualities in objects but perceptions in the mind."[1]

The conclusion is that "To diminish, therefore, or augment any person's value for an object, to excite or moderate his passions, there are no direct arguments or reasons which can be employed with any force or influence".[2] It is true that the intractability of moral attitudes is not entailed by this view; mutual accommodation between people passing different value judgements is to some extent possible, for "though the value of every object can be

---

1. <u>Treatise of Human Nature</u>, Bk. III, Part I, Section I.
2. This quotation is from his essay, <u>The Sceptic</u>.

determined only by the sentiment or passion of every individual, we may observe that the passion, in pronouncing its verdict, considers not the object simply as it is in itself, but surveys it with all the circumstances which attend it",[1] and because of this relationship between the movement of passion and the features of the situation we can quell the passion by pointing out that the features of the situation were other than the person supposed. For example, a man transported by joy on account of his possessing a diamond, does not experience joy simply because of the glittering stone before him. He also considers its rarity, and it is in large measure from this consideration that he derives joy. Thus, by pointing out that the stone is not a diamond, or that it is a fake, or that a new mine has been opened up, we can change his reaction to the situation: the circumstances will no longer elicit the passions. Since Hume much ingenuity has been displayed in developing this possibility,[2] and the resulting theory has often been called a theory of moral argument, but it always remains true that contradiction is impossible; persuasion or discussion are perhaps the categories appropriate for describing the process. "The result of nature and the constitution of the mind"[3] always retain their right, and while their requirements can/no doubt be suppressed or manipulated, they can never be shown to be logically inappropriate, i.e. wrong or bad or wicked.

It would seem, then, that a satisfactory account of obligation cannot be attained so long as a problematic logic makes the connections we achieve between our moral and political ideas a matter of arbitrary association. The word "association" itself indicates clearly enough the underlying assumption that reasoning consists of coupling intrinsically separate and unrelated facts with other facts, or with values. The doctrine of the concrete universal, in one of its aspects, aimed to establish that our practical judgements are as objective and as rational as the judgements of "fact" with which they are often contrasted. By their critique of the logic of classical empiricism the idealists hoped to prepare the way for this by showing that moral and

---

1. The Sceptic.
2. S.C.L.Stevenson, *Ethics and Language*, Yale University Press, 1945.
3. Hume, The Sceptic.

political words are not defective because no corresponding external objects can be found to which they might refer, or which might generate them.

c) We may turn now to the metaphysics of classical empiricism. In its metaphysics we find the implications of its epistemological and logical doctrines for the treatment of the problem of political obligation made most clear. At the beginning of chapter XI of the <u>Leviathan</u> Hobbes remarks that "there is no such finis ultimus, utmost aim, nor summum bonum, greatest good, as is spoken of in the books of the old moral philosophers." Elsewhere he states that there is no natural knowledge of another world. The chain of being is truncated at the level of human sense-perception. The hope of a transcendental anchor for political obligation - through participation in the agathon or through knowledge of God's will - is dead, and obligation can only appear as an unfortunate concomitant of the wretchedness of the human circumstance; it reveals no rational necessity grounded in the structure of the universe and of human nature.

For empiricism, the causal relationship is the chief ground for postulating a reality beyond sense. Hobbes argued that "...the acknowledging of one God Eternal, Infinite, and Omnipotent, may more easily be derived, from the desire men have to know the causes of natural bodies, and their several virtues, and operations, than from the fear of what was to befall them in time to come. For he that from any effect he sees come to pass, should reason to the next and immediate cause thereof, and from thence to the cause of that cause, and plunge himself profoundly in the pursuit of causes; shall at last come to this, and there must be (as even the Heathen Philosophers confessed) one First Mover; that is, a First, and an Eternal cause of all things; which is that which men mean by the name of God".[1]

Since sense cannot have any "imagination" of anything answering to the words "spirit" and "incorporeal", "men that by their own meditation, arrive to the acknowledgement of one Infinite, Omnipotent, and Eternal God, choose rather to confess he is Incomprehensible, and above their understanding; than to define his Nature by Spirit Incorporeal, and then confess their definition to

---

1. <u>Lev</u>. chap XII.

be unintelligible."[1] The word "God", then, means "First Cause", and nothing more. Any richer conception would require more of our senses than they can offer, which is knowledge of the finite alone. The empiricists were given to emphasizing the fact that no positive conception of infinity is possible. When we add the word infinite to qualities such as magnitude, swiftness, force, power and so on, in an attempt to predicate these qualities of God, "we signify only, that we are not able to conceive the ends, the bounds of the thing named; having no Conception of the thing, but of our own inability".[2] This does not mean that such ways of speaking are illegitimate. It implies that we are concerned to honour God; we then speak not as philosophers, "but Piously, to honour him with attributes, of significations, as remote as they can from the grossness of Bodies Visible."[3]

The place of God in Hobbes' thought is, notoriously, a much contested matter. Without wishing to minimize the difficulties or to distort the picture by gross abridgement, we will try to pin down one further doctrine of Hobbes, which is perhaps his most profound and interesting one. It appears that if God is accepted as the transcendental source of an ethical theory, it is only because man has made him so, by contracting with some individual to recognize him as God's spokesman. The relevance of this doctrine for the interpretation of the person of Christ is obvious. Such a view would seem to follow from Hobbes' general teaching as to the nature of authority: only an artificial person can wield authority, and an artificial person is created when he is acknowledged as their representative by covenanters. It would seem to be implicit in such a statement as the following: "...all formal Religion, is founded at first, upon the faith which a multitude hath in some one Person, whom they believe not only to be a wise man, and to labour to procure their happiness, but also to be a holy man, to whom God himself vouchsafeth to declare his will supernaturally".[4] On the other hand, Hobbes speaks of God

---

1. *Lev.* chap XII.
2. *Ibid.*, chap III.
3. *Ibid.*, chap XII.
4. *Lev.* chap XII.

being king of all the earth by his power,[1] yet he has said that the word "God" means only "First Cause", and that "to call this Power of God, which extends itself not only to Man, but also to Beasts, and Plants, and Bodies inanimate, by the name of Kingdom, is but a metaphorical use of the word".[2] And if God were the author of natural law by virtue of his power, that law would not be law in Hobbes' sense of rightful command since reason discovers only hypothetical and not categorical truths. But to try to resolve these competing statements would take us further afield than is necessary for the present purpose.

Locke followed a different line of argument in attempting to prove God's existence. His proof turns upon the assertion that "as for <u>our own existence</u>, we perceive it so plainly and so certainly that it neither needs nor is capable of any proof. For nothing can be more evident to us than our own existence...If I doubt of all other things, that very doubt makes me perceive my own existence, and will not suffer me to doubt of that". Abandoning his doctrine, that we know only the ideas of things and not things themselves, Locke claims that "we have an intuitive knowledge of our own existence and internal infallible perception that we are".[3] Given this certain intuitive knowledge, we can proceed to deduce from it God's existence: and this deduction will be equal to mathematical proof in its degree of certainty.[4] Although we have no innate idea of him, God has not left himself without witness in our experience, and that witness is the knowledge we have of our own existence. Moving from this assertion, Locke holds that man knows, by an intuitive certainty, that bare nothing can no more produce any real being than it can be equal to two right angles. It follows that "If, therefore, we know there is some real being, and that nonentity cannot produce any real being, it is an evident demonstration that from eternity there has been some-

---

1. E.g. chaps. XII and XXXI.
2. <u>Lev</u>. chap XXXI.
3. <u>Essay</u>, Bk IV chap IX, 3.
4. <u>Essay</u>, Bk IV chap X, 1.

thing, since what was not from eternity had a beginning, and what had a beginning must be produced by something else."[1] There are at least three assumptions here which go beyond what is known to experience as Locke conceived it. There is, first, the assumption that everything is caused; secondly, there is the assumption that the idea of cause, with the anthromorphic conceptions of agency and responsibility with which it is insuperably bound up, can significantly be predicated of the universe; and, thirdly, there is the assumption that words such as "eternity" have a positive meaning for us. But Locke wishes to go even further; he is not content to characterize God as a mere cause, like Hobbes, but wishes to conceive of him positively. He therefore adds that (1) "what had its being and beginning from another must also have all that which is in and belongs to its being from another also", and hence the eternal being must be the most powerful; and (2) since a man finds in himself perception and knowledge, we can be certain that there is not only some being, but some knowing, intelligent being in the world.[2]

In so far as the idea of cause was the central one in empiricist metaphysics, it was once again Hume who pulled the ladder away. His criticism was simple: we never see cause and effect but only the movement and meeting of different entities, hence there is no possibility of applying these categories to reality itself.

Locke's discussion of infinity is of significance for an understanding of his conception of the limits of natural knowledge. It is intended to establish that "even the idea we have of infinity, how remote soever it may seem to be from any object of sense or operation of our mind, has nevertheless, as all our other ideas, its original there."[3] Locke's main point is that our idea of infinity is only quantitative, being primarily an attribute of things which have parts and are capable of increase or diminution by the addition or subtraction of a part. Such are the ideas of space, direction and number.

---

1. *Essay*, Bk IV, chap X, 3.
2. *Essay*, Bk IV, chap X, 4.
3. *Essay*, Bk II chap XVII, 22.

Thus "when we apply to that first and supreme Being our idea of infinity, in our weak and narrow thoughts, we do it primarily in respect of his duration and ubiquity, and, more figuratively to his power, wisdom and goodness, and other attributes".[1] The idea of infinity itself does not come from the senses, but these do yield the simple ideas from which it is subsequently composed. The senses give us the idea of portions of extension and of succession, and we find that we can always repeat these ideas, without ever coming to an end, thus arriving at the idea of infinite space (immensity) and of eternity (infinite time). The impossibility of conceiving of ideas other than those of space, time and number arises from the fact that other ideas are not divisible into parts; for example, "to the perfectest idea I have of the whitest whiteness, if I add another of a less or equal whiteness (and of a whiter than I have, I cannot add the idea), it makes no increase, and enlarges not my idea at all; and therefore the different ideas of whiteness, etc., are called degrees".[2] Locke is careful to distinguish between the idea of (e.g.) the infinity of space, which we may have, and the idea of an actual space infinite, which is impossible to attain: "the first is nothing but a supposed endless progression of the mind over what repeated ideas of space it pleases; but to have actually in the mind the idea of a space infinite is to suppose the mind already passed over and actually to have a view of all those repeated ideas of space which an endless repetition can never totally represent to it; which carries in it a plain contradiction".[3] In other words, any positive idea we may have of infinity is still finite; the idea is never completed. To the extent that the idea is completed it is indeed positive, but of the remainder we have no positive distinct idea. When God is spoken of as eternal, then, this means only that we have the idea of the negation of a beginning, and this "being but the negation of a positive thing, scarce gives me a positive idea of infinity."[4]

---

1. *Essay*, Bk II chap XVII, 1.
2. *Essay*, Bk II chap XVII, 6.
3. *Essay*, Bk II chap XVII, 7.
4. *Essay*, Bk II chap XVII, 17.

Revelation was left as the last source of a transcendental ground for obligation. Hobbes showed that it was based on a contract which did not differ in logical status from any other contract, and Locke brought it within the sphere of reason. If revelation makes known more than natural reason could discover, it is still the case, for Locke, that reason has to judge whether or not it is a true revelation. Thus the limitations in Locke's account of revelation are identical with those of his account of reason, which has already been considered.

One important side of the doctrine of the concrete universal, particularly in the form in which the doctrine was developed by Green, was the attempt to provide a new intellectual foundation for Christianity.[1] In Green's case this enterprise had a very intimate connection with his moral and political thought. With the passing of the Victorian age, this side of the Idealist doctrine might seem to have lost ground, although A.E.Taylor wrote in 1924 that "The one thing of all others I have had it long on my conscience to say, is that I have always wished my book to be understood in a definitely theistic, indeed, in a definitely Christian sense. I have never disguised it from myself that when I speak of the 'Absolute' I mean by the word precisely that simple, absolutely transcendent, source of all things which the great Christian scholastics call God."[2] It would perhaps be more accurate to say that a more modest account of the nature of the absolute and its relationship to practical experience has been developed.

We have now fulfilled the first part of our intention, which was to bring out the more general philosophical position underlying the problem of political obligation, whilst illuminating at the same time the doctrine of the concrete universal by setting out the philosophical doctrines in opposition to which it emerged. Having specified the concern of idealist metaphysics negatively we will endeavour to distinguish briefly the main issues involved in the philosophic doctrines which the idealists opposed to classical empiricism.

---

1. M. Richter, *The Politics of Conscience, T.H.Green and His Age*, Weidenfeld & Nicolson, 1964; chap I, *Idealism and the Crisis of the Evangelical Conscience*.

2. *Elements of Metaphysics*, 1st ed. 1903; Preface to 7th ed., Methuene, p xiii.

PART B.

THE CONCRETE UNIVERSAL

Chapter 3

The Issues

English idealism presents the aspect not so much of a monolithic intellectual structure as of a continuing dialogue. The continuity of the dialogue is indeed vouched for by the participants themselves. Bosanquet studied under Green and Nettleship at Balliol after arriving there in 1867, and Bradley too attended Green's lectures on moral philosophy.[1] To the end of his life, Bosanquet refused to recognise that any fundamental disagreement existed between himself and Green, and always retained the greatest respect for Bradley's philosophical position, a respect which was reciprocated by Bradley. The philosophical tradition remains unbroken when we come to Oakeshott, who expresses his indebtedness to the work of Hegel and Bradley.[2]

We speak of a "continuing dialogue" because the idea of a dialogue suggests that there is a certain framework (a theme or themes) which provides the discussion with an ultimate unity, without minimizing the fact that positions taken up within the framework may differ very greatly. Specifically, we wish to acknowledge that there are differences of opinion among Green, Bosanquet and Oakeshott on first-order questions and that it is impossible to extract a single agreed doctrine upon the nature of the concrete universal from their writing. But we wish also to maintain that the English idealist tradition has a basic unity, and to characterize the identity of this philosophical tradition by specifying three central theses, considered by us to be those around which the philosophical debate about the nature of the concrete universal has centred. We will indicate which would be accepted and which denied by each of the philosophers to be examined, but would wish to make clear immediately that we are aware that the sense in which the different philosophers understand any one of the theses has yet to be clarified. The same applies, of course, to the grounds for their acceptance or rejection of any particular thesis. These problems will be dealt with in what follows.

---

1. A.E.Taylor, <u>Francis Herbert Bradley</u>, Proceedings of Brit. Academy, Vol. XI, 1924-25, p.464.
2. <u>Experience and Its Modes</u>, p.6.

The three theses are these:
1) that subject and object are identical since both fall within one whole, and that within this whole degrees of reality may be distinguished;
2) that within this whole there is a movement of an absolute self towards self-recognition;
3) that individual human personality is not absolutely real.

The only substantial area of agreement amongst all three of the philosophers with whom we are concerned is on (1), i.e. the unity of thought and reality. Only Bosanquet was concerned with the question of degrees of reality: Green never developed his system to the point where degrees become discernible, and Oakeshott does not find it profitable to pursue the question. Green and Bosanquet would agree in maintaining also (2), i.e. that the universe may be understood as a self, although Bosanquet was much more reticent about this than Green. Only Green would deny (3), and assert the absolute reality of the individual human personality: Oakeshott would see it as a modified conception, while Bosanquet would break down its exclusive aspect by emphasizing the content of experience.

In the following three chapters we will flesh out the skeleton just erected, examining in detail each of the three idealist systems. The nature of the idealist critique of classical empiricism will then be more adequately represented, and it will also help us to make evident (at a later stage) that both the strengths and the weaknesses of the treatment of political obligation offered by each idealist are to be traced to their several systems of general philosophy.

One word of explanation is called for. Because we consider that the first section of Oakeshott's book *Experience and Its Modes* presents shortly and lucidly what might be called a minimal formulation of idealism – i.e. a statement of at least the formal character of thought, truth and reality in accord with the general tenor of idealist opinion – we have chosen to leave an extended consideration of these subjects until we come to that volume. Furthermore, we have not attempted to section off the consideration of the three metaphysical systems in accordance with the issues distinguished (above) as central to the idealist debate, because this would have created distortion through failure to follow the internal development of each system as it developed in the mind of its creator. Enough will be said at appropriate points, however, to indicate how their theories bear on the three issues.

It is in the fact, then, that each of the English idealists defined his philosophy externally against the tradition of classical empiricism and internally around the above three issues that we find the unity of the idealist tradition and the context of the idealist treatment of political obligation.[1]

---

1. Useful discussions of the issues involved in English idealism, and of possible classifications, are to be found in J. H. Muirhead, <u>The Platonic Tradition in Anglo-Saxon Philosophy</u>, op.cit., especially the conclusion, "What is Dead and What is Alive in Idealism?" p 413 et seq; G. W. Cunningham, <u>The Idealistic Argument in Recent British and American Philosophy</u>, The Century Co., New York and London, 1933, chap XIV, "Arguments and Issues", and chap XVIII, "Underlying Issues"; Francois Houang, <u>Le Néo-Hegelianisme en Angleterre: La Philosophie de Bernard</u> Bosanquet, Paris, 1954; Hirolal Haldar's <u>Neo-Hegelianism</u>, London, 1927, is not very helpful from this point of view, since he contents himself with essays on individual thinkers; I find myself closest to Jean Pucelle, who refers in <u>L'Idéalisme en Angleterre</u> to "Les trois principaux thèmes de l'idéalisme anglais: le moi, la liberté; la synthèse de l'objet et du sujet; la totalité organique", Neuchatel, 1955, p 126.

Chapter 4

T. H. Green

T. H. Green's philosophical inquiry took its rise from the conviction that "to be free to understand, to enjoy, is the claim of the modern spirit." This claim, Green believed, was being thwarted by sophistry. The Platonic overtone is not unintentional. While the modern equivalent of Plato - Kant - has dislodged the sophistical mode of thought from philosophy, it remains afoot in the world at large in what Green calls "the popular philosophy", referring by that name to the system of ideas derived by the Aufklärung from Locke and inherited by the nineteenth century, and comprising in particular naturalism and hedonism. The central tenet of sophistry, both ancient and modern, is the belief that "man, the sensitive man, is the measure of all things." Now the doxic soul - the soul of the sophist and his victim - can know no peace, for it is divided against itself. It can never be at home in the world, for it does not recognize itself there. It considers itself locked up in an attitude of pure receptivity, submerged in the natural order of phenomena and subject to the laws which determine their every movement. In short, in spite of the conquest of nature by science, nature remains for the sophist "a labyrinth in which he has wandered at will till he has lost the clue, and which at the same time is so much his own that in its perplexities he seems at war with himself".[1]

To what extent Green's own philosophy encouraged the modern spirit to be free and to enjoy will be considered later: the limitations he imposed on these delights were in fact rather severe. The importance of the sophistry in opposition to which his philosophy emerged lies in the fact that it seeks the spirit in a world of sensation, thereby preventing men from recognizing the common nature they shared through participation in God, and so destroying that knowledge of man's vocation which is essential for a right ordering of human affairs at both the individual and the social level. Immersion in the senses, further, bred a type of ethical theory which puts an uncritical seal on individual egoism, encouraging men to disregard their obligations to their

---

1. All refs. to <u>Works</u>, Vol. III p 92-96.

brothers. Only when men have been enabled to recognize once again what they are and how they are related to each other can a sound discussion of the place of the state in life take place, for "Among a people who have no sense of a law superior to their own wilfulness" there can be no conception of "permanent being or of absolute will..."[1] and without these conceptions a stable social order is impossible.[2]

We must note immediately that Green opposes to the popular philosophy the thought of Kant, and not that of Hegel; and it is important to consider why this is so. Green's contention is that "it was...impossible for him ((Hegel)) to present the absolute reality of the world to himself as thought, without introducing into his conception of that reality certain determinations which are really inappropriate to it. In the absence of any positive predicates by which the absolute could be defined, certain attributes of thought as we know it, which can in truth be no longer attributes of such thought as could be identified with the absolute, were tacitly allowed to take their place." Hegel argued, illegitimately, that the merely human process of thinking, as manifested above all in philosophic thinking, could be regarded as "a sort of absolute movement of thought." Thus Green rejects the Hegelian dialectic. However, in the course of his review of J. Caird's *Introduction to the Philosophy of Religion*, where the discussion of Hegel occurs, he attempts to indicate the direction of inquiry which would establish a truly absolute idealism. In establishing the unity of thought and reality we must proceed, not from an analysis of the processes of our intelligence, but from an analysis of the objective world, or things themselves. Beginning from these, and not from our thought, we must show what Hegel correctly concluded (though by the wrong method), that things *are* thought and that thought *is* things. Specifying the appropriate method more carefully, Green maintains that since all things known by us have their being in relations, and since relations are only held together by the unifying activity of a thinking consciousness, it follows that wherever there is being there is a unifying con-

---

1. *Memoir*, Vol. III, p.xxvii.
2. Cf. *Pro.* sect. 245.

sciousness constituting it. When these questions are pursued, he considers that three conclusions are forced upon us, which are that

"there is one spiritual self-conscious being of which all that is real is the activity or expression; that we are related to this spiritual being, not merely as parts of the world which is its expression, but as partakers in some inchoate measure of the self-consciousness through which it at once constitutes and distinguishes itself from the world; that this participation is the source of morality and religion."[1]

These conclusions embody the metaphysical programme which Green undertook to carry out in the Prolegomena to Ethics. The first two books raise the question: is a natural science of man possible? In the first book Green endeavours to extract the intellect from the trammels of materialism by an analysis of the conditions of knowledge; his aim is to show that "the experience of connected matters of fact, which in its methodological expression we call science, ((presupposes)) a principle which is not itself any one or number of such matters of fact, or their result."[2] The natural or phenomenal order is never apprehended by us without the mediation of thought. What is experienced is never mere matter or motion, never the mere particulars of a series, but always a number of relations or qualities held together in unity; and this unity is not itself reducible to, or derivable from, the spatio-temporal series of feelings which it unifies. It is in fact the condition of such series.[3] Thus in an important sense Kant was correct in holding that understanding "makes" nature.

Science, then, presupposes another order of knowledge and reality. But what is the precise relationship between these two orders? Does the scientific world merely veil reality, or does it represent a positive manifestation of reality? At this point Green's Platonism enters and makes it impossible for him to attribute any significance to the scientific world. We may illustrate this, and at the same time show how Green's metaphysics reflects his

---

1. All refs. to Works, Vol III, pp 142-146.
2. Pro. Sect. 8.
3. Pro. sects. 9 and 32.

personal reaction to what he called the sophistry of the age, by referring to his essay on *The Influence of Civilization on Genius*. Green sees in all knowledge other than that of "the divine idea" itself only limitation. The divine idea, he writes, "is manifested in every created thing under certain limitations from which it is evermore working itself free;... the mind of man is the only manifestation which can enjoy the consciousness of its perfect original...this apprehension in its highest and most general form is the property of all the truly good."[1] The "perfect original", the "highest and most general" knowledge, are arrived at by a process of evacuating from experience its specific forms. It is to the eye of faith that the absolute appears; Green quotes with approval, "By faith they understand that the things which are seen were not made by things which do appear." The truly good man, the man who possesses this faith, is thereby made aware that God has a purpose in his life, and thereafter he travels through this mortal life as a citizen of a better land, conscious that his home is with God.[2] However, not only the man of faith, but the man of genius achieves this condition, although in a different way: he "apprehends the idea through the medium of his intellectual faculties".[3] He is, however, necessarily doomed to failure in the end, for he recognizes the divine idea only through the limitations which inevitably attach to his human nature. Green emphasises that the intellectual faculties of the man of genius grasp a truth which cannot be arrived at merely by generalization from external facts, or by scrutinizing the structure of ordinary thought: he has a "truth from above" to reveal to mankind.[4] This man Green describes as seeing the universal in the particular, and as avoiding separations and false abstractions in his thought. He is the man who has attained the truly concrete position. This is perhaps too hasty a conclusion. Precisely what this man has learnt, and what way of life his "entrance into the inner shrine of the counsels of God"[5] might involve, why he or anything

---

1. *Works*, Vol. III, p.11.
2. *Ibid*., Vol III, p.11.
3. *Ibid*., Vol III, p.12.
4. *Ibid*., Vol III, p.12.
5. *Ibid*., Vol III, p.12.

else should exist at all - all these questions have been left unanswered. We are considering, indeed, an early essay, but we would suggest that Green's later and more systematic work left open all the gaps which are apparent in this picture, merely embroidering more exquisitely the tapestry now before us.

The essay on *The Influence of Civilization on Genius* reveals clearly the confusion and hostility which Green felt in the face of the emerging competitive society. His main concern was the impact of the competitive and commercial spirit upon genius, and he was provoked by it to write "Better an old age of poverty and neglect, with five pounds for the poem to keep the poet alive, than a literary life in a time when the intellect is vexed with the spur of competition, and the inspiration of heaven is bargained away in the dearest market".[1] In his metaphysics he sought to find a corner where such intrusions could not occur: what he theorized was those "heaven-sent moments...with which no external system may intermeddle..."[2] The concrete embodiment of the divine idea he found in

"that free spirit with which Shakespeare walked this earth, drinking in every hue of many-coloured life, and plunging into the common stream of human existence unfettered by the consciousness of superiority".[3]

The competitiveness of the age is to be abandoned in favour of a "common stream of existence", and this is theorized ontologically as a leap from the divisions and separations of the world of sense with its trials and blindness to things spiritual into the peaceful unity of the divine idea, the leap being facilitated by revelation, since "all truth partakes of the nature of revelation".[4] Politically, it is to be theorized (we shall see) as the movement of the individual into the general will, for "isolation is the death of genius", i.e. of the truly good man, since "it is when we see it manifested in the common affections of man that we most lovingly and

---

1. *Ibid.*, Vol. III, p.19.
2. *Ibid.*, Vol. III, p.14.
3. *Ibid.*, Vol. III, p.18.
4. *Ibid.*, Vol. III, p.15.

reverently apprehend the divine idea."[1] As a statement of fact this is of course open to question: one might well love the divine idea more as it reveals itself in other forms.

Green's hope of uniting the intellectual and moral side of our natures by displaying the connection between the eternal and the temporal in a concrete synthetic position was made even more difficult to realize by the way two structural concepts in his system became intertwined with Platonic (or Christian) ideas. These were his concepts of teleology and of truth. Green thought that from the consciousness of potentialities in ourselves, unrealized but constantly in process of realization, we may infer a plan of development in the world.[2] Without pursuing the question of whether we are justified in attributing our ideas directly in this way to the universe, it may be observed that Green found in the idea of development an implication which would in fact render development quite inexplicable. For he held that one implication of the idea of development is "the eternal realization for, or in, the eternal mind of the capacities gradually realized in time".[3] The problem this presents is of understanding why what is eternally realized should yet develop. The presence of this difficulty in Green, however, would not in itself seem to justify W.D.Lamont's view that "the real difficulty... ((is)) to understand what is meant by the identical thing which develops through different stages," and is not "the so-called problem of relating 'eternal reality" to 'actual existence'".[4] Green himself did not think that only a piece of conceptual clarification was at issue, although it is true that he could not get very far without that.

Green had set the man of genius an impossible task; he wrote that "... till he can achieve the impossibility of entirely freeing himself from the spirit of his age, ((the faults of the general mind)) must check the free development of his power, if it be only by rousing him to constant rebellion against them".[5] But even if the man of genius had in fact managed to jump

---

1. Ibid., Vol.III, p.18.
2. Pro. sect. 186.
3. Pro. sect. 187.
4. W.D.Lamont, Introduction to Green's Moral Philosophy, Allen & Unwin, 1934, pp. 205-6.
5. Works, Vol. III, p.17.

out of his own skin in his endeavour to get back to his perfect original, he would not have achieved the truth which was his goal. We must explain why. In his endeavour to establish the reality of an eternal self Green rested heavily on what he considered to be the implications of our distinction between an objective or real world and a purely conceptual or illusory one. He takes the example of a railway-driver who mistakes a signal. A mechanical analysis of his perceptions will not enable us to find anything which distinguishes this situation from the situation in which he perceives the signal correctly. Where, then, are we to find the difference between a real and an illusory perception? It lies in the interpretation which the railway-driver gives to his sensations: he relates them to other ideas or interpretations of sensation, and it is the consistency or inconsistency of his interpretation with these other interpretations which constitutes reality and unreality.[1] Experience of an objective world thus forces us to conceive of the world as a single system of relations, and further, to recognize that the concepts of truth and reality presuppose an underlying order of unalterable relations; to know a real object is to know it as always the same in the same relations.[2] It is the unalterable character of true and real relationships which prevents us from "making" nature in accordance with our whims and fancies.

The difficulty with Green's account of truth and reality is that a thing which sought objectivity in unalterable relations would lose all reality by becoming a bare identity, which is the only thing which never alters. In effect, Green commits himself to saving reality by depriving it of all its appearances. There is, however, a suggestive tension in his theory. On the one hand it appears to lead in the direction of a "coherence" theory, and this was to be the side of it which Bradley and Bosanquet pursued (and the view which Oakeshott also adopts). On the other hand, Green himself does not pursue the idea of logical coherence as the criterion of truth and reality, pre-

---

1. *Pro.* sect. 12.
2. *Ibid.*, sects. 13-14.

ferring to use his analysis as the basis for a metaphysical leap to the idea of an eternal consciousness which synthesizes the objective relations between phenomena.

It will be evident that Green has already extended the Kantian doctrine of the transcendental unity of apperception beyond the point to which Kant himself took it. Kant's own doctrine ended in the conception of the thing in itself and involved no reference to an eternal order of relations present to an eternal consciousness and in part known to us. Green of course knew this perfectly well, and in fact considered his most important advance upon Kant to be the elimination of the dualism introduced by the thing in itself. How does he escape the dualism which is the enemy of absolute idealism? He endeavours to show that understanding not only "makes nature" in the sense of enabling us to conceive that there is such a thing, but also in the further sense that "it is the source, or at any rate a condition, of there being these relations ((viz. which we form into a single system))", thereby avoiding the postulation of a pre-established harmony between our conception of the order of nature and that order itself.[1] Kant erred at the point where he drew an absolute distinction between the form and the matter of our knowledge of nature. By "form" he understood the categories of intuition, space and time by which the self renders nature a unified system of experience; by "matter" he understood the pure sensation which precede all relationships. This distinction necessarily creates the possibility that our experience of thing may not correspond with things as they are in the world itself. By it Kant was led to hold that the matter (our sensations) is the result of the unintelligible operation upon our senses of unknowable things-in-themselves. Like the empiricists, he thought of experience as ultimately resting upon an externally given experience. Green has no difficulty in showing the inconsistencies in which Kant thereby became involved. He asserted, for example, a causal relationship between the manifold of sensation and the originating thing-in-itself, while maintaining at the same time that causality is one of the transcendental categories within the self by which it creates the unified order of

---

1. *Pro.* sect. 19.

of nature. In short, he was unable to hold appearance and reality completely apart. In criticising Kant's position, Green commences from the position he has so far developed. It has been shown that sensations, to become sensible objects or events, must be related by a self-conscious subject. He generalizes this position, maintaining that "the same or an analogous action is necessary to account for any relation whatever - for a relation between material atoms as much as any other".[1] In other words, if we are to maintain that things, and not only our ideas of them, have that unity which constitutes their existence, we must recognize as a condition of such a reality "the action of some unifying principle analogous to that of our understanding".[2]

For these reasons Green concludes that a study of knowledge and reality leads to a conception of experience in which knowledge is recognized not as the effect of the action of an external nature upon a passive human subject, but as "the concrete whole, which may be described indifferently as an eternal intelligence realized in the related facts of the world, or as a system of related facts rendered possible by such an intelligence, partially and gradually reproducing itself in us, communicating piece-meal, but in inseparable correlation, understanding and the facts understood, experience and the experienced world."[3]

The eternal consciousness lies behind the world of appearances. Although Green writes that we cannot "suppose that which we only know as a principle of unity in relation, to exist apart from a manifold through which it is related",[4] his main view of the eternal consciousness is best reflected in the passage in which he asserts that "the 'punctum stans', to which an order of time must be relative that it may be an order of time, cannot itself be a moment or a series of moments in that order; nor can the 'punctum stans' <u>in consciousness</u>, necessary to the punctuation of time, be itself a succession in consciousness."[5] The most sympathetic way of regarding these conflicting

---

1. <u>Pro</u>. sect. 29.
2. <u>Pro</u>. sect. 29.
3. <u>Pro</u>. sect. 36, 54.
4. <u>Ibid</u>., sect. 66.
5. <u>Ibid</u>., sect. 81, his emphasis.

statements seems to be that of Lamont, who suggests that religious habits of thought prevented Green from overcoming a tendency to think of the universe in terms of the product a transcendent creative mind.[1]

Perhaps the most cogent criticism of Green's argument is that made by Seth, who would convict Green of committing what he terms the "realistic fallacy." This fallacy is committed not only by Green but by all the idealist philosophers who start from the Kantian analysis of knowledge and end with "a confusion between logic or epistemology and metaphysics or ontology".[2] The realistic fallacy occurs when "the imaginary object of the theory of knowledge is hypostatised by the Neo-Kantians as the one ultimately real Thinker. Hegel's metaphysical logic may be taken without injustice as the culmination of this tendency." In other words, Green errs in trying to extract existence from mere logic. Furthermore, Seth argues, the attempt to unify the divine and the human subject is ultimately destructive of the reality of both, for "if....the theory deprives man of his proper self by rendering him, as it were, to an object of a universal Thinker, it leaves this universal Thinker also without any true personality." If we attempt to conceive of the divine self, in Green's fashion, as the eternal sustainer of an objective world, "such a purely objective consciousness is not in any true sense of the world a self; it is no more than an imaginary focus into which an objective system of relations returns".[3] And the endeavour to hold such a self in one whole with the human self must destroy that self by denying its "imperviousness", because it becomes merely a predicate of the universal self.

It is difficult to defend Green against the charge of failing to render intelligible the nature of the eternal self, which does appear to be "no more than an imaginary focus into which an objective system of relations returns." It is a device, in other words, for rescuing objectivity from the subjectivism towards which his doctrine that the understanding makes nature leads

---

1. W. D. Lamont, Introduction to Green's Moral Philosophy, op.cit., p.190.
2. Hegelianism and Personality, 2nd ed., Blackwood, 1893, p.231.
3. Ibid., p.233.

him. Sidgwick would support Seth in holding that Green makes too much out
of our experience of objectivity in using it to move immediately from the
affirmation of an analogous action of consciousness in the universe to the
affirmation of identical quality.[1] But where Seth himself is vulnerable is
in respect of the reasons with which he supports his criticism of Green. Is
there, we may ask, a "realistic fallacy"? Is it in principle impossible,
that is, to pass from thought to reality, or from logic to metaphysics?
Seth does not demonstrate that it is impossible to press thought until it
becomes identical with reality: he merely assumes that it is. Green, then,
may have been shown to have sketched his system too rapidly: but he has not
been shown to have adopted an intrinsically futile method. And the position
from which Seth works in fact displays some of the very difficulties which
he finds in Green and other idealists. Thus he begins by allowing that "the
mere individual" is a fiction of philosophic thought, and that reality is
consequently to be thought of as a suprapersonal world: "There would be no
interaction between individuals unless they were all embraced within one
reality; still less could there be any knowledge of one individual by others
if they did not all form parts of one system of things." And yet in the same
passage the individual self is described as "in its nature perfectly imper-
vious to other selves in a fashion of which the impenetrability of matter is
a faint analogy." Clearly he himself has gone beyond the Kantian epistemology to which he wishes to confine Green.[2] But, what is more important than
Seth's own inconsistency is the fact that his claim that Green destroys the
human and the divine selves depends upon the "faint analogy" between the impenetrability of matter and the imperviousness of the individual. That Seth
himself fails to retain for the individual his imperviousness is naturally a
point strongly in Green's favour. And in any case, Green's intention (as
distinct from the import of his doctrine) was not of course to destroy either
the human or the divine self; he wrote that "It is clearly of the very

---

1. *Mind*, Vol. IX, 1884, p.171.
2. I owe the last point - viz. Seth's inconsistency - to J.H.Muirhead's
    Platonic Tradition, op.cit., p.217.

essence of our doctrine that the divine principle, which we suppose to be realizing itself in man, should be supposed to realize itself in persons, as such."[1] It is, however, too sympathetic to Green to suggest, as W. H. Fairbrother has in effect suggested in The Philosophy of T.H.Green,[2] that Green's difficulties arise because he has delved so deeply into the nature of the universe that he has encountered its inner mysteries.[3] His difficulties arise more from the internal limitations of his philosophic system than from the structure of reality, as may be seen (for example) from the difficulties Green encountered with the notion of teleology.

Green's claim to have established the foundations of a truly absolute idealism is made even more doubtful by the presence in his system of a further difficulty, which illustrates his tendency to recognize and eliminate one abstraction while replacing it immediately with another. Green made the following criticism of Aristotle:

"Having apparently idealised the world as a series of the 'thoughts of God,' which we may think after him, and of which each is in necessary relation to, and qualified by all the rest, he cannot sustain himself at this conception, but habitually treats the world as subject to conditions, which have a reality other than as objects of thought, and so cease to form an organic whole, which is the negation of each in particular".[4]
Unfortunately, the same criticism appears to apply to Green himself. His criticism of Kantian dualism aimed at rejecting the distinction between the form and matter of experience which has led to the thing in itself. To this end Green appears to argue at times that mere sensation is an analytical abstraction, with no corresponding reality in the world: "mere sensation is in truth a phrase that represents no reality. It is the result of a process of abstraction".[5] But at other times he refers to "that large part of our own

---

1. Pro. sect. 182.
2. Published by Methuen, London, 1896.
3. pp. 163-164.
4. Works, Vol. III, p.86.
5. Pro. sect. 46.

sensitive life which goes on without being affected by conceptions",[1] and implies that there must be sensations external to our consciousness, and working upon it as an exciting cause, if perception is to occur. A perception of colour, for example, requires sensation arising out of a stimulus of the optic nerve by a particular vibration of ether.[2] This reversion to dualistic thinking makes the nature of the eternal consciousness even more difficult to comprehend, because the operation of consciousness becomes unintelligible when it is not located in an animal organism. Yet to attach an animal organism (in the sense in which it is subject to external stimuli) to the eternal consciousness itself is impossible, because this would make it dependent upon something external to itself, and thereby reduce it to finitude. More generally, Green's attitude towards external stimuli seems to imply the existence of those immediate, unrelated particulars whose reality he was most concerned to deny. In a way he could hardly avoid this assumption: his whole analysis arose from the impact made upon him by Kant's discovery that the mind is active in both cognition and volition, and the concept of action itself suggests the presence of prior data to be worked upon.

Green has so far advanced two considerations which would lead to the conclusion that there is an eternal consciousness; he has endeavoured to show that this is presupposed by (1) our knowledge of nature and (2) by the existence of nature. The second book of the *Prolegomena* reinforces the argument for the necessity of assuming the existence of an eternal consciousness, and brings also the transition to moral and political philosophy. Just as in the sphere of the intellect the materialist could not answer the question, What is a fact? so he cannot answer, in the sphere of action, the question, Why ought I to do X? When man is thought of as merely part of the physical order, the conceptions of free will, conscience and moral obligation become inexplicable; an injunction to conform to a rule is meaningless if action is determined by laws of nature.[3]

---

1. *Ibid.*, sect. 48.
2. *Ibid.*, sects. 59-60.
3. *Pro.* sect. 7.

In the first book Green's aim was to demolish the separation made by the popular philosophy between the intellectual judgment and sensation. In the second book the main target is the separation between feeling and reflection. It is at this stage that Green's direct attack upon Utilitarianism commences, for in common with all the popular theories of morals, Utilitarianism regards feeling as "the exhaustive account of all modes of consciousness with which it is associated".[1] The treatment of the reason/feeling dichotomy involves not only the demonstration of the freedom of the will but also an examination of the true nature of the unity of the self.

Green argues that human action is not motivated by wants but by the consciousness of wanted objects. The self distinguishes itself from its wants, and in so doing creates the gap between a world which is and a world which ought to be. Further, in being more than a succession of wants - in being that which unifies the succession - the self appears as a persisting identity which can only find satisfaction in an organized whole, and not in this or that particular satisfaction.[2] Green uses the term "motive" to describe "an idea of an end, which a self-conscious subject presents to itself, and which it strives and tends to realize".[3] It is the fact that moral action derives from motives and not from physical causes (or wants) that entitles it to be called free. That wants present the occasion of moral action does not alter the fact that want as such never figures in a motive, which only exists precisely because the moral agent distinguishes himself from his wants. Thus wants may continue in existence alongside of motives, without having been in any way altered, while yet contributing in no way to determining the action undertaken, for which the supervening motive is entirely responsible.[4]

The concept of a motive forces us to recognise once again the existence of an eternal consciousness, for the act of adopting desired objects "is the act of a subject which has not come to be; the act itself is not in time,

---

1. *Works*, Vol. III, p.97.
2. *Pro*. sect. 85.
3. Ibid., sect. 87.
4. Ibid., sect. 89.

in the sense of being an event determined by previous events".[1] In reply
to the objection that the kind of motive which moves the self is conditioned
by the temporal order - by its circumstance and character - Green argues
that every stage in character-formation the self has been an object to itself, and that circumstances affect action only through the medium of a
motive.[2] If it is further objected that circumstances are often not of the
agent's own making, Green replies that nothing can influence a man except
through the medium of his conception of personal good; only through this can
climate or social circumstances come to bear upon his character. The
imminence of the same danger will make a hero of one man, a slave of another,
a miser of a third.[3] And because it is impossible to hold that action is
physically caused by motive, character or circumstance, it follows that the
determinist thesis cannot stand. Finally, Green argues that in connection
with the world of practice, there can be no equivalent to the problem which
arose in relation to our knowledge of nature, viz., Does it correspond to
the natural order itself? This problem cannot arise in the world of practice
because its constituents "are objects of which the existence in consciousness,
as wanted, is prior to, and conditions, their existence in reality".[4]
Practical reality, in other words, exists only in and for practical consciousness - the moral world is created by man himself.

Having supplemented his argument for the existence of an eternal consciousness by the consideration of the will, Green has a third consideration
to advance. Not only our knowledge of nature and the very existence of
nature require us to recognize the existence of such a consciousness but
(setting philosophy to one side) the most ordinary intellectual and moral processes are found to be unintelligible without this conception. In the case

1. Pro. sect. 101.
2. Ibid., sect. 99.
3. Ibid., sect. 106.
4. Ibid., sect. 86.

of knowledge our experience of the cumulative growth of knowledge in the learning process, and in the case of will our desire to be better, require us to acknowledge that an eternally complete and perfect consciousness is gradually reproducing itself in the animal organism which it has taken as its vehicle.[1]

The problems which appeared in Green's metaphysic of knowledge reproduce themselves in his metaphysic of morals. The division between the temporal and the eternal order is paralleled by a division between the intellectual and the desiring parts of the finite self. Desire is not fully integrated into the self since, like the "matter" of knowledge, it is what is presupposed as the datum on which the moral consciousness operates. Further the tension which appears as a result of Green's desire to retain two centres of absolute value - the finite self and the eternal self - makes it difficult to recognise the ultimate ground of obligation. If the eternal consciousness is morally perfect then it is impossible to see why we should engage in a pointless reproduction of it; and, at a deeper level, the attainment of moral perfection by the finite agent would seem to involve both his own extinction and that of the eternal consciousness itself, as Seth suggested. This, of course, was not the result Green intended (as we have already noted). The most sympathetic interpretation of Green's conflicting views is that of Bosanquet. While agreeing with Green that "our ultimate standard of worth is an ideal of _personal_ worth. All other values are relative to value for, of, or in a person",[2] he argues that a distinction must be drawn between the given self and the self when taken with all its contents, for "...in a personal consciousness we have already accepted a standard that goes beyond the states of consciousness of a conscious being. By a person, or a being partaking of individuality...we presumably mean some sort of a whole.." And he further insists that the real question is whether two or more so-called persons can be members of the same whole or unity for purposes of valuation.[3] Elsewhere, in discussing Green's belief in personal immortality,[4] he returns to the subject of Green's apparent valuation of the mere form of

---

1. _Pro_. sects. 67, 114.
2. _Pro_. sect. 184.
3. _Principle_, p.312.
4. Green's discussion of this subject is to be found in _Pro_. sect. 185.

finite personality and argues that Green really conceives of the goal of development as <u>a</u> personality and not <u>our</u> personality; and that his doctrine is therefore compatible with a conception of the absolute as more than a personality, so long as in it all that constituted a self can have fuller justice done to it than it could have when accepted as a merely given self.[1] Bosanquet's ingenious interpretation of Green's conflicting statements suggests that Green's system is more flexible than might at first appear, but the impression gained from the whole corpus of Green's work is that Green himself understood personality in the immediate sense. He does appear, that is, to assign value to a bare identity, or else to the conscious states of conscious beings: in either case an abstraction is encountered. A judgment upon the possibility of reconciling Green's different opinions by adopting Bosanquet's suggestion must necessarily anticipate the next chapter, but it may be said that Bosanquet's own view of the absolute was not fully coherent and that his interpretation of finite personality is therefore problematic.

Green's metaphysic of morals is vulnerable in a further respect. His view that our experience of moral development implies the existence of one eternally perfect being suggests that he confused the logic of comparative terms with the logic of relative ones. A comparative term involves reference to a standard; to say "X is good" is to compare X with things which are bad, but in the light of a standard which is not exhausted in X and in the bad things. This standard is constituted by whatever considerabilities are contained in the notion of the best possessed by the person comparing. Thus, while good implies best, this best does not entail the existence of an eternally perfect being. A relative term, on the other hand, involves no reference to a standard; it involves only a contrast with its own correlation. A "fast" car is only fast by contrast with ones which are slower. To call a car fast is not to imply the existence of an absolute standard which must be surpassed before the term fast can be used.[2] It is clear, then, that even the logic of comparison would not be enough to prove the existence of an eternally perfect consciousness.

---

1. <u>Value</u>, p.282.
2. On the distinction between comparative and relative terms, see Collingwood, <u>The New Leviathan</u>, O.U.P., 1942, sects. 38.39 - 38.42.

Conclusion

Green's intention was to unite the moral and intellectual sides of our nature and by so doing to provide a foundation for his treatment of the problem of moral and political obligation. Beginning from the Kantian philosophy he hoped to move from it to absolute idealism, and thereby to retrieve the source of obligation from the inscrutable noumenal sphere into which Kant had thrust it. But Green's absolute idealism failed to disengage itself completely from the philosophical assumptions made in the tradition of classical empiricism, with the result that Green ends with a foot in both camps and disastrous ambiguity on practically every level. On the one hand he believed in the unity of all reality within a single teleological process: nature and spirit are continuous, so that nature without spirit or spirit without nature is unthinkable. This is essentially a dynamic picture, in which the individual and his career are reduced to details of the embracing conception within which they fall. This side of Green's thought is clearly Hegelian in inspiration. On the other hand, Green was never able to regard matter as, in the end, more than a limitation upon spirit, with the result that absolute reality was made into a static centre of perfection behind the world of matter, flesh, and becoming. Because this philosophical position led him always to reason from a Kantian conception of the cognitive and volitional situations, he never felt happy about replacing the dualism of subject and object which was contained in the starting point by a monistic theory, which made a process, and not the individual, the ultimate reality.

Because of the confusion between these two positions Green never achieved a clear conception of the nature of selfhood, and this makes his general philosophy an unsatisfactory basis for his political theory because it provides no conclusive means of eliminating those antitheses of classical empiricism to which Green directed his attention. In the chapter on his politics we will attempt to exhibit the ways in which those antitheses reassert themselves by showing how the dualism of spirit and nature is carried over from his metaphysics into his social theory.

In terms of the schema we adopted at the beginning of the section on the concrete universal we may say that Green (1) wished to assert the identity of thought and reality but failed to show that what we take to be reality is anything more than a creation of our own minds; and that (2) while he wished to attribute personality to the absolute he did not find a sense of "personality" which would render such a usage fully intelligible, nor one which would enable us to see clearly how human personality is related to the absolute self; and (3) that he did not explain how it is possible to attribute complete perfection to the absolute while maintaining at the same time the absolute reality of human personality.

Chapter 5

Bosanquet

Daisy Chain was considered by Bosanquet to be a most successful book. He compared Miss Yonge's novel with Zola's *Nana*, and the latter came off very badly. The English authoress, he wrote, "...has in the main expressed the motives and experiences through which great things are done in the world and great communities are strong and valuable, while in the other case we find an analysis of morbid growths which are not typical and which if removed from the world by a miracle would not be missed."[1]

A brief glance at Miss Yonge (1823-1901) and her work will facilitate our study of Bosanquet, and has the added interest that we appear to be in the middle of a Yonge renaissance. It is, admittedly, a very feminine renaissance - the three works on her which have appeared since 1940 are all by ladies,[2] and the *Charlotte M. Yonge Society* founded in 1961 has an all-female membership. One of the members gives some idea of the spirit which pervades the Yongian enthusiast: in an essay on *Charlotte Yonge's Ethics: Some Unfashionable Virtues*, Katharine Briggs writes that:

"...it is for want of these virtues ((i.e. those extolled by Miss Yonge)) that our whole civilization is sick. Because so few of our young people understand why they should be chaste, our sex life is falling back into savagery; pride has hurried us into two world wars and still makes us greedy for status symbols and for more good than we can use or enjoy".[3] Miss Yonge herself did indeed keep her sex life free from any trace of savagery. Even Georgina Battiscombe, a great admirer of hers, confesses that love-scenes in her novels make clear that Charlotte was not, at any rate, very experienced in proposals. Thus when Percy Fotheringham proposes to Theodora in *Heartsease*, his proposal concludes with the statement that "Together we would crush the

---

1. *Suggestions*, p.225.
2. *Charlotte Mary Yonge: The Story of an Uneventful Life*, by Georgina Battiscombe, Constable and Co., London 1943; *Victorian Best-seller: The World of Charlotte M. Yonge*, by Margaret Mare and Alicia C.Percival, Harrap and Co., London, 1947; *A Chaplet for Charlotte Yonge*, edited by Georgina Battiscombe and Marghanita Laski, The Cresset Press, London, 1965.
3. *A Chaplet for Charlotte Yonge*, ed. by Battiscombe and Laski, op.cit., p.29.

serpents, bring forth all that is excellent", to which she replies, "in an odd sort of voice", that "I think there might be a chance for me with you".[1] Miss Yonge's inexperience in such matters may have arisen in large measure from her opinions on dress, for she was not unattractive. Her indifference to dress even provoked Mrs. Sumner, founder of the Mothers' Union, to protest.[2] Mrs. Sumner had in mind a volume of essays entitled Womankind in which Miss Yonge expounded upon the subject of dress and warned her readers in particular against one evil:

"Exposure of the face is one of the great tendencies of the time; and though it is not exactly indelicate in itself, yet the bold confronting of notice that is involved in going out with a totally unprotected countenance, thrown into prominence by the headdress, cannot be modest in itself; nor does a veil coming close over the nose materially alter the matter".[3]

Of her novels as a whole, Mare and Percival write that they are "crowded with instances great and small of...self-sacrifice, and in raising this motive to the dignity of a principle she was thoroughly in tune with her surroundings."[4] This was perhaps what appealed to Bosanquet about Daisy Chain, which was first published in book form in 1856. One approaches this novel, which is a chronicle of the May family, with some trepidation, since Georgina Battiscombe concludes her enthusiastic analysis of it by assuring us that of its admirers "Some are born mad, some achieve madness, and some, the unfortunate husbands, brothers, or sisters of these maniacs, have the Mays thrust upon them."[5] Obviously, it is very difficult to fit Bosanquet into this scheme. The central figure is Ethel. Ethel is at first inconspicuous, but emerges to occupy a position in which the whole May family comes to depend upon her when it is rendered motherless. Ethel's life is summed up in two lines

---

1. Quoted in Charlotte Mary Yonge, by Georgina Battiscombe, p.100.
2. Ibid., p.101.
3. Ibid., p.101.
4. Victorian Best-Seller, op.cit., p.282.
5. Charlotte Mary Yonge, p.97.

she composes:

> Purer than breath of earthly fame,
> Is losing self in a glorious aim. 1

Her progress is made by self-discipline; as Battiscombe puts it, "Character... and not circumstance, was the real power that went to the making of Ethel".[2] Ethel's great aspiration (the alternative title of the book was _Aspirations_) is to build a little church, and this she eventually manages to do when (unexpectedly) the sailor lover of her sister dies in the south seas, and in his will leaves all his money to be spent on a church.[3] Of course, she takes none of the credit, giving it all to the dead sailor and her sister, who is named Margaret; Georgina Battiscombe remarks that "...every lover of _The Daisy Chain_ will remember the episode where Margaret gives her engagement ring to be set round the stone of the chalice belonging to Cocksmoor Church."[4]

For the purpose of understanding Bosanquet's thought, and the basic appeal of _Daisy Chain_ to him, two further comments from Katharine Briggs' essay on _Charlotte Yonge's Ethics_ are of especial value. The first is that "The particular power that she had, which is rather rare among novelists, was to create people of delightful goodness," and the second (which Briggs' attributes to Marghanita Laski) is that "...the main theme of Charlotte Yonge's writings is the Kingdom of God."[5]

We have now encountered one Bosanquet, the Bosanquet for whom (like Miss Yonge) black is black and white is white, with healthy (and heavenly) lives on the one side and "morbid growths" on the other. The "central experiences" (an idea which Bosanquet had elevated a few years earlier to a central position in his metaphysics)[6] grasped by Miss Yonge remain unblemished. This is the Bosanquet who admired Plato and, surrendering himself to the erotic attraction of the agathon, defined logic as love;[7] who in the first chapter

---

1. _Daisy Chain_, MacMillan, London 1901, p.18.
2. _Charlotte Mary Yonge_, p.95.
3. Ibid., pp.95-96.
4. Ibid., p.93.
5. _A Chaplet for Charlotte Yonge_, op.cit., p.21 and p.29 respectively.
6. _Principle_, Chap.1.
7. _Value_, p.9.

of his metaphysics dismissed the self as "a dangerous immediate";[1] who spoke of the "over-lapping of selves",[2] with the implication that the world might be better (or no worse) without selves like Nana; and who, obsessed with the "nisus towards the whole" which he found everywhere, convinced himself that the world could not possibly be intended to culminate in beings like himself.

But there is a second Bosanquet. This Bosanquet could end his course of lectures on metaphysics by quoting at length and with approval a passage from William James in which James describes his reaction to a week spent at the Assembly Grounds on the borders of Chatauqua Lake, in the U.S.A. There, James said, "You have...a foretaste of what society might be, were it all in the light, with no suffering and no dark corners."[3] He found it a "middle-class paradise, without a sin, without a victim, without a blot, without a tear."[4] And yet - and this is the point which Bosanquet chooses to emphasise - he was glad to get back to "the big outside worldly wilderness with all its sins and sufferings".[5] For this Bosanquet Nana would not be a non-contributory self: she would become an essential part of the universe, in which good only occurs because evil exists. She would be able to establish her right to a place in the scheme of things by appealing to a doctrine which Bosanquet developed almost at the outset of his first volume on metaphysics, viz. the doctrine of the concrete universal.[6] She would be able to do so because on this view a premium is placed upon diversity. In Bosanquet's own language, the doctrine of the concrete universal implies that "It takes all sorts to make a world..."[7]

We encounter at the outset, then, two different directions of thought in Bosanquet's metaphysics, with the tension between them quite apparent. Our particular aim must be to determine to what extent they are brought into harmony and, in the absence of some synthesis being achieved, to discover which controls Bosanquet's theory of the state.

---

1. *Principle*, p.13.
2. *Value*, pp.53-54.
3. Quoted by Bosanquet in *Value*, p.323.
4. *Ibid.*, p.323.
5. *Ibid.*, p.324.
6. *Principle*, chap.II.
7. *Ibid.*, p.37.

The notion by which Bosanquet sought to relieve the tension just mentioned was the idea of individuality. We must explore this idea because Bosanquet also makes it the principal means by which he seeks to break down the opposition between the self and others, in which he sees the origin of the problem of political obligation. The adoption of this idea as the central one for metaphysical inquiry constitutes his principal break with Green's philosophy, for Green had laid the stress not on individuality but upon personality. Individuality is possessed by a thing in the degree to which it is inclusive and internally non-contradictory. Bosanquet's Gifford Lectures, his most ambitious venture into metaphysics, represent an effort to apply the criterion of individuality in a way which would weld experience into a unified whole, within which different degrees of reality may be distinguished. It was on this point - the question of degrees of reality - that Bosanquet found Bradley's Appearance and Reality unsatisfactory, for Bradley had not ended with the structured monism which his acceptance of the criterion of individuality seemed to imply, but with a hostility to thought and relations. Bosanquet believed that Bradley's conception of the perfect individual - the absolute - lacked concreteness because Bradley began by finding the unity of thought and reality best exemplified in the unity of feeling. In his opinion many passages of Bradley must inevitably leave the impression that the absolute lies beyond experience, or else is to be found only in the most impoverished kind of experience, viz. feeling. Bosanquet therefore rejected feeling as a dangerous immediate and began instead from the conviction that "we experience the Absolute better than we experience anything else".[1] It should perhaps be added that he came to believe in the unity of thought and reality only after the publication of Appearance and Reality. 'In his earlier work he had not distinguished logic from metaphysics.[2] Without pursuing the detail of his intellectual biography we will merely suggest that in the works which

---

1. Ibid., p.27.
2. His own account of the development of his thought is to be found in the essay Science and Philosophy, in the volume entitled Science and Philosophy.

primarily concern the political philosopher - the metaphysical ones - Bosanquet has clearly abandoned the epistemological foundation which Green had sought to provide for idealism and has moved on to pursue the ontological criterion of individuality.[1]

To reject Bradley's concern with feeling and intuition would not in itself create a concrete metaphysics, although it might well be a precondition for such a metaphysics. Bosanquet did have an idea, however, which went beyond anything which Bradley had entertained; it is in some ways his most interesting (and also his most Hegelian) idea. This is the idea which he refers to as "negativity".

By negativity Bosanquet means that "experience is always beyond itself... It is what has been spoken of under the name of self-consciousness as the nature of a being which is itself, and its other in one".[2] His contention is that "negativity...is fundamental in all that is real".[3] This may not be very illuminating so far; but if we now notice that the idea of negativity is defined in contradistinction to the idea of contradiction then things become clearer. A large part of Bradley's difficulties in achieving a concrete conception of the absolute arose because he confused negativity with contradiction. In Bosanquet's view, contradiction is an unsuccessful or obstructed negativity; negativity is a successful or frictionless contradiction.[4] For example, it is a formal contradiction if you say that "this colour is both beautiful and ugly, i.e. not beautiful". It ceases to be a contradiction if you say, "this colour by daylight is beautiful and by candlelight is ugly."[5] In other words, contradiction only exists when predicates are brought together on an inadequate basis of distinction - it exists when a systematic whole has not been developed to accommodate them. The presence of contradiction is incompatible with truth and reality, but it does not follow that to attain to truth and reality we have to obliterate contradiction; what is required is

---

1. Cf. Letters, p.26, where Muirhead discusses his use of the argument a contingentia mundi.
2. Principle, p.231.
3. Ibid., p.231.
4. Ibid., p.231.
5. Ibid., p.224.

that the subject of the conflicting predicates should be expanded until it can hold the predicates together in a harmonious and differentiated whole. In short, by distinguishing contradiction from negation, Bosanquet is able to show that differentiation is not incompatible with unity: contradiction must indeed be removed, but in such a way that it leaves behind it a determinate unity and not a substance with no predicates. On this basis he concludes that "negative and affirmative grow pari passu",[1] this being the idea which lies behind (for example) his sympathy for William James' critique of the heavenly life of Chatauqua Lake.

The idea of negativity brings Bosanquet closer than any other English idealist to an acceptance of something like Hegel's concept of dialectic; for Hegel had found in the negation of the negation the clue to the working of the universe. But Bosanquet does not apply the idea of negativity very systematically: it remains confined in his thought to epistemological, moral, and aesthetic conjectures and never establishes itself as the basis of a coherent ontology. We are given many illustrations. One of them has already been mentioned, viz. "this colour is both beautiful and ugly", and many references are made besides to other ordinary experiences to show that we do place a positive value on what might at first sight appear to be non-contributory to moral development, and in that sense purely negative. The general principle involved in moral experience is that "....suffering and privation are also opportunities...This is the simple and primary point of view, and also, in the main, the true and fundamental one."[2] No number of illustrations, however, amount to a serious attempt to show that anything more than suggestive analogies are being advanced.

Perhaps the origin of his failure to get beyond a string of analogies may be traced to his refusal to conceive of philosophy as affording absolute knowledge. For him "philosophy is in the first instance a purely theoretical activity".[3] That is to say, it cannot stand upon its own foundation: it

---

1. Ibid., p.232.
2. Ibid., p.21.
3. Value, p.230.

presupposes a subject-matter outside itself upon which it can work. Because it is "the theoretical interpretation of experience as a whole",[1] it will find the higher experiences the most rewarding to study, but this does not release it from its dependence upon them. Religion too falls short of absolute experience. It is conditioned by its place in the world of will, for "as it takes definite shape through adoration of an object and community of will with its will, (it) tends to become engaged in the specific conflict between good and evil, and though it transcends this, yet (it) remains determined by this particular transcendence".[2]

Bosanquet is particularly sympathetic towards the claim of aesthetic experience to be the absolute experience, but in the end that also is found to be defective. Nonetheless, he concludes the <u>Principle of Individuality and Value</u> by taking Dante's <u>Divine Comedy</u> as a "remote analogue of the Absolute".[3] In this analogy it is clearly recognisable that the idea of negativity has given way before the idea of an overlap of selves; a static picture replaces a dynamic one, and the differences within the temporal order are (by implication) merely dissolved into the pervasiveness of the spiritual world. What Bosanquet suggests is that, just as the mind of Dante includes the external (spatial) world of Italy, without thereby destroying its otherness; just as, also, his mind includes the selves which figure in the poem, without destroying their distinctness; so the absolute may be considered to hold together an organic unity differentiated into nature and mind.[4] Elsewhere Bosanquet speaks of Shakespeare and Dante overlapping many selves without being as careful to emphasise the ultimate distinctness of those selves.[5] Ability to overlap means, of course, greater reality and value - for comprehensiveness is the test of both. Cunningham generalizes the problem involved when he writes of the absolute idealist that he "tends to forget

---

1. <u>Ibid</u>., p.230.
2. <u>Ibid</u>., p.311.
3. <u>Ibid</u>., p.379.
4. <u>Principle</u>, pp.380-382.
5. <u>Value</u>, p.51

that content apart from a centre is an abstraction...."[1] François Houang echoes this criticism when he finds Bosanquet's most disastrous assumption to be that identity of contents in two selves implies the identity of those selves,[2] and also when he maintains that Bosanquet's monistic doctrine of individuality seems "d'avoir trop subordonné l'activité particulière des sujets de l'expérience au contenu objectif et universel de celle-ci".[3] Substantially the same point was made long ago by another critic, Tsanoff, when he suggested that Bosanquet's conception of the absolute was as defective as Bradley's, since his method was to pronounce one appearance after another incomplete and so to be transcended, in the sense of extinguished, in the absolute.[4]

The discussion so far has focussed upon Bosanquet's difficulties in developing a coherent metaphysical conception of individuality. It has not yet grasped the nerve of his philosophy - the master-conception, the vision, has yet to be explored. We will now determine what this master-conception is, and will try to show how it is vitiated by Bosanquet's failure to incorporate the concept of negativity into the structure of reality. This bodes ill for his politics.

Jean Pucelle speaks of Bosanquet's philosophy as a "drame du salut transposé en termes philosophiques",[5] and Bosanquet himself uses the phrase "the Pilgrim's Progress of Philosophy".[6] It is conducted, as we have already noticed, through an examination of the "sane and central experiences". But we will get the flavour of what is at stake beneath the complex language of his metaphysics if we first notice what is being criticised and rejected. Bosanquet was no more pleased with the age than Green. He too feared that the popular philosophy might sink men into the world of the senses, and so breed apathy about improvement. His metaphysics, like those of Green, are an attack upon sin, which reveals itself in the form of "a mood of false absoluteness and self-satisfaction".[7] We are exhorted, lengthily and in philosophic

---

1. G.W.Cunningham, *The Idealist Argument in Recent British and American Philosophy*, op.cit., p.534.
2. *Le Néo-Hégélianisme en Angleterre*, op.cit., p.217.
3. *Ibid.*, p.214.
4. *Philosophical Review*, 1920, p.74.
5. *L'Idéalisme en Angleterre*, op.cit., p.270.
6. *Principle*, p.7.
7. *Value*, p.20.

depth, to give up the materialism and self-absorption which pervade modern industrial or "mechanical" civilization. In the first lecture of <u>The Value and Destiny of the Individual</u> the following passage is encountered:

"...we must say, I think, that the mood of false absoluteness and self-satisfaction in finite attainment is of sin, and the value of what is so attained, though contributory to the Absolute, is not offered to it, and therefore does not attach to its author, just in so far as he claims it for his own. The mood in question corresponds especially today to the aberrations of a mechanical civilization, which has lost in the accumulation of means that recognition of the end which is one with the true sense of the nature of the finite".[1]

What we need to know, then, is the true nature of the finite; and Bosanquet's view of this is most quickly gathered from a quotation from Keats which he gives at great length. We will cite only the most relevant passage, in which the "drame du salut" emerges as the theme of Bosanquet's philosophy:

"The common cognomen of this world among the misguided and superstitious is 'a vale of tears', from which we are to be redeemed by a certain arbitrary interposition of God and taken to Heaven. What a little circumscribed straitened notion! Call the world if you please 'The Vale of Soul-making'... Then you will find out the use of the world..."[2]

Taking Keats' reference to "the Vale of Soul-making" as his point of departure, Bosanquet proceeds to present the universe (in Houang's metaphor) as the stage on which a cosmic drama is played out, a drama in which the absolute writes the script, directs the action, takes every part, comprises the audience, moves the scenery, and creates the sets.[3] The soul-making upon which the whole action centres is the achievement of freedom by finite creatures who are called upon to transcend themselves in an endeavour to realize a more comprehensive identity.

---

1. <u>Ibid</u>., p.20.
2. <u>Ibid</u>., p.64, quoted by Bosanquet from A.C.Bradley, <u>Oxford Lectures</u>, p.222.
3. <u>Le Néo-Hégélianisme en Angleterre</u>, op.cit., p.139.

Bosanquet's answer to those who followed Rousseau in finding modern civilization too complex and too rough for them would be a frank recognition that soul-making is not a pleasant matter. He was fond of describing the world as a furnace, having in mind "Ibsen's man with the ladle in Peer Gynt, who comes to recast those who have not proved themselves to possess a self really of their own".[1] But it is a thing to be welcomed, for (as we have seen) suffering and privation are also opportunities.

This doctrine could obviously lend itself to social quietism: too much insistence on suffering as one's chance to make something of oneself might produce that very acquiesence in the condition of the mass which both Green and Bosanquet were so concerned to dispel. To what extent it did produce this result in Bosanquet's hands will be more extensively discussed in the chapter on his politics, but it must be noticed immediately that Bosanquet was very hostile to those who could not recognize that in the existing order of reality they have everything they could really desire. Their difficulties, he feels, arise because they judge the universe from the standpoint of individualistic justice. Such a standpoint inevitably leads to pessimism, a pessimism which asks, for example, What had this man done or his parents that he was born blind? Such narrowly-conceived questions find no answer,[2] and produce a "wearisome sentimentalism" which seeks a compensation to be found in a life beyond the grave.[3] They find no answer because the juridical framework which they presuppose is inadequate to express that real unity enjoyed by each of us with God, man, and nature which is the essence of the matter, whatever the appearance.[4]

It may well be true that those who refuse to believe that this is the best of all possible worlds are guilty of adopting an abstract juridical standpoint, but this criticism does nothing to justify a more optimistic view; in itself it is quite negative. The ultimate basis of Bosanquet's answer to the pessimists is a disputable personal conviction, according to which "... the sense of unity and reconciliation with the world beyond us is a far larger

---

1. Value, p.324, n.3.
2. Ibid., p.146.
3. Ibid., p.156.
4. Ibid., p.xxv.

factor in our awareness of selfhood....than is the sense of collision with the not-self."[1] To Bosanquet, however, this conviction did not appear disputable; its truth was "quite plain".[2]

Although Bosanquet applies the idea of negativity to the struggle for salvation he does so only at the individual and moral level. The struggle, is conceived of in purely personal terms, in spite of his strictures upon an abstract, juridically-conditioned individualism. It is true that the formal subject of the three stages through which the struggle for salvation passes is "mind", and not the individual mind, but the first and third stages which this subject is intended to comprehend remain problematic. The first level, at which "selves" are not yet present and sentience is the highest form of consciousness,[3] requires an all-embracing teleology for its justification, yet Bosanquet is very obscure in his discussion of this crucial concept. At the beginning of the Principle of Individuality and Value he states firmly that teleology cannot be applied to the whole, because "it can express nothing but a necessity for change founded upon a whole which constitutes the situation to be modified, and, in that, the need for modification".[4] In The Meeting of Extremes in Contemporary Philosophy, on the other hand, Bosanquet elaborates a teleological view which does apply to the whole, although only at the cost of rendering its appearance in time unintelligible. There the absolute is described as the source of the spatio-temporal world, and as being suggested everywhere in it, but as lying beyond it, since "this is not in ultimate reality a universe of time and change".[5]

If the first stage in the journey of mind towards self-knowledge and salvation is obscure, the third stage is no less obscure. The main difficulty is to determine how far Bosanquet is prepared to go in characterizing the absolute as a self; he is much more reserved on this question than Green. That he would be prepared to go a considerable way in the direction of so doing is suggested by two considerations. In the first place, he criticises that sense

---

1. Principle, p.248.
2. Ibid., p.248.
3. Value., p.76.
4. Principle, p.16.
5. Meeting, p.216.

of self which Bradley had condemned as purely finite (on the ground that it always implied an "other"), and instead takes self-consciousness as being "the recognition of self *in* others as experienced in cognition, practice, the aesthetic attitude, and religion".[1] To be a self, in Bosanquet's view, is not to be an object to oneself as subject, but is "the recognition in externality of a counterpart, whether discordant or harmonious, with its own principle".[2] When this view is taken in conjunction with his insistence that the infinite is the finite perfected, it appears to suggest that the absolute is a self.[3] In the second place, he expresses the hope that his lectures on metaphysics may have opened the way "to a deeper conception of reality, formed at least on the analogy of self-consciousness".[4] Against these considerations, however, must be set his conviction that the absolute transcends all forms of finite experience. Probably the best way of characterizing his position on this question is to say that he is less ambitious than Green and less sceptical than Bradley and, we may add, than Oakeshott.[5]

We appear, then, to be left with only one intelligible stage - that of the hazards and hardships of the self which considers itself (falsely, in Bosanquet's view) to be self-sufficient. Bosanquet's endeavour to convict this stage of complete abstraction is unconvincing because the condition which is portrayed by contrast as the concrete reality is itself abstractly conceived. His attack upon individualism, in short, remains without an ultimate anchor.

Although the unity of self which Bosanquet finds at the end of the Pilgrim's Progress may be too blank and problematic to be gladly welcomed, we noted at

---

1. Principle, p.221, note 1; emphasis added.
2. Ibid., p.221, note 1.
3. Cf. Houang, Le Néo-Hégélianisme en Angleterre, op.cit., p.212.
4. Principle, p.222.
5. An anticipatory remark may be in place at this point. It is in Oakeshott's philosophy that the distinctive contribution of English thought to idealist metaphysics - viz. the notion of individuality as the criterion of truth and reality - is most clearly discernible, for there the criterion of individuality is completely disengaged for the first time from the influence of Hegelian philosophy which led Green and, to a lesser extent, Bosanquet and Bradley, to associate perfect individuality with absolute selfhood. The consequence of so doing remains to be seen.

the outset that there is an aspect of his thought which appears to be capable of providing a counter to the charge that he places no value on the finite self and begins by failing even to recognize the reality of the subject-matter of social theory, viz. the existence of separate selves. It is not a very effective counter because it is a logical doctrine in the narrow sense, i.e. it has no necessary implications for reality. The doctrine referred to is Bosanquet's conception of the concrete universal. It may be approached most easily through his theory of knowledge.

The movement of knowledge towards concrete individuality, or comprehension of the central experiences, passes through three phases or levels. There is (1) the common sense assertion; at this level the object is the concrete of sense, which is an apparently self-existent individual, e.g. a tree. The object has not yet been sundered by the activity of intellectual analysis. (2) At the second level we have generalization or scientific law; this level is characterized by its hypothetical affirmation of reality. It occurs when an attempt is made to bring the particulars of sense-perception into some relationship with each other. Bosanquet refers to the object of thought at this level as the "abstract of reflection". (3) Finally, there is the categorical assertion of ultimate reality in systematic thought. The concrete of thought is its object, and this is "a self-existent individual or one as nearly so as anything can be". As examples of the concrete of thought Bosanquet instances the universe, the soul, the British Constitution, the state of the moral world. In these entities a far higher individuality and concreteness and self-existence are achieved than is the case with a tree or house.[1] At the third level finite spirit includes far more of its not-self than it does at the other levels: it is this fact to which Bosanquet refers in speaking of the concrete of thought as more "self-existent" than the concrete of perception or the abstract of reflection. How far finite spirit can include its other, and hence approximate absolute experience, is a question we will consider shortly.

The main obstacle to the attainment of concrete knowledge of the finite

---

1. Letters, ed. Muirhead, p.186.

self and to an understanding of the nature of value is the prejudice which "sees in the individual not a positive cosmos, with its own logic and organisation, expressive, in spite of its immediate unity, of a determinate being, but an empty and exclusive point, whose spontaneity and purposiveness mean an initiative that draws upon no positive source, and focusses in itself no positive striving of the universe".[1] In philosophy this prejudice expresses itself in the determination to find release from contradiction in generalization. Generalization, however, is inadequate to grasp concrete reality, for a generalization never speaks of things in their whole and fundamental nature. It always fixes upon a particular aspect of things, some shared quality, and ignores their other features. It pursues identity apart from difference.[2] In order to take account of things in their full determinacy, we must abandon the idea of a generalization or class and work with the idea of a cosmos or world. Bosanquet explains the difference between these two conceptions as follows:

"A world or cosmos is a system of members, such that every member, being ex hypothesi distinct, nevertheless contributes to the unity of the whole in virtue of the peculiarities which constitute its distinctness. And the important point for us at present is the difference of principle between a world and a class. It takes all sorts to make a world; a class is essentially of one sort only. In a world, the difference is that the ultimate principle of unity or community is fully exemplified in the former, but only superficially in the latter. The ultimate principle, we may say, is sameness in the other; generality is sameness in spite of the other; universality is sameness by means of the other".[3]

This then is the doctrine of the concrete universal, conceived (as we have noticed) rather narrowly, as a phenomenon of thought alone. This narrowness makes it difficult to assign any great significance to the predicate "concrete", but Bosanquet considered that the doctrine is particularly valuable

---

1. *Principle*, pp.80-81.
2. *Ibid.*, pp.31-35.
3. *Principle*, p.37.

for the explanation of society. It provides him, in particular, with a means of determining the limitations of the different standpoints from which society may be studied; some of the standpoints work with categories which make it impossible to comprehend the nature of social unity and therefore render the problem of political obligation intractable. Bosanquet criticizes in particular the standpoints adopted by sociology, psychology, economics, and jurisprudence, and contrasts their abstractness with the concrete nature of philosophical method. Sociology and psychology originate as extensions of the method of the natural sciences to a field previously denied to it. Both claim to be value-free or impartial in their study of mind, impartiality being taken as a characteristic of natural science.[1] Both thereby make the mistake of explaining the higher forms of life by reducing them to the level of those which are commonly held to be the lower.[2] Both deal with the laws of aggregation and of the behaviour of aggregates as such, although sociology deals with social aggregates while psychology deals with mental elements. In other words, both treat their subject-matter as composed of atoms, and therefore use the concept of class to explain it (for laws are generalizations about classes). Bosanquet regards political economy as "still the only part of ((sociology)) which is obviously and indisputably successful as a science of explanation",[3] but denies its claim to be the absolute science of society since this involves elevating distinctions into separations; in other words, activities connected with earning a living are isolated from the complexity of the life of which they are aspects and are then turned into "material causes" of the other elements in that life.[4] Jurisprudence is more satisfactory than the empirical disciplines just mentioned since it does not deny reality to the normative aspects of society: the idea of law involves the idea of something which ought to be obeyed. But jurisprudence is nonetheless abstract, since "the legal personality already presupposes a stage of

---

1. Science, p.238.
2. Ibid., p.238; P.T.S. pp. 20 and 46.
3. P.T.S. p.26.
4. P.T.S. p.28.

individuality which transcends it. Legal personality represents the social machinery, the mechanism of definite co-operation. But the social spirit which sustains it must be beyond the system which it sustains".[1] Only in philosophy, then, does one find a mode of explanation which takes account of the full nature of things, and so does justice to the ethical aspect of the state. Only by philosophy is the state recognized as a <u>concrete</u> universal.

We began the discussion of the concrete universal by remarking that it provided Bosanquet with a counter to the charge of destroying the finite self, since the doctrine appears to emphasise variety rather than sameness; we had in mind in particular Bosanquet's contention that "it takes all sorts to make a world." We have noticed one objection to the doctrine, viz. that it is not really very concrete, but there is another. It is that, in the last resort, Bosanquet turns even the concrete universal into only a further means of destroying finite selfhood. This happens because the idea of concrete universality is developed by him in conjunction with the criterion of individuality. This means that concreteness is identified with comprehensiveness or inclusiveness (i.e. with the maximization of individuality), with the consequence that we find once again that we must recognize a "dangerous immediate" in what we ordinarily call our self.

It is now fairly clear which of the two Bosanquets, identified at the beginning, gains the upper-hand in his metaphysics. It is the first Bosanquet for whom the emphasis always falls upon the whole, the Bosanquet who found in <u>Appearance and Reality</u> a work only "telling him his own dream" because he saw in it a modern restatement of the doctrines expounded by Plato in the <u>Republic</u> and the <u>Symposium</u>.[2] We may indicate the result which follows from the triumph of the Platonic Bosanquet by referring briefly to an illustration of the implication of his theory on individuality given by Bosanquet in the course of his treatment of value.

---

1. <u>Principle</u>, p.285.
2. <u>Letters</u>, ed. Muirhead, pp.26-27.

In order to show the falsity of any view which maintains that individuals "... cannot be unified in their contributions to a common experience",[1] Bosanquet takes the theory of slavery which, he writes, "applies in principle to all imperfection and reciprocal supplementation of consciousness in all society whatever".[2] This is a surprising statement; not many philosophers would single out the theory of slavery as presenting the clue to all social organization. According to the theory of slavery, slaves "...severally take on the character of that to which they are instrumental, in as far as each of them, by thought and loyalty (not merely as a means), transcends its immediate self and is absorbed in the total result."[3] In the same way the loyal servant of the statesman or scholar takes a value from the latter's work - "he is in and through it a participant in the perfection of the whole..." This is an argument which (we shall see) will recur frequently in Bosanquet's political thought. What is left in doubt is the status of those who do not "by thought and loyalty" transcend their immediate selves and immerse themselves in the total result. Are they merely distinct centres, and as such without value? The suspicion that they are gains ground when Bosanquet writes, a little further on, that the example is intended to illustrate that "It is possible for a consciousness to have, its end, its explanation and value, in what it shares with another consciousness, and what is incompletely present in itself alone";[5] This suspicion is further confirmed when Bosanquet makes clear, in the same paragraph, that he is following Plato. "All this", he writes, "is involved to a careful reader in the class-system of Plato's Republic".[6] And to leave no doubt about what is involved in Plato's Republic he writes that "When you have admitted the necessity of the person with himself, it is impossible to stop short of his unity with others, with the world, and with the universe; and the perfection by which he is to be valued is his place in the perfection

---

1. *Principle*, p.314.
2. *Ibid.*, p.314.
3. *Ibid.*, p.314.
4. *Ibid.*, p.314.
5. *Ibid.*, p.314.
6. *Ibid.*, p.315.

of these greater wholes".[1] Although Bosanquet modifies his position at one point and acknowledges that we have in the ideas just mentioned only "a partial theory of the slave's position," a theory which "does not excuse the special incidents of slavery",[2] the theoretical foundation for this modification is not discussed, and hence there is nothing to compel us to qualify the foregoing remarks.

Conclusion

It appears, then, that Bosanquet's conviction that "...social life and experience is that of one mind in a number of bodies, whose consciousnesses, formally separate, are materially identical in very different degrees",[3] seriously erodes the reality of the finite self. The objection to this is not primarily the moral one, that it tends to minimize the importance of individual consent in social relationships; it is the logically prior one, that by depriving the finite centre of its ultimate character Bosanquet begins by getting rid of the very datum from which morality and politics arise. If there are not really different _persons_, but only one mind in different _bodies_, then there is no political problem; or if it is believed that there really is a political problem, even though there are not different persons but only one mind in different _bodies_, then that problem must arise from selfishness, from failure (that is) of selves to realize that they are really one and to act accordingly. In either case politics (terrestrial politics, at any rate) are not respectable, and Bosanquet must take it as the premiss of all political discussion that politics are a transient phenomenon, to be abolished as soon as possible. This, then, is the result of the triumph of the Platonic Bosanquet, the Bosanquet who admired Charlotte Mary Yonge.[4]

---

1. _Principle_, p.315.
2. Ibid., p.314.
3. Ibid., p.314.
4. It may be helpful to summarize Bosanquet's attitude towards each of the three theses around which the idealist argument has centred. (1) He accepts the unity of subject and object, although he maintains that absolute experience is beyond the capacity of finite beings. (2) He appears tempted at times to identify the absolute as a self, but hesitates to do so. (3) His acceptance of the criterion of individuality places the stress upon the content of experience and involves a rejection of the ultimate reality and value of human personality.

Chapter 6

Oakeshott

If Seth is right - and we think that he is - in maintaining that "the nerve of Neo-Hegelianism is supplied by Hegel's professed exhibition of existence as the process of a (universal) self",[1] then Oakeshott must be regarded as having introduced a radical modification into English idealism.[2] Even Bradley, whose sceptical mood makes him the closest to Oakeshott of all the English idealists, concluded Appearance and Reality on a note which leaves him very much closer to Hegel than to Oakeshott: he wrote that "...my whole view may be taken as based on the self; nor again could I doubt that a self or a system of selves, is the highest thing that we have".[3]

Taking the three theses which we distinguished at an earlier stage, we find that while Oakeshott (1) accepts that the real is the rational, and seeks to demonstrate the identity of thought with reality, he denies (2) that experience may be considered as a process in which greater recognition of its nature is achieved by a universal self, and denies also that (3) the individual personality is absolutely real or valuable.

It would be extremely difficult to determine in detail the extent of Oakeshott's indebtedness to other philosophers, but some general directions of sympathy may be discerned. To Green, it may be observed immediately, he owes nothing. From Hegel and from Bosanquet he appears to take the conception of experience as thought or judgment, departing in this respect from Bradley's emphasis upon immediate experience or feeling as our sole means of access to reality. From Hegel, again, he takes the conception of philosophical experience as absolute experience, refusing to follow Bradley and Bosanquet in maintaining the ultimate inability of thought to comprehend reality. But he rejects Hegel's conception of experience as the movement of Geist, accepting

---

1. Hegelianism and Personality, op.cit., p.225.
2. Cf. J.H.Muirhead, The Platonic Tradition in Anglo-Saxon Philosophy, op.cit., p.420: "The emphasis on the idea of the Self, as something primary in experience and providing the basis of an ontology, may be said to be the keynote of modern as contrasted with ancient and medieval philosophy."
3. Appearance and Reality, 2nd. ed., reprinted 1962, p.497.

instead the criterion of individuality (or principle of non-contradiction) developed by Bradley and Bosanquet. While abandoning the Hegelian dialectic he refuses, however, to follow Bradley and Bosanquet in seeking to distinguish degrees of reality: his position on this question resembles that of Bradley in those more sceptical moods in which he negated one appearance after another, without hope of taking each up in a process in which an abstract position is sublated in a relatively more concrete position. Instead of an ascending scale of experiential forms, Oakeshott finds in experience a number of modes, each of which is unrelated to the others and makes no positive contribution to absolute experience. But although he resembles Bradley in emphasising, in the end, the negative character of each mode, he differs from him in an important respect. In Oakeshott's thought the emphasis on negation does not (at first sight) produce the final divorce of appearance from reality with which Bradley concluded. He thus escapes (to some extent) the charge that Caird brought against Bradley, that Bradley's knife was "all blade and no handle".[1]

By the conception of modality, again, Oakeshott endeavours to perform a rather remarkable feat, when dealing with the individual self. He manages to adopt a position which is distinguished both from personal idealism and from absolute idealism, in that he manages to maintain the indefeasibility of the finite centre of consciousness without destroying its universality, and to maintain its universality without "extinguishing" the finite centre in the absolute.

The development of a philosophic system may be likened in some respects to the creation of a model which becomes progressively more complicated as additional pieces are added to it. In the mind of the maker the model is complete and concrete from the start, but the actual framework as it first appears is bare and has to be filled in. So it is with Oakeshott's argument. His concern is to take the broadest of all categories, experience, and to develop and enrich it until it can accommodate every philosophical question put to it. His initial contention that experience is the concrete whole is

---

1. Jones (Sir H.) and Muirhead (J.H.), The Life and Philosophy of Edward Caird, 1921, p.206.

necessarily an anticipatory remark - the category, like the framework of the model, remains stark and unhelpful until the structure and detail have been completed. The contention, specifically, is that "'Experience' stands for the concrete whole which analysis divides into 'experiencing' and 'what is experienced'".[1] The difficulty confronting us in comprehending the significance of the term experience as here used arises from our tendency to think of it as the empty vessel created by abstracting all the contents or objects which we begin by presupposing to be outside it. For Oakeshott, however, this is not the case: the key word in the definition of experience is "analysis". Experience itself is a unity, a one, a whole, and any divisions made within it are analytical abstractions, useful within their limits and for their purpose but always liable to be mistaken for entities existing separately. We thus encounter at the outset a central theme of idealism, that of the difference between "separating" and "distinguishing". The great failure of previous philosophy, all idealists from Hegel onwards agree, was to create separation and hence antithesis in inappropriate fields. Some referred to this error as the peculiar vice of what they called "the Understanding" or "the Popular Philosophy".[2] The problems which resulted they would recognize as in some sense "pseudo-problems", if we may be permitted to apply to them a phrase which has acquired wide currency in recent philosophy.

Oakeshott's method throughout his treatment of the nature of experience is fundamentally simple: it is to take the things or concepts which have been held to be separable (as opposed to being distinguishable) and to show that absurdity or contradiction necessarily results from such separations. Examples of concepts which have been treated as separable are subject and object, experience and thought, thought and reality. A necessary postulate of this method is that the real is the rational,[3] which may also be expressed as a

---

1. Ibid., p.9.
2. See, for example, Green's essay, Popular Philosophy in Its Relation to Life, Works, Vol. III, p.92.
3. Experience, p.58.

commitment to the law of non-contradiction as the governing principle of metaphysics. It should immediately be added that this postulate or commitment does not remain such - it is eventually taken up and examined, in no sense being left as an ultimately arbitrary axiom of philosophy. The method, again, might quite appropriately be referred to as dialectical, but we shall see that Oakeshott himself finds nothing in the nature of experience to justify the pregnant sense which the word dialectic has in Hegel. His initial category of experience does not have built into it anything resembling Hegel's theory of Geist. On the contrary, the determinations or specific qualities which experience assumes are set on one side by Oakeshott as arrests or blind allies to be fervidly eschewed by the determined philosopher; they are not to be welcomed as increasingly fruitful developments in the eternal game in which Hegel took Geist to be engaged. But now the current flows too fast and we must pause to consider in detail the ways in which Oakeshott uses his philosophic method to clarify the character of experience. His first topic, the separation of subject from object, provides a good example.

Within experience two sides may be distinguished, those of an experiencing subject and an object experienced. But to <u>separate</u> the two sides must result in absurdity or contradiction, for "the character of what is experienced is, in the strictest sense, correlative to the manner in which it is experienced." Thus whatever is true of the one side will be true also of the other. Oakeshott next turns to consider the consequences of further divisions or separations which have been made in experience; he pays particular attention to the division which has sometimes been made between thought on the one hand, and mere consciousness, sensation, perception, volition, intuition, and feeling, on the other hand. Without denying the legitimacy of these distinctions for appropriate purposes, Oakeshott's concern in each case is to show that contradictions result when thought is taken as simply one part of experinece and as absolutely distinguishable from the other parts. Specifically, his thesis that "experience is a single whole, within which modifications may be distinguished, but which admits of no final or absolute division; and that experience everywhere, not merely is inseparable from thought, but is itself a form of thought."[1] Thought is identified with judgment by Oakeshott at the outset. Judgment is not one form of experience, but is itself the concrete whole of experience.[2] It is difficult perhaps to see what might entitle judgment as such to this claim of concreteness, but Oakeshott in emphasizing the identity of experience with thought or judgment avoids the divorce which Bradley had opened up between thought and reality when he defined judgment as "the act which refers an ideal content (recognized as such) to a reality beyond the act".[3] We may elaborate a little upon the relation between Oakeshott's and Bradley's theory of the judgment, for it was this theory of the judgment which had determined what Bradley took to be the true nature of dialectic,[4] and consequently the mode of progression in the argument of Ethical Studies; we may also touch briefly upon their differences over the possibility of immediate experience and of intuitive knowledge of it.

For Bradley, all judgment took the form of a subject and predicate. Thought or judgment is an attempt to attach a predicate, which has been separated from existence by thought, to a subject. We come immediately to Bradley's problem of relations: all thought must be essentially relational, since the predicate is always the adjective of existence and never existence itself. This meant, for Bradley, that knowledge of the Absolute (which is a unity) must be intuitive knowledge, for the relational character of thought will prevent the unity of the Absolute from being grasped by it. Intuitive knowledge, then, is knowledge in which relation gives way to identity. Bradley's argument, we fear, must be regarded as specious. The source of his difficulty lies close to hand. While belabouring the assumptions of contemporary empiricist logicians, he has obviously ended by himself accepting their basic assumption, viz. that judgment is to be identified with the proposition, which is itself based upon the sentence. Hence his obsession with the subject-predicate distinction, a distinction never to be transcended as long as thought (which is essentially propositional in form) exists. Oakeshott does not explicitly

---

1. Ibid., p.10.
2. Ibid., p.11.
3. Principles of Logic, op.cit., p.10.
4. This is discussed by R.W.Church, in Bradley's Dialectic, Allen & Unwin, London, 1942.

make these criticisms of Bradley, but that they would convey his view is clear from his remark that "Judgments, in the sense of propositions in which predicate and subject are separate and remain separated from beginning to end, are the mere deposits of concrete experience."[1]

If we bear in mind that Bradley's attack on the form of the judgment (or proposition, taking the term in its denotation for him) was inevitably an attack on the structure of reality, we have the background to some sentences by Oakeshott which might well puzzle those not conversant with idealist literature. Thus when Oakeshott writes that "Thinking is not the mere qualification of existence by an idea; it is a qualification of existence by itself, which extends, in the end, to a qualification of the whole of existence by its whole character",[2] and that "In its full character thought is not the explicit qualification of existence by an idea, but the self-revelation of existence",[3] he is only denying that reality or experience can be seen as a bare indeterminate unity, and is claiming that the very relational character of thought impugned by Bradley is a necessary feature of thought which seeks to be adequate to reality; it is not to be mistaken for a mark of thought's poverty. Of course, thought and reality are not _merely_ relational, but the source of the unity of relations is a question we will ignore for the moment. Relating the foregoing to the view which holds that we can have intuitive knowledge of immediate experience, we are now in a position to recognize that the conception of reality which lies behind intuitionism is such as to reduce it to a nonentity, by making reality so free from thought that it disappears.

Experience, however, is not merely thought: it is always a "world of ideas". It is through the idea of a world that Oakeshott eventually presses experience to the point where it ceases to be merely "ours" and becomes identical with truth and reality. The notion of a world, when elaborated, turns out to be eseentially identical with the criterion of individuality used by Bradley and Bosanquet; it must, of course, be supplemented with the ideas of comprehensiveness and non-contradiction before it becomes the master-key to concrete reality.

---

1. _Experience_, p.24.
2. _Ibid._, p.24.
3. _Ibid._, p.24.

Oakeshott first seeks to establish that "Truth is the condition of the world of experience in which that world is satisfactory to itself".[1] At least we are not to be asked to jump out of our skins, as it were, in order to find it. The method by which Oakeshott establishes this conclusion is already familiar in its general character: any other position is shown to be absurd because it separates truth from experience, thereby rendering the word meaningless. The advantage of the coherence theory of truth, including Oakeshott's form of it, is that it makes it possible for us to recognize that as thought advances beyond what at first merely presents itself, we are not really moving from contact with reality into an abstract world but are recognizing the given more accurately, and in so doing are nearing (and not departing from) truth. Bertrand Russell, a critic of the coherence theory of truth, has argued that it allows anything at all to be called true provided only that we can think of some other proposition, which would entail what we wish to assert.[2] But Oakeshott has an answer to this: Russell's difficulty arises because he confuses coherence with conceivability.[3] We can indeed conceive of anything we wish, but the coherence theory requires us to bring in the idea of completeness or system: a true proposition must harmonize with the whole of experience, and not only with some isolated piece of it:

"...no particular idea can be true, for particular ideas are abstractions such as cannot be supposed to afford satisfaction in experience".[4]

We have seen that in all experience there is judgment, and also that truth is not destroyed by being experienced or known. We come now to Oakeshott's third and final step: thought (or experience) and reality are identical. Oakeshott can only understand how they ever came to be separated by referring once again to the difference between distinguishing and separating: analytical abstractions were mistaken for existent entities, "with the result that knowledge becomes one unit and reality another, and we

---

1. Ibid., pp.27-28.
2. B. Russell, Philosophical Essays, London 1910, p.156.
3. Experience, pp.35-36.
4. Ibid., p.48.

are puzzled how to relate them".[1] What Oakeshott wishes to establish is that "Reality is experience, not because it is made real by being known, but because it cannot without contradiction be separated from knowledge".[2]

Oakeshott rests considerable weight upon the argument that to deny reality can be known, is itself to assert a piece of knowledge about reality.[3] He must therefore meet the objection raised by Russell in The Problems of Philosophy,[4] that the argument rests upon a confused use of the word "knowledge". Russell distinguishes between knowledge by actual acquaintance with things and knowledge about things, in order to show that things could exist (i.e. be real) apart from our experience and knowledge.[5] But Russell's concept of knowledge by acquaintance, on which his argument depends, is knowledge without judgment,[6] and such knowledge has already been shown by Oakeshott to be incompatible with the nature of experience; and Russell's position also involves the more radical claim that we can never know anything as it really is.[7] Oakeshott finds such a position quite meaningless; it involves restricting the real arbitrarily, when the truth is that "reality, whatever else it is, cannot be a thing amongst things; it must be everything, and has not even the alternative of being nothing".[8] No part of reality can be thrust outside experience without absurdity.

If thought and reality are identical, can we then conjure "things" out of thought? Oakeshott thinks we can, but there is no magic involved. What is to be avoided is the pursuit of thinghood apart from relations.[9] But Oakeshott also recognizes that a unifying principle is required: nothing can be constructed wholly out of relations.[10] Unifying principles differ, of course:

---

1. Ibid., p.49.
2. Ibid., p.50.
3. Ibid., p.50.
4. H.U.L. London, 1912.
5. Ibid., pp.69-70.
6. Ibid., p.73.
7. Ibid., p.75.
8. Experience, p.50.
9. Ibid., p.62.
10. Ibid., p.62.

Oakeshott distinguishes several in *Experience and Its Modes*, and they are what create the different modes, in each of which different things appear. The principle upon which the relations in any particular mode are unified is located by establishing the presuppositions of that mode. In this way Oakeshott gets over the problem of relations encountered by Bradley at the beginning of *Appearance and Reality* and never solved by him. Bradley began with a lump of sugar (a thing) which dissolved into its qualities of whiteness, sweetness and hardness before his gaze; he was never able to put it together again because he could not find the principle of its unity.[1] Oakeshott's solution would be to point to the fact that an individuating principle (that of will) is already contained in what Bradley took to be a mere object on the one hand and pure relations on the other: hardness, sweetness etc. can only occur (for Oakeshott) where the presuppositions of the world of practice are already present. The only perfect thing, of course, will be the absolute, for the quality of thinghood is the attribute of unity and totality.[2] There are, consequently, degrees of reality or thinghood, although Oakeshott is not concerned to distinguish them: he is content to claim that whatever is not absolutely real is (whatever degree of reality it may have) completely unsatisfactory, from the standpoint of absolute experience. He tries to prevent the philosophical destruction of things which are less than absolutely real by allowing that they are real from another standpoint, that of some arrested phase of experience. It is in this way that he seeks to avoid Bradley's ruthless scepticism.

What is the relationship between thought, truth and reality? We said at the beginning that philosophising is like constructing a model: the early stages of the construction are incomplete in relation to the final construction. This brings out a point of great significance, which is that we have not moved aimlessly between three different standpoints from which experience may be regarded but have moved from positions in which less than its due was given to experience (the positions from which it appeared as mere thought or as true,

---

1. *Appearance and Reality*, 2nd ed. 9th impression, reprinted 1962, p.16.
2. *Experience*, p.62.

but true only _for us_), to that in which experience was recognized to be always some one's experience and yet to be true or false, real or unreal, in spite of what anyone in particular may think. The first two standpoints were, in fact, abstractions from the concrete position yielded by the third standpoint.

What emerges from the argument so far is a convincing refutation of the notions of metaphysics, logic and epistemology which we outlined in chapter 2. The division between subject and object and the view of ideas which give rise to the epistemological problem; the conception of isolated propositions as capable of truth or falsity, and of the association of ideas as the means by which we move from one proposition to the next; and the conception of reality as lying beyond common ken - all these conceptions are overturned. This we may refer to as the critical phase of Oakeshott's thought, and of idealism in general, in so far as he can be said to have stated its _minimal tenets_. We think this phase is completely successful. But what has Oakeshott to offer by way of a positive contribution? Before we can answer that we must consider the concept of modality developed by Oakeshott.

To be told that thought, truth and reality become identical in coherent experience is helpful, but it sheds no light on the main problem of philosophy, which Oakeshott refers to as "the fact of diversity".[1] To our disappointment the question which every ambitious metaphysician has sought to answer, _why_ there is diversity in experience, Oakeshott sets aside as "beyond my purpose".[2] In fact, he does not really set it aside, for he does have an answer, which soon reveals itself. Diversity in experience occurs when the effort to achieve complete coherence in experience fails. Failure results in the creation of an abstract world of ideas, and what philosopher can become interested in a determinacy which is synonymous with abstraction? The mode, however, differs from absolute reality only in its degree of coherence. Because there are no absolute divisions within experience every mode is the whole of

---

1. Ibid., p.69.
2. Ibid., p.70.

experience, but the whole as seen from a particular standpoint. Diversity, then, presents two aspects. Under the first of these aspects it appears as an arrest in experience, the arbitrary abandonment of the pursuit of coherence at a particular point. To call experience arrested is only possible, of course, when the standpoint from which it is being viewed is the absolute or concrete one of philosophy. Under the second aspect diversity appears as a specific world of ideas, a world which claims to be considered as it exists for itself. In this perspective it is self-contained and bears no relationship to other modes of experience or to philosophy. The same point may be put in other ways. When a mode is considered as it exists for itself, it is real. When it is considered as it exists for philosophy, it is demoted to the level of appearance. Or, again, when it is considered as it exists for itself, we only consider its explicit character and criterion of reality, whilst its presuppositions or its implicit character are ignored. When the implicit assumptions are explored we have reverted once again to the pursuit of absolute coherence — we have returned, that is, to philosophy. Once more, the mode may be described as philosophy or as concrete experience, but as possessing this character only in potentiality.

Two further characteristics of Oakeshott's conception of modality require to be noticed. There is, in the first place, no theoretical limit to the number of possible modes.[1] Secondly, Oakeshott differs from Hegel and Bosanquet in rejecting any conception of modes "as necessary to experience and unavoidable".[2] This contention is perhaps the most sceptical and controversial element in his philosophy, and more will be said about it when the exposition of his argument has been concluded.

We must now consider how Oakeshott understands the relationship between the modes themselves. On this question too he differs radically from Hegel and those influenced by him, notably Bosanquet, and Collingwood in Speculum Mentis. Oakeshott's answer is simple: there is no direct relationship at

---

1. Ibid., p.75.
2. Ibid., p.75.

all between the modes. Specifically, he seeks to establish two propositions, viz. that each abstract world of ideas is, as such and as a world, wholly and absolutely independent of any other; and that each, in so far as it is coherent, is true for itself.[1] The second proposition has already been touched upon; the first should not be taken to imply that the unity of experience has collapsed into mere diversity: that the modes have no direct relationship to each other does not make them ultimately separable realities. They are related indirectly through their common source in concrete or philosophical experience. Like the spokes in a wheel, they do not touch each other but are related through their meeting-point at the hub. The cardinal sin, for Oakeshott, is irrelevance or confusion, and this arises (in one form) when argument passes unwittingly from one mode to another. Thus the person who believed that the conclusions of science invalidated religious experience, or the historian who thought that history could prove the divinity of Christ, would be guilty of ignoratio elenchi.

We must now examine in detail the practical mode of experience. This will serve both to illustrate the general philosophical difficulties raised by Oakeshott's treatment of determinate being and also to effect the transition from his metaphysics to his political thought.

The Practical Mode: the presuppositions of action, including political activity.

We must now endeavour to bring out the implications of Oakeshott's argument in Experience and Its Modes for the philosophical understanding of politics. Two things at least we know already. That politics is real follows from the fact that it falls within experience. This may not appear to be a very substantial conclusion, but it will not appear so banal if we recall that Plato (for example) reached precisely the opposite conclusion. For him, politics was merely an incident in the world of change and becoming, and as such had no reality. In the second place, we know that political reasoning is possible - for everything which falls within experience is susceptible to questioning and assessment in terms of truth or falsity. Nothing is merely a matter of taste, and that he may choose to regard a thing as such redeems no man from the charge of vulgarity (or the encomium of elegance). This

---

1. Ibid., p.75.

conclusion is, once again, not startling. To appreciate it we must recall that Hobbes and Hume, with others, arrived at a different conclusion. Or it may be sufficient if we simply recall the wealth of sceptical implication in the common man's retort, "That is your opinion", or in the academic's more sophisticated "But that is a value-judgment". To have grasped that experience is always a world, and as such is governed always by the iron laws of implication and not solely by the fortuitous canons of taste and association, is to have made some progress. Thirdly, we know that political philosophy in the strict sense is, for Oakeshott, impossible. In the strict sense political philosophy is the attempt not merely to exhibit the place of politics in the map of experience, but to demonstrate the *necessity* of its occupying that place. Hegel is the only modern philosopher who has a well-established claim to have demonstrated that reflection on the nature of experience or the universe would, logically, force one to the conclusion that reality would be less than real if it did not contain within it the determinations of objective mind, of which the state is the highest. A more limited philosophical enterprise, such as that of Hobbes, contents itself with demonstrating the relative reality of politics by showing its irreducibility to other forms of experience: thus, for Hobbes, it is logically impossible to analyze the state without distinguishing between a natural and an artificial person, and without further distinguishing between artificial persons, the state being characterized by the possession of sovereignty. But in the end Hobbes fails to accommodate himself to the criterion by which all philosophy is to be judged: he fails to exhibit necessity, for what answer has he for the person who denies that either natural or artificial persons are ultimately real? To that extent he fails to find the place of politics in the map of experience or reality. What is clear, at any rate, is that an enterprise in political philosophy as ambitious as that of Hegel is, for Oakeshott, doomed to failure. Politics occurs within the practical mode, and, as a modal phenomenon, it is simply accepted by Oakeshott as something which may (and does) occur, but which cannot be shown to be necessary: reflection on the nature of experience, in his view, leads to no suggestion that it must be so, that reality, without the state, would be imperfect. The occurrence of politics cannot be heralded as a positive achievement on the part of the universe, or Geist, as it was by

Hegel and Bosanquet. For Oakeshott it is, from the standpoint of concrete experience, abstract, a mere distraction, and totally non-contributory. The state cannot, on his view, be said to be an essential part of the scheme of things.

Such is the character of Oakeshott's political scepticism. The label of sceptic would however, if unqualified, be inappropriate. What follows from his general philosophical position is scepticism at the metaphysical or philosophical level. And even then, (i.e. at the philosophical level) Oakeshott would, over certain areas, be optimistic if compared, say, with Hume. For he does not, as we have seen, believe that political and moral argument is merely the statement of one's own sentiments; it is possible, on his view, to argue, as opposed to talking past one's opponent.

We must now consider the implications of Oakeshott's philosophy for the problem of political obligation. He never discusses the problem as such, but it is possible to extrapolate a treatment of it from his writings.[1] The first question to be asked must be, What kind of problem would Oakeshott take it to be? This is important to decide because the answer will determine the kind of solution considered to be appropriate. If, for example, it is a philosophical problem, then only the philosopher can deal with it. On the other hand, if it is a practical problem, the solution will be practical. Oakeshott gives clearest expression to his view of this matter when discussing the nature of ethics, which he terms an indeterminate mode of experience. And his analysis of the status of ethical inquiries may legitimately be extended to political philosophy because he himself explicitly assigns "the same general character" to both inquiries.[2] We must consider, then, Oakeshott's view of the nature of ethics and, by implication, of political philosophy, but before doing so another germane difficulty must be removed. We have seen that several general conclusions about the nature of politics followed from the fact that it fell within experience. But we have not so far considered

---

1. As has been done by Benn and Peters, in Social Principles and the Democratic State, op.cit., pp.312-18.
2. Experience, p.335, footnote.

what, in Oakeshott's view, is the _specific_ character of practical knowledge, reality and truth. When, for example, we speak of the individual and of the state, what is the precise nature of their reality? Are these concepts merely embodiments of values, "the individual" being a sentiment of the liberal and democrat and "the state" being a predilection of the collectivist? Oakeshott recognizes that the general criterion of reality (the principle of coherence) renders no help in resolving such difficulties: what is required is "a detailed criterion for determining what, in experience, is abstract; and we require the detailed and conscientious application of this criterion to the actual world of experience."[1] It will eventually become clear that the examination of Oakeshott's view of political philosophy as an indeterminate arrest in experience is closely related to his examination of the criterion of reality in practice. This connection arises because, in his view, ethics and political philosophy in their most complete form are no more than the pursuit of such a criterion. When they fail to rise to this level of inquiry an arbitrary halt has been made in the process of philosophical questioning, a halt which is inspired by an unwillingness to abandon the understandable but philosophically indefensible commitment to the ultimate satisfactoriness of reality as it appears in the practical mode. This, in bare outline, is the sphere within which political philosophy is possible, for him. Its ultimate limitation is that of philosophy as a whole - the impossibility of establishing the necessity of any form of modified experience.

The next step, then, is to determine the criterion of individuation in the practical world, and to determine the relationship between reality and value. At first sight, it must be admitted, Oakeshott's analysis of these problems in Experience and Its modes appears to contain nothing of especial significance for the theory of society, for he is not explicitly concerned to discuss there whether any particular style of politics or set of political arrangements has an overriding claim to be considered as the most appropriate - he is merely concerned to ask what it is that makes anything (whether it be the Polis, the Res Publica Christiana, the Regnum, or the Individual or State is a matter of indifference) real. In short, we appear to have a purely for-

---

1. Ibid., p.83

mal analysis with no implications favouring one content rather than another. Yet this is not so.

The two fundamental themes of Oakeshott's political essays, traditionalism and rationalism, are closely related to his treatment of practice, and are most intelligible when regarded, not as elements in an independent corpus of writings, but as an extension and development of that treatment. In the case of Oakeshott's concept of tradition, the connection arises through the notion of practical coherence: the claim of a traditionalist style of politics turns ultimately upon the view that only through it is maximum coherence achieved in the world of will. In the traditionalist style the gap between "is" and "ought" is most nearly closed. Yet the nature of practice is to be unending, and the gap between is and ought can never be finally removed. This idea, developed in full only in Experience and Its Modes, leads to Oakeshott's critique of rationalism, the main objection to which is that it entirely mistakes the character of practice. In particular, it fails to realize that an end to practical problems cannot be contemplated: utopianism is not merely a moral error, it is a logical mistake. Furthermore, (which is only to put the same thing another way), rationalism ignores what, in Oakeshott's view, is the presupposition of all practice, (and hence the necessary presupposition of political activity), viz. the ultimate separateness of the entities which occur within it. This proposition requires elucidation, and will receive it in due course, but for the moment it may be noted that Oakeshott's premise of the selfishness of man rests upon this logical ground and not upon a moral one; thus it is this logical characteristic of the nature of practice which he has in mind when he writes that politics is an activity which is prepared to accept "the permanent (but not exclusive) egoism of human behaviour",[1] and that "the necessity, for the conduct of life, of maintaining the integrity and separateness of the self, which to a dramatist like Hebbel, a novelist like D.H.Lawrence, or a moralist like Kant is a matter of psychological observation or moral conviction, for us is a matter of psychological observation or moral conviction, for us is a matter of definition."[2] In short, the concept of tradition is merely the fleshing

---

1. C.J. Vol. I, 1947-48, p.355.
2. Experience, p.271.

out of the criterion of practical coherence developed in Experience and Its Modes, or, as Greenleaf puts it, a tradition "is, in fact - though Oakeshott does not use the term - what the idealists call a concrete universal";[1] while rationalism is an essentially contradictory attitude towards practice - contradictory because it fails to accommodate its aspirations to the necessary limitations of all action.

We will now consider Oakeshott's treatment of practice, with a view to illuminating the remarks just made. We will then consider the conception of ethics as an indeterminate arrest in experience, in order to clarify the logical status (for Oakeshott) of the problem of political obligation, leaving the examination of Oakeshott's detailed consideration of politics in the essays (together with such aspects of them as appear relevant to the problem of political obligation) until a later chapter.

We have already observed that certain general characteristics of the world of practice may be deduced from the fact that it falls within experience. These may be summarized in the proposition that practice is a world of ideas and hence can be known and rationally criticized, but such a summary can only be ambiguous both as to what it denies and what it asserts. It will not then be unprofitable to follow in a little more detail Oakeshott's account of the implications of this proposition. In the first place, it denies the contention that practice is concerned with action, and that action is not thought, and that practice, therefore, cannot be a world of ideas. Oakeshott's objection to such a position has been delineated in the previous chapter and need not now be elaborated. It is that anything which is not thought, anything which claims to be absolutely immediate, must be a nonentity. To act or to will is not to engage in a non-ideational process; it is itself to think.[2] More serious, however, is the objection which allows that the stuff of practice is ideas, and yet maintains that practice is not a world of ideas. Such is the belief of those who argue that in practice we find only instincts, intuitions, or mere opinions. This is the view of practice which was attributed to classical empiricism in chapter 2,[3] a view to be found most clearly

---

1. Oakeshott's Philosophical Politics, op.cit., p.55.
2. Experience, p.251.
3. Above.

expressed in Hobbes and Hume, and it amounts in essence (as was said there) to the claim that practical experience is a collection (and not a world) of ideas. Oakeshott himself, it may be noted, would reject this attribution, in the case of Hume at least, on the ground that Hume did allow the possibility of practical knowledge,[1] but there would be no serious disagreement here: the model constructed in chapter 1 was modified to take account of the sphere within which practical knowledge (and hence practical reasoning) was possible for Hume. He appears to be directing his critique more in the direction of philosophers such as G.E.Moore. The objection to any conception of experience which maintains that it can ever be reduced to a collection of ideas is, once again, already known to us. On such a view ideas are taken to be mere ideas, without relation to or implication for any other ideas, and no idea is so poor that it descends to this level. Oakeshott's refutation, then, turns upon his view that experience is always a world of ideas, and to conceive of it in terms which deny this is to assert a contradiction.[2]

Turning from the general character of practical activity, Oakeshott's next business is with the particular character of practical experience which distinguishes it from other worlds of experience. As a first approximation he offers a definition of practice: "Practical life comprises the attempts we make to alter existence or to maintain it unaltered in the face of threatened change."[3] The experiences which are to be considered as parts of the practical world include ones which may, to the ordinary man, appear unrelated to practice as he understands it. Thus "a poet, a religious mystic or an evangelist are not commonly considered 'practical' persons, and yet their lives are certainly active and consist wholly in attempts to change or maintain existence."[4] In one important respect Oakeshott subsequently modifield his view in this connection. He later distinguished a poetic mode of experience, distinct from the practical (and all other) modes of experience.

---

1. <u>Ibid.</u>,p.252.
2. <u>Ibid.</u>, p.253.
3. <u>Ibid.</u>, p.256.
4. <u>Ibid.</u>, p.257.

This development, although it has implications for the understanding of politics, may be disregarded for present purposes. The important point is that the contravention of ordinary usage and ideas never, as such, invalidates a philosophical argument. The philosopher's concern is not with what we think, in the sense of what we are conscious of thinking, but with what is implied in what we think. His endeavour is to establish the necessity of the ideas with which he is concerned, and not to prove that his view coincides with that of the ordinary man.

The initial definition, however, is inadequate as it stands. Practice is not the mere alteration of existence: it is the alteration of existence in the light of an unrealized idea, a "to be" which is "not yet". This cleavage within the world of practice, this discrepancy between the given and that which is to be achieved, is the main characteristic of the world. And it is important to realize that the discrepancy always exists, even when there is no apparent concern for explicit change but only for the maintenance of "what is". For the desire to maintain the situation is itself an idea, as yet unrealized, within the situation or "what is". Practice, or action, is the endeavour to close this gap by changing "what is" in such a way as to realize what is "to be".

Oakeshott is concerned to remove a misconception which may arise from this view. It is very difficult to avoid thinking of action as the translation of mere ideas into an external world of things. Doing a thing is thereby assumed to be of an entirely different nature from thinking about it. But the idea to be realized is never a mere idea, and the action is never a merely external or physical thing: "What volition requires and presupposes is a world in which change is possible and significant, a finite world in this sense, and not in the sense of a world which is not a world of ideas."[1]

The particular character of the world of "what is" which is presupposed in practical activity must receive more detailed consideration. It may be considered in its three aspects as practical fact, practical truth and practical reality. The outstanding characteristic of each of these aspects of the

---

1. *Ibid.*, p.259; his emphasis.

practical world - a characteristic which disconcerted Greek philosophers and Plato in particular - is their ability to be fact, truth, or reality on one day, and no fact at all, untrue or unreal the next. This apparent paradox arises necessarily from the fact that only what is transient or unstable can find a place in the world of practice. The world of practical fact is the world which is here and now: it is not only present experience (for all experience is present), but present experience as such. From this arises its vulnerability, its subjection to change: what is here and now or simply present, is forever disappearing, being replaced by another here and now. Yet a fact which loses its place in the here and now of practical existence does not thereby lose its factual character: it would only do so if action took us totally beyond the given, but it never does so, for "wherever there is action there is presupposed a world which action may modify, but which it can never wholly and in principle transform".[1] What was present fact yesterday is not present fact today: but it nonetheless remains part of the practical world, deriving its factual character from its place in that world as a whole. Practical truth, as we would expect, is the world of practical fact as a coherent whole. The acceptance of this view cannot be reconciled with a pragmatist doctrine in any of its forms, for the deficiency of that philosophy (and its close relation, Utilitarianism) is its division of experience into ideas, on the one hand, and their consequences, on the other. Such a procedure results in the destruction of any criterion of truth at all, for we are always left with the question, why are the particular consequences selected as the criterion themselves true?

In the course of his consideration of practical truth, Oakeshott appends a short footnote which is most illuminating on the question of his relationship to Hegel, Bosanquet and Green. At the outset of this chapter we said that the conception of experience with which Oakeshott commences had not the richness which the idea of Being had for Hegel. The notion of Geist, of spirit seeking to know and enjoy itself through a progressive (dialectical) development, is lacking. Why is this? the nearest Oakeshott comes to an explicit answer is in this footnote, in which he discusses the relationship between

---

1. _Ibid._, p.261.

practical truth and freedom. For Hegel and Bosanquet and Green the concept of freedom has been central not only to their moral and political philosophy but also to their metaphysics. This extended usage of the word by the more ambitious of the idealist philosophers is completely rejected by Oakeshott, and his reason for rejecting it perhaps provides the basis of his general scepticism, and (specifically) of his unwillingness to take up the problem of deducing determinacy from the nature of concrete experience (the question of *why* there should be modes, we saw, he set aside). His reason is that "Freedom I take it, is a practical idea, an idea which has relevance in the practical world of activity and nowhere else".[1] It follows from this that freedom and necessity are terms which only have meaning when they are used to describe conditions of the mind which has achieved (or failed to achieve) practical truth. In short, "they have neither meaning nor relevance for the self in scientific experience or in history, and are certainly meaningless when attributed to the universe as a whole".[2] A criticism of Oakeshott's view of the scope of the concept of freedom would have to begin by breaking down completely the basic structure of his system. It would have to show, in particular, that the modes are not mere abstractions but are essential to the concrete whole of experience, and also that they imply one another. Only in the light of such an extensive critique could intelligibility be restored to the idea of freedom when predicated of the universe as a whole. The present writer cannot attempt it, and must be content to observe that within the framework of Oakeshott's own argument, the idealists who were closest to Hegel were guilty of ignoratio elenchi: they argued from the nature of the mode to the nature of the concrete whole.

It is in the course of Oakeshott's consideration of the practical world in its aspect as practical reality that the implications of his view for politics become clearest. He chooses to cast the problem in the form of the question, What in the practical mode of experience is real or a thing? The answer is at first sight a little puzzling: "The world of practice is a world

---

1. *Ibid.*, p.267, note I.
2. *Ibid.*, p.268, note.

of things and individuals which are designated, not defined. And, consequently, the explicit criterion by which the individual is determined is that of separateness, rather than of completeness: what is fixed upon is that which is self-contained, and not that which is self-complete".[1] The difficulty is to see how the fact of designation directly implies the criterion of separateness. It does so because designation always leaves at least some questions about the nature of the thing designated unexplained, whereas definition is achieved only when every aspect of the thing has been accounted for. In other words, definition is the prerogative of philosophic experience. All non-philosophic experience ends in designation, that is, in an incomplete account of reality. Now, when fully defined the thing or individual becomes the whole: nothing is left outside it, for then the explanation or definition would be incomplete (a mere designation). And in becoming the whole it loses its individuality, for individuality implies the existence of other individuals. If the individual is expanded so as to include all other individuals, to become self-complete, then the world of practice is necessarily destroyed.

Separateness, then, is a presupposition of the practical world. Oakeshott does not himself expand this presupposition so far as to deduce the necessity of politics within the practical mode, but we can see that, while the separateness of individual persons is a fact which they may safely ignore over substantial areas of life, its existence must be recognized (and will force itself upon them) at some stage. And when separateness as such is the problem to be dealt with, we have the occurrence of politics - where the problem is that of finding some mutually acceptable set of arrangements for living together. Taking the matter a step further, we may say that Oakeshott's account of life or practice has the virtue of containing within itself a necessary place for conflict, the natural concomitant of separateness. From this logical position, as was remarked earlier, stems his opposition to rationalism, more especially in its utopian forms. Any theory (whether of love or of socialism or of religion) which demands the total sacrifice of

---

1. *Ibid.*, p.268.

individuality is not merely open to the charge of moral obnoxiousness - it can be convicted of logical absurdity: it offers a theory of the conduct of life while making life itself impossible. It is only a further application of the same argument to point to the fact that the occurrence of the problem of political obligation must be, for Oakeshott, a permanent possibility. It is logically impossible to visualize a condition of things in which there could be a final resolution of the "individual-state" antithesis. This is true of course at the theoretical level: what is not asserted is that a resolution within practice itself is impossible. Indeed, the practical political problem is precisely that of devising a set of arrangements which does not jeopardize the well-being of the individual or the community. The only significance for Oakeshott of the problem of political obligation would be, consequently, that its emergence indicated failure or incoherency in the practical world. These themes are drawn together in the following important passage:

"The practical world, because it is a world of activity and change, is a world of oppositions to be balanced (because they cannot be unified), of contradictions which (because they cannot be resolved) must be co-ordinated. The practical self and its interests can never give way before the interests of 'others'; the relationships into which it enters are external to itself; and, since in practical experience the practical self is the very embodiment of reality, its dissolution is a contradiction and inconceivable".[1]

It has been assumed in these remarks that the practical human self, as a constituent of the world of practice, is created upon the same principle of individuation as the practical individual in general. This is in fact Oakeshott's contention. There is, however, one important feature of the practical self which is lacking in other practical concepts. This is its dual aspect. The practical self is both the self which thinks practically and at the same time, the self which practical thinking recognizes in others.[2] To be aware of one's own existence is, ipso facto, to be aware of the reality of others. In other words, the self is essentially social, in the very general sense that "the will operates in a world of wills".[3]

---

1. Ibid., p.270.
2. Ibid., p.269.
3. Ibid., p.271.

Why is it that Oakeshott, unlike Hegel for example, does not try to deduce the specific social forms which the practical self must assume? Why do we not find any dialectical development through the ideas of property, contract, crime, and so on, to such concrete social forms as those of the family, civil society and the state? The answer to this question has already been adumbrated and follows from Oakeshott's general view of modality and of the scope of political philosophy. The specific entities which are recognized as real in the practical world are ultimately arbitrary. There can be no question of deducing the necessity, for example, of the practical self from the character of absolute experience. Thus Oakeshott writes, in discussing the practical self, that "It is determined, not by the inclusion of all that belongs or is related to it, but by the exclusion of all that can be shown to stand outside an <u>arbitrarily selected centre</u>."[1] The world of practice, with all its presuppositions, is (for Oakeshott) a mere occurrence, whose nature may be explored but whose raison d'être remains always unintelligible.

One of the most interesting aspects of Oakeshott's argument is its implication for the subject of free-will, a subject which idealists have never felt able to ignore in treating of the problem of political obligation and in dealing with the subject-matter of political philosophy in general. Green, for example, felt that a decision in this court must be attained before any further questions could be considered or even meaningfully stated. Freedom of the will is, for Oakeshott, a presupposition of the practical world: hence it requires no justification, no more than the mechanical conception of nature held by the scientist does. Freedom belongs to the will by definition.[2] To deny it is to call into question the autonomy of the world of practice, and this is impossible. It is impossible because the whole of Oakeshott's argument is directed to establishing that the concepts of the present as such, of change, of practical individuality, together provide a possible way of conceiving of reality, and in the end the determinist is faced with the task of showing that they do not. All denial of the freedom of the will would be an ignoratio elenchi, an attempt to import the standpoint of one of the other

---

1. <u>Ibid</u>., p.270, emphasis added.
2. <u>Ibid</u>., p.270.

modes or of philosophy into the practical mode.

The general implications which have been remarked of Oakeshott's conception of practice for the nature of political activity and the problem of political obligation are further clarified and reinforced when we turn to consider his treatment of the world of value. This reveals once again the logical grounds for Oakeshott's opposition to utopian forms of rationalism and, by implication, for his view that the problem of political obligation rests on terms which cannot be finally resolved into the one or the other without the destruction of practice as a world. In the form so far considered the antithesis between the individual and the state was one concomitant of the separations which were inevitable features of practical entities in general. In the following analysis of value, the inevitability of the same antithesis is further emphasised by being exhibited as a concomitant of the gap between is and ought, or fact and value. Hence any resolution of the problem of political obligation which requires the obliteration of this distinction (through a once-and-for-all achievement of the valued state of affairs) is a contradiction in terms. The analysis of value also reveals the logical ground of Oakeshott's predilection for piecemeal change rather than revolutionary upheaval, for it will become clear that in his view action is necessarily confined to the "<u>point-by-point</u> qualification of 'what is here and now' by 'what ought to be'" and that "Any attempt to resolve the discrepancy generally... must be made without the sympathy of practice".[1] We will see, in addition, that the practical world is not identical with concrete experience, and in this connection Oakeshott has some remarks to make which are of great importance in determining whether his attack on rationalism is a polemic[2] against any reasoning whatsoever about the conduct of moral and political life. Specifically, there will be occasion to note his contention that "It is one thing to say that there is a kind of reflection, that there are modes of thought, which will paralyse moral sensibility and make a man less, rather than more capable of leading his life, but it is quite another to say that the less a man thinks about how he is acting the more satisfactory will be

---

1. <u>Ibid</u>., p.290, emphasis added.
2. As some have taken it to be, e.g. M.Postan, Revulsion from Thought, <u>C.J</u>. I, 1947-48, pp.395-408.

his way of living".[1]

The world of value, like the world of practical fact, is a presupposition of the world of practice. Without it there would be no activity. But what is the precise character of this presupposed world of value? Oakeshott is concerned to establish four propositions which he takes to characterize it: (i) the world of value is a world of experience, it implies an assertion of reality; (ii) valuation is thinking, the attempt to make coherent a world of ideas; (iii) value is a world of being, and a judgment that "This is valuable" is, in the end, a judgment that "This exists in a certain way"; and (iv) the world of value is a mode of experience, an abstract world of ideas, an incomplete assertion of reality.[2]

The first proposition, that the world of value is a world of experience, is an inference from Oakeshott's general view of the nature of experience. Its significance lies in the rejection it implies of two opposite views of value. It implies, first of all, the rejection of any view which claims that value is objective, in that sense of objective which would make value something completely unrelated to consciousness. Any such view must fall before the objection that anything which is experienced is experienced, and anything which is not experienced is a nonentity. This argument by reductio ad absurdum is already familiar to us. Secondly, the view which goes to the opposite extreme and concludes that, because everything in experience is experienced, value (which is experienced) is therefore subjective is also to be rejected. Subjectivism in this context means a figment of our own minds, a mere idea without any relation to reality. Subjectivism in this sense was (we saw in an earlier chapter) the position towards which empiricism inevitably moved. Oakeshott distinguishes several variations within the subjectivist theory of value, according as value is identified with what interests us, with what we desire, or with what contributes to our happiness. In every case the objection is the same, viz. that in experience there are no mere ideas, no ideas which are completely subjective. There is also the further objection,

---

1. _Experience_, p.303.
2. _Ibid._, p.274.

that the subjectivist makes value a matter of mere opinion, thereby denying any place to reason in practical experience, and making disagreement about judgments of value a logical impossibility. But this cannot be so for we have seen that experience is always a world or system, and to take it for something less involves a contradiction. It is by virtue of this characteristic of experience (viz. its systematic nature) that value must also be seen to involve an assertion of reality: whatever is more than a mere idea, whatever has meaning or the power to coerce us logically, must be real (in some degree) ipso facto. The real, (we have seen) is the rational.

About the second proposition, that valuation is thinking, the attempt to make coherent a world of ideas, little need be said. Every denial of it must rest upon the assertion that the experience of value is, in the end, an immediate experience, and it has already been shown that no experience is immediate. Nothing can escape what Oakeshott refers to as "the despotism of significance". And what is valuable, is valuable, not because it corresponds with some standard external to experience, but because it is required to make coherent the world of "what ought to be". It follows from this that no value(s) can be absolute; every value is logically conditioned by its place in the world of value as a whole: "Whatever virtues there be, whatever judgments of value, each must submit itself (and does submit itself in the mind of anyone who leads an 'examined life') to the world of value as a whole, and from that it derives both its status and its truth".[1]

It may, however, be asked what is meant by speaking of each value as logically conditioned by its place in the world of value. Oakeshott himself never pauses to illustrate his argument, so we must think of our own. A good example is the section on abstract right in Hegel's *Philosophy of Right*. There it is shown very clearly that anyone who values property is presupposing (inter alia) the ideas (or values) of contract and personality. Thus anyone who said that property was an absolute value, something to which all else in the end should be sacrificed, would be speaking unreflectively. He would be failing to recognize that his insistence on this particular value necessarily committed him to valuing the keeping of contracts also.

---

1. *Ibid.*, p.278.

The third proposition, viz. that value is a world of being, and a judgment that "This is valuable" is, in the end, a judgment that "This exists in a certain way", is particularly interesting because it brings directly before us the problem of the relationship between the world of practical fact and the world of value (i.e. between is and ought). Oakeshott's argument on the matter amounts to this: there is a gap or discrepancy between the two worlds, and this discrepancy never disappears in any circumstances whatsoever; on the other hand, the gap is never absolute. This is the position which we must now explicate more fully. When a thing is judged to be valuable it is judged to be worthy of being in the practical world.[1] That it is so judged, Oakeshott is at pains to emphasise, is not the ground of its being valuable. What makes a thing valuable, we saw when examining the second proposition, is the fact that its presence is required in the world of "what ought to be" in order to render that world coherent. Putting the same point more loosely, we might say that every judgment of value involves the assertion that the practical world would be a less valuable place if it lacked the particular thing valued. This does not mean, of course, that the practical world does in fact lack that particular thing. For example, when I value ice-cream, the ice-cream which I am valuing may well be in front of me, in which case it is not only worthy to be, but in fact also is in the practical world; and if it is not before me, if I am therefore valuing something which is "not yet", then my valuation remains related to the practical world because it necessarily convicts that world of deficiency in a particular respect (viz. in its not containing ice-cream). The point is, then, that value differs from practical fact, but is no less real than it (although its reality is of a different order). The world of value only detaches itself absolutely from the world of practical fact when "what is here and now" as such is contrasted with "what ought to be" as such, but this discrepancy between practical fact and value does not prevent the world of value from occupying the world of practical fact, even though it is not reducible to it and does not qualify it.

Oakeshott is aware that his identification of the idea of ought with the idea of value is open to objections. Above all it will be said that not

---

1. Ibid., p.278.

everything which is valued ought necessarily to be realized in the practical world, and that Oakeshott's identification of ought with value implies the opposite. But there is nothing in Oakeshott's view which commits him to denying this. To define what is valuable or what ought to be as what is worthy of being (or ought to be) in the practical world, is not to imply that there is a duty or obligation to do anything about it. Value only becomes obligation or duty when two conditions are met, conditions which make the valued object more than merely valuable. Since it is obviously of great importance that we should understand Oakeshott's view of the nature of duty, especially as confusion often results from failure to distinguish between what it is that makes an action valuable, and what it is that makes it a duty, his formulation of these conditions may therefore be given in full:

"The apprehension of a merely other perfect world, standing over against our world of what is here and now, carries no obligation with it. It becomes duty, an obligation to realise what is judged to be valuable, not merely and only because it is seen to be valuable, but when and because it is seen to be necessary for the completion, the coherency of 'what is here and now'. 'What ought to be' must be seen as the 'ought' of this particular 'is', this particular 'here and now', and must be seen also as fitting within the competence of my volition, before it becomes obligatory to realize it. And it is this which distinguishes obligation from a mere judgment of value".[1]

The fourth proposition, that the world of value is a mode of experience, an abstract world of ideas, an incomplete assertion of reality, brings before us the question of the relationship of the world of value to absolute reality. This question is not to be confused with that of the relationship between the world of value and the world of practical fact. It arises necessarily because one characteristic of every experience, in the view of all idealists, is the claim which it makes to be the whole, or the absolute reality. Science, history, art, religion - each claims that the knowledge it offers is all that there is to know. No experience can avoid making this claim because if it did so it would have lost its distinctive logical character; it would have become self-critical and in so doing would pass into philosophy. The specific

---

1. Ibid., p.280, note 1.

claim made by the world of value is that the world of "what ought to be" is in fact the real world, and that the discrepancy between "is" and "ought" (between the world of practical fact, of "what is here and now", and the world of value) is the discrepancy between "what is here and now", and what really and absolutely is. Oakeshott's ground for rejecting this unqualified identification of value with reality is implicit in what has gone before. The judgment of value asserts that a thing is worthy of being in the practical world, and is therefore tied to the structural concepts of that world. In other words, it has to accept the principle of individuation upon which that world is constituted. And we have already seen that this principle emphasises separateness and will not withstand any attempt to turn the self-contained practical individual into a self-complete one. The world of value, like the world of practical fact, must content itself with designation; for it to seek the definition which concrete reality demands is suicide. We will return to this problem shortly.

Having examined in detail the structure of the two worlds presupposed by practice, Oakeshott returns to the subject of the general nature of practice. In the course of drawing out the implications for practice of its presuppositions there emerge two conclusions which are relevant for understanding his view of the nature of political activity. The first is that the goal of practice can never be total change: "the alteration which practical activity produces is never absolute".[1] The second is that neither politics nor morality can be regarded as the highest level of practical experience: "Religion...is practical experience pursued to its conclusion; in it all subordinate attempts to establish the harmony, unity or coherence of the world of practical experience - attempts such as politics and morality constitute - are swallowed up and superseded".[2] These conclusions are arrived at in the following way. Practice or action is the alteration of "what is here and now" so as to agree with an idea of "what ought to be", but the state of affairs achieved - no matter how much of the detail and content of the practical world it alters - never differs in kind from the original world of practical fact.

---

1. Ibid., p.289.
2. Ibid., p.309.

The aim of practice is to overcome the gap or discrepancy between "is" and "ought", but each success brings with it only one more "here and now" requiring further change. (The world of value itself, of course, contains within itself no potency, no force making for its realization in the world of practical fact: if it did, action would be unnecessary. The world of value is distinct from the world of practical fact, and depends upon practice for its realization in that world). To contemplate a final resolution of the discrepancy is absurd because it is, in effect, to contemplate the destruction of the world of practice itself. From this position Oakeshott is able to condemn (by implication) all extreme forms of political utopianism: "Even if we suppose a condition in which everything was as it should be, that could never be more than a momentary condition...Nowhere in practice is there uninterrupted progress or final achievement."[1] Further, change is always specific change; the very nature of action is such as to generate success only when the limited "point-by-point qualification of 'what is here and now' by 'what ought to be'" is purposed.

Turning to the relationship between politics and religion, we may note first of all that Oakeshott's analysis assumes the ethical order of the modern world, in which politics is not understood to be identical with morality and religion (as it was in the ancient world). Politics is an activity in which the endeavour to realize the world of value is not at its maximum intensity: it must confine itself to realizing (for the most part) values shared by a whole community, and will create excessive incoherency in the world of (social) practical fact if it tries to realize all the particular values of every individual. Views of this kind constitute the background to Oakeshott's remarks in The Tower of Babel where, having said that "The pursuit of perfection as the crow flies...is an activity suitable for individuals, but not for societies," he continues: "For a society....the penalty is a chaos of conflicting ideals, the disruption of a common life, and the reward is the renown which attaches to monumental folly",[2] and adds, in a lighter vein, that "human life is a gamble; but while the individual must be allowed to bet

---

1. Ibid., p.291.
2. Rationalism, p.60.

according to his inclination (on the favourite or an outsider), society should always back the field".[1] Religion is what practice becomes when it is taken most seriously, it is "practical life in its most concrete mood".[2] As such, it differs from moral and political experience only in degree. It is interesting to consider the consequent significance of the concept of God for Oakeshott. He does not mention the word, but the meaning and status he would give to it are clear. A man's religion is the way he leads his life,[3] and a man's God will be the object (or value) to which he attaches most importance. It will be whatever constitutes the unifying purpose of his life, and thus may just as well be a motor-cycle or a woman as the Christian deity. Such a definition of God would, no doubt, startle some, but there is nothing unacceptable or obnoxious about it, and it even corresponds with some ordinary expressions (e.g. "he worships his wife"). The main deficiency of Oakeshott's account of religion lies elsewhere, in his general conception of the nature of modality. For Oakeshott religion is, in the end, a mere distraction from the pursuit of concrete experience; it has to be set distinctly to one side, together with all other practical experience, by the philosopher. It has no necessary place in the scheme of things.

A natural consequence of Oakeshott's recognition of the futility of setting one's sights perpetually on some future state of affairs (conceived of as perfect and final), to be produced perhaps by the revolution to end all revolutions, is his conservatism. This is grounded in the determination to enjoy the world of practice, to the best of one's ability. To accept the analysis of the presuppositions of practical experience does not, of course, unequivocally entail conservatism, but it does imply that the radical will find it quite impossible to find a rational basis for his conception of happiness as the attainment of a condition which does not contain within itself the possibility of change. What is at once the core of Oakeshott's own conservatism and of his opposition to rationalism, is a dispos-

---

1. *Ibid.*, p.60.
2. *Experience*, p.292.
3. *Ibid.*, p.292.

position which has as its central characteristic "a propensity to use and to enjoy what is available rather than to wish for or to look for something else; to delight in what is present rather than what was or what may be.... What is esteemed is the present..."[1] Thus, although Oakeshott nowhere in the political essays attempts a systematic defense of conservatism, contenting himself merely with the observation that he does not share the common belief that such a defense or explanation is impossible,[2] the general character of the considerations he would adduce in its support is clear enough.

We are left now with the task of considering whether Oakeshott is committed by his conception of the nature of practice to opposing any form of reflection in the conduct of moral and political life. At first sight it might appear that he is, for is not the endeavour to realize the world of "what ought to be" in the world of "what is here and now" to be confined to action, with all theorizing occurring only as a distraction which will "seduce and make flaccid [the] will"?[3] And he asserts also that "any attempt to resolve this discrepancy generally or _theoretically_ must be made without the sympathy of practice".[4] His opposition to rationalism, if it were complete, would lead to the longing for the completely unreflective or "natural" way of life desiderated by Rousseau in one of his moods. The consequence of adopting such a position would be disastrous: it would mean that, as a political theorist, Oakeshott would have nothing of any relevance to offer us; he would be in no position to offer an account of a type of social order, or way of life, which might provide stability for the modern community by harmonizing the different values it cherishes. He would therefore have nothing of significance to say about the problem of political obligation, because at some stage an adequate treatment of it must include an account of the institutional order which would reconcile the conflict of values which generate it (in its practical form). His irrelevance would follow from his starting-point, the mere dismissal of the most universal feature of the modern consciousness, viz. the desire not merely to act, but to know explicitly why one is acting as one

---

1. On Being Conservative, in Rationalism, p.168.
2. Rationalism, p.168.
3. Ibid., p.290.
4. Ibid., p.290.

does, and to be able to act upon principles or inner conviction. In Hegelian terms, there would be no recognition and mediation of particularity, but merely the negation of it. However, we need not take the matter further because such pure reactionism is entirely alien to Oakeshott. He explicitly rejects the ideal of the primitive life: "For the complete exemplification of this life ((viz. the practical)) we do not, I think, require to turn to the life of primitive men".[1] He allows that the life of the primitive is indeed practical from end to end, that in it the intellect is directly subservient to the will. But this life cannot be regarded as the fulfilment of all the potentialities of the practical world, and is deficient for that reason: in it "the possibilities of practice remain undeveloped".[2] Further, that the world of practice is the world of will and action does not imply that reflection and thought have no place in it. The opposite is true - for action is thinking. And Oakeshott explicitly maintains that "there is no reason why ((a man)) should be denied the use of reflection if that be required to coordinate his experience".[3] However, the important point to emphasize is that, if coherence in practice is achieved with the help of reflection, the criterion of that coherence is not to be identified with the presence of the reflection.[4] We will see later that the political essays abound with examples of failure to comprehend this. A good one is that of the Victorian clothing designers who felt that the product they designed for ladies who wished to cycle - bloomers - was rational simply because they had reflected upon the activity of cycling.[5] Conversely, it follows that practice without reflection is not, on that account, deficient. Oakeshott insists upon this conclusion: it is not those whose life appears to be ruled by "a happy instinct" who fail to achieve coherence in practice: this rather, "is the condition of the practical experience of those who pass a futile and feverish existence endeavouring to make their random desires and capricious hopes conform to some preconceived

---

1. Ibid., p.296.
2. Ibid., p.296.
3. Ibid., pp.302-303.
4. Ibid., p.302.
5. Rationalism, p.81.

system of general maxims".[1] Once again we see how the roots of Oakeshott's better known conceptions and concerns in the subsequent political essays are to be found in the treatment of practice in Experience and its Modes: the final phrase in the last quotation, "some preconceived system of general maxims", is very like the definition of the ideological consciousness in Rationalism in Politics, where that consciousness is characterized as the conviction that rational activity is "behaviour in which an independently premeditated end is pursued and which is determined solely by that end".[2]

We must now return briefly to the question of the ultimate reality of the world of practice. Every world demands to be judged from the absolute standpoint, for it does not claim merely that its truth is true for itself alone, but that it is absolutely true. It claims to give an account, not simply of a part of experience, but of the whole of experience. From this fact arises the ultimate contradiction upon which practice rests. For although practice can explain everything, its explanation will only take account of a certain dimension of the thing to be explained. Its explanation, specifically, will only take account of that dimension of the thing which falls within the world of practice itself. Since the practical mode is reality as it appears under the category of change, this category itself must remain unexamined by practice, and is presupposed by the terms of the explanation it offers. In this lies the unsatisfactory character of practical explanation as an ultimate explanation of the universe. By calling practical explanation unsatisfactory (or "a contradiction", to use the stronger word employed by Oakeshott), what is meant is that change is only incidental to some aspects of reality, and therefore their full nature is not adequately comprehended under that category alone. When I dig my garden, my activity is practical through and through. But when I adorn the handle of my spade and rejoice in its beauty, the differentia of this new experience (which certainly involves a change in my here and now and hence falls within the world of practice in one of its aspects) cannot be given through a specification of its nature in terms of the category of change alone.[3]

---

1. Experience, p.302.
2. Rationalism, p.83, essay on Rational Conduct.
3. Cf. Bradley, Essays on Truth and Reality, O.U.P. 1914, p.105.

The category, we might say, is too impoverished to contain the experience of beauty in its fullness. The matter is even more obvious if we take philosophy itself. To write or to think about philosophy is of course to engage in practice, it is to alter existence. But it is not merely that. For more must be said about the alteration I achieve in existence than that something has been changed, if the specifically philosophical character of my activity is to have justice done to it. We can now recognize that, in rejecting practice as a contradiction, something essentially simple is being emphasised, which is that no activity is merely or barely practical. There is no denial of the other truth, that the whole of reality may be seen in terms of practice: there is only the necessary supplementation of it. We may accept, then, that the whole cannot be adequately conceived in terms of the practical world, but where Oakeshott is most vulnerable is in his insistence that we must place before ourselves the problem of the adequacy of practice from the concrete standpoint in absolute terms: "I must insist, once more, that this is a question which must be accepted or rejected with an absolute affirmation or an absolute negative". Similarly, his view (which follows from his general view of the nature of modality) that practice has no direct relationship to other modes is open to question on the kind of grounds which we indicated briefly with reference to the world of science when conceived of as a purely quantitative world. In the present case, our difficulty arises in the following way. It is not to be denied that the merely practical (like the merely quantitative or scientific) would be nothing real. It would be (as Bradley puts it) the maintenance and alteration of existence in complete abstraction from the quality of the existence and the change. Its end would be to produce the greatest quantity of bare doing.[1] This granted, it appears that the endeavour to establish the autonomy of the world of practice, after Oakeshott's manner, by erecting it upon the category of change alone, is inherently impossible. It is impossible because the very consideration of the differentia of that world, viz. change, forces us to think of more than change, it forces us to recognize that other worlds of experience are so intimately involved in

---

1. Ibid., p.101.

the world of practice that that world cannot be given the independence from
these which Oakeshott assigns to it. We may rest for the moment on this
point because its cogency may be assessed as it stands - the establishment
of its validity does not commit us to demonstrating precisely what other
worlds of experience are involved in the world of practice.

Oakeshott's conception of political philosophy.

It was said at an earlier stage that an answer to the problem of political obligation always presupposes a particular view of the logical status
of that problem, and that this view will determine the sort of considerations
which are relevant to the solution. For Oakeshott, the very phrase "problem
of political obligation" would be laden with the interests and concerns of
the practical world. This would indeed be true of all the problems of political and moral philosophy. But he recognizes that the issue is more complex
than that: the problem of political obligation does not fall completely
within the practical world, being susceptible only to practical reflection.
It may be, and has been, the subject of philosophical explanation also. We
may come to perceive his view of its status more clearly by examining his conception of an indeterminate arrest in experience. He illustrates it most
thoroughly through a consideration of moral philosophy, but in a foot-note[1]
he ascribes the same general character to Theology, to "so-called Political
Philosophy," and (with some hesitation) to Psychology, so we will not be going
astray if we accept what is offered and draw our conclusions from it as to
Oakeshott's view of the nature of political philosophy.

We have seen that in experience complete intelligibility may be pursued
or that satisfaction may be sought in the acceptance of the partial intelligibility which is yielded by a modal standpoint. In spite of its abstractness the modal position offered a specific and homogeneous world of ideas,
and was self-contained because it contented itself with the category upon
which it rested. Oakeshott proceeds now to argue that we find in experience
not only philosophy and specific modality, but also indeterminate arrest. He
writes that "There is not only abstraction as a special process, but abstrac-

---

1. *Experience*, p.335, n.1.

tion as a mere inadvertence. The failure to achieve what is satisfactory in experience may be merely implicit as well as explicit and formulated. There may be mere falling short as well as determinate arrest".[1] An indeterminate arrest in experience therefore lacks specific identity: it has no category into which it can withdraw when faced by philosophical criticism, permitting it to disregard such criticism as irrelevant. Of course, not even a determinate arrest can, in the end, avoid passing over into philosophy, in virtue of its character as experience as such. But it can do so as long as it insists on its right to be recognized as a *specific* form of experience (a right not possessed by indeterminate arrest) and not merely experience as such. To indeterminate arrest in experience Oakeshott gives the name pseudo-philosophical experience. Unlike determinate arrest it cannot withstand direct philosophical criticism, and it is because it lacks any specific character that it is philosophical in a sense in which any specific world of abstract experience is not philosophical.[2] Lacking any specific character of its own, then, indeterminate arrest falls within philosophy, but what makes it pseudo-philosophy? It is the fact that, while a philosophical idea knows the world to which it belongs, a pseudo-philosophical one is ignorant of its world.[3] Thus, for a pseudo-philosophical idea to be converted into philosophy proper, "What is required is that the arrest should recognize the whole to which it explicitly as well as implicitly belongs".[4] Political philosophy, then, is certainly philosophy, but the predicate "political" indicates that it has not become fully aware of all that this status commits it to. Expressing it more strongly, political philosophy is philosophical error or defect.[5] To illustrate the general character of all pseudo-philosophical experience Oakeshott takes ethical thought, and his thesis is that "ethical thought is nothing if not philosophical, but in so far as it remains 'ethical' it is a modification

---

1. *Ibid.*, p.331.
2. *Ibid.*, p.333.
3. *Ibid.*, p.334.
4. *Ibid.*, p.334.
5. *Ibid.*, p.334.

of philosophical thought".[1] His definition of it would be that of political philosophy also: "Ethics I take, in general, to be thinking about the world of values, the consideration of judgments of value",[2] although moral philosophy would naturally place its emphasis on a different range of values. But the difficulty is to know from what standpoint this consideration of values takes place. We may leave to one side the questions of whether an historical or scientific consideration is possible and how such consideration differs from that attempted by political and moral philosophy, and concern ourselves with the problem of whether every consideration of the practical world must itself be practical in character. The view that ethics - and of course political philosophy - are themselves practical is a view (Oakeshott observes) which is widely spread, and has enjoyed respectability since the time of Aristotle. On this, the task of the moral and political philosopher is to construct a world of values, to determine what is right order in private and in public life, to establish that courage is a virtue and that representative government is the best form of government, and so on. On the other hand, there is another element in our tradition of moral and political philosophy, which holds that they are concerned to <u>define</u> the notions of "value", of "good", of "right", of "ought", of "law", of "state" and of "justice". On this view the result must be a world of non-practical ideas, for "Agreement that certain things are good, or that certain actions are right involves neither agreement nor disagreement about the ultimate reason why some things are considered good and others bad, some actions right and other wrong".[3] When these two views are combined in one enterprise, there results only "a hybrid and nondescript mode of thought without legitimate issue or valid conclusion".[4] Moral and political philosophy, then, must abandon one of their masters if their life is to become harmonious, and in Oakeshott's opinion the choice must be made against the former master and in favour of the latter. For ethics to opt for the former is to lose its existence by becoming indistin-

---

1. <u>Ibid.</u>, p.335.
2. <u>Ibid.</u>, p.335.
3. <u>Ibid.</u>, p.333.
4. <u>Ibid.</u>, p.339.

guishable from practice and "popular and pedantic".[1] If what is strong and disciplined in ethical thought is to survive, it must recognize more clearly that its nature is philosophical, and that its destiny lies in discovering and defining "the ultimate character of moral and practical concepts ((and in ascertaining)) the relation of practical judgement to reality".[2] In short, moral and political philosophy reduce themselves to an enterprise of the kind undertaken by Oakeshott in his analysis of practical experience.

Conclusion

We are now in a position to attempt a general criticism of Oakeshott's position. It was said earlier in the chapter that Oakeshott's conception of the general nature of experience represented the critical (or negative) side of his philosophy and was the most successful part of it; now we have to assess the adequacy of his treatment, not merely of experience as such, but of determinate experience.

The main deficiency of Oakeshott's philosophy is, in the first place, his selection for emphasis of the abstract aspect of all determinacy. His identification of modality with abstraction is, in the end, purely arbitrary. He does not, that is to say, indicate why non-philosophical experience cannot be regarded as constitutive of concrete experience itself, as opposed to a mere distraction or arrest in experience. As Greenleaf puts it, "He seems to accept them ((viz. the modes)) as in some way given, or even fortuitous".[3] To regard determinate experience in this way is not merely an arbitrary (in the sense of unjustified) element in his system: it tends to reduce the system to absurdity. For Oakeshott presents philosophy as _critical_ experience, or experience without arrest, and yet wishes to refer to it also as _concrete_ experience. It is difficult to see how these two predicates can co-exist outside a system such as Hegel's, where "criticism" becomes "concrete" because it involves taking in determinate experience, and not merely the avoidance of it. To dismiss the modes as absolutely unsatisfactory from the standpoint of

---

1. Ibid., p.340.
2. Ibid., p.340.
3. Oakeshott's Philosophical Politics, op.cit., p.94.

philosophy, or of absolute reality, is to strip reality or concrete experience of all its concreteness. When Oakeshott claims that his standpoint is the single, concrete whole of experience, he is really standing on bare nothingness, notwithstanding all his protestations to the contrary. Although he himself recognizes that a unity which is to claim reality must be a differentiated or determinate unity, he yet hastens to thrust from him, as treacherous distractions, everything which would afford such differentiation. When philosophy conceives of determinacy as so completely alien to reason, merely fortuitous and unnecessary, it certainly acquires for itself a high degree of purity - but a purity so ethereal that it passes into nothingness rather than into the world of concrete reality. Oakeshott does show awareness of this difficulty, but he only addresses himself to it at a very late stage in his argument, and then only in the form of a non-committal footnote. He writes: "Neither here, nor anywhere else, am I asserting that in this concrete whole of experience there is no differentiation. The concrete world is, perhaps, single in, through and by virtue of an intrinsic variety. On that point I have ventured no opinion".[1] If we accept his disclaimer, then he must be prepared to accept the consequence, viz. the incoherence, arbitrariness and ultimate absurdity which will infect his thought.

It would seem indeed that in the years since the publication of <u>Experience and Its Modes</u>, Oakeshott himself has come to feel the weight of this objection. In an essay written in 1959 entitled <u>The Voice of Poetry in the Conversation of Mankind</u>, Oakeshott speaks of all human intercourse as occurring within a "conversation" in which there is no concern with truth, no proof of propositions, no conclusions to be sought, no debates to be won, and no inquiry to be carried through.[2] It is the role which he assigns to philosophy in this conversation which interests us:

"Philosophy, the impulse to study the quality and style of each voice, and to reflect upon the relationships of one voice to another, must be counted a parasitic activity; it springs from the conversation, because this is what

---

1. <u>Experience</u>, p.348, note.
2. <u>Rationalism</u>, p.198.

the philosopher reflects upon, but it makes no specific contribution to it".[1]

The point of interest lies in the fact that Oakeshott no longer speaks of philosophy as "concrete" experience: it is now recognized to be parasitic. We find it impossible to understand how Oakeshott ever came to feel that the term "concrete" might be the appropriate one for his position.

In the second place, we may attempt to extract a more general lesson from Oakeshott's deficiency. Both Bradley and Oakeshott attempted in their philosophies, not to attain to a complete system, but to find a criterion of reality; as Oakeshott puts it, "What is required is a point of view from which the relative validity of any world of experience can be determined; what is required is a criterion".[2] But the criterion turns out to be philosophy, or experience without arrest: and we have just seen that a criterion which does not become a complete system leaves its own veracity and adequacy in question. In other words, Oakeshott treats coherence as a metaphysical criterion, by which certain modes can be treated as abstract, but it is _in fact_ a bare _logical_ criterion. Thus, if Oakeshott's argument points to any more general lesson, it must be that the attempt "not to formulate a system, but to see clearly and to grasp firmly a single idea - the notion of philosophy as experience without arrest or reservation",[3] is doomed to failure: the criterion remains abstract and fails to meet the full obligations of experience.

In the third place, we may say something about the modes. We have seen that philosophy itself cannot be concrete, because deprived of all content. But if this is true, then the modes themselves cannot significantly be termed "abstract". For if Oakeshott has not found in philosophy a concrete whole then the modes cannot be compared with it and found to be partial and abstract. It may indeed be possible to describe philosophy as the whole of experience and to compare the modes as partial, but it remains true to say that they cannot therefore be called abstract: and to point to the presuppositionless character of the whole of experience only misses the point, which is that

---

1. _Rationalism_, p.200.
2. _Experience_, p.2.
3. _Experience_, p.3.

Oakeshott's "experience without arrest" is only achieved by sacrificing all content. In a more sympathetic vein we might put it another way: Oakeshott's concept of philosophy as critical experience may be regarded as a minimal (and hence as an abstract, and therefore inadequate) specification of the nature of philosophy. Philosophy, as we said above with reference to Hegel, is indeed critical, but not with a view to destroying all content.

There is a further point to be made in connection with the concept of modality. We may question the possibility of conceiving of the modes as totally independent of one another. Oakeshott insists that the modes are different from one another, and this may immediately be granted. But his insistence on this matter neither demonstrates nor implies what he takes to be demonstrated and implied, viz. that difference implies exclusion, or the impossibility of ever moving from one mode to another.

Perhaps the simplest way of illustrating the difficulty inherent in Oakeshott's conception of the modes as mutually exclusive is to take the scientific mode, which is "a world of purely quantitative experience"[1] and to ask whether it is not in fact meaningless to speak of such experience. That quality, for science itself, is something external, is not of course denied. What is to be emphasised is that science cannot be conceived of as differentiated from other modes by adopting mere quantity as its differentia, for quantity as such is totally undifferentiated substance or matter. Science as such may endeavour to ignore quality, but it cannot do so completely: it must have a subject-matter and the specification of this will inevitably involve quality. As far as science is concerned it is indeed a matter of indifference whether the things quantified have this or that quality - "five horses are five horses whether they are brown, or white, or black. A mile is a mile whether it is a mile of metalled road or a mile of telegraph wire"[2] - but the quantity must be a quantity *of* something; it cannot be pure quantity. This criticism admittedly does not take us very far in a positive direction: it does not indicate the precise character of the other (qualitative) mode

---

1. Experience, p.172.
2. W.T.Stace, Hegel, Dover, U.S.A., 1955; p.156.

or modes to which science is related. But it may serve to show that something like Collingwood's attempt to arrange aesthetics, religion, science and history in a scale of forms is not in fact precluded by Oakeshott's scepticism, and is indeed necessary if full intelligibility is to be achieved in experience.

We may refer, finally, to Oakeshott's extension of the concept of modality to characterize political philosophy as an arrest in experience. It is important to notice that Oakeshott does not preclude or disparage attempts to delineate a social order in which the problem of political obligation would be resolved: his concern is with the status of the body of theory which would result from such an attempt, and his contention is that it would not, and could not, be philosophical writing. And this conclusion, we think, cannot be avoided once the general framework of the system from which it proceeds is accepted. However, if a more sanguine view than Oakeshott's of philosophy's scope were taken, it would be possible to argue that the problem of political obligation when treated philosophically does not inevitably dissolve (like all other problems in moral and political philosophy) into a more general inquiry into the presuppositions of the practical world and their adequacy from the standpoint of concrete reality. In particular, a view of experience which endeavours to establish necessity throughout its modes or appearances (not contenting itself with pointing, in the end, to their contingent, even if unavoidable, character), would not be satisfied with a delineation of the bare _form_ of the practical world; it would insist on a deduction of the specific things or individuals which occurred within that form, i.e. a deduction of its _content_, and this would restore to philosophy (inter alia) the task of exhibiting the necessity of a certain form of social organization, instead of leaving such matters in the hands of the man of practical wisdom. In other words, instead of saying only that "these are the presuppositions of the practical world, and this is the point at which they fail to characterize reality adequately", it would be argued that "the practical world is a necessary appearance of reality and the precise content it must assume is as follows." This latter position is that of Hegel and (in a less systematic way) of Green and Bosanquet.

PART C

POLITICAL OBLIGATION

Chapter 7

T. H. Green

Sin

Nettleship wrote of Green that "the noblest feature in his character is a serious sympathy with the wrongs and sufferings of the poor",[1] and there can be no doubt that the plight of the mass of humanity was indeed a central preoccupation with him. But the nature of Green's sympathy for the masses was shaped by a still more comprehensive preoccupation and one which provides the key to his moral and political reflection. Above all he dreamt of personal salvation and release from sin, and of a society where there would be no trace of that selfishness which subjection to the animal (or natural) side of our nature brings. Throughout this dream there is observable the dualism of spirit and nature which characterized his metaphysics, now particularized but still unresolved. For example, at one extreme we find Sir Henry Vane taken as the exemplar of the pure reflective soul, with Cromwell as the virtuous man of action; at the other extreme there is "the dandy or diner-out",[2] the exemplar of the flesh.

In Green's eyes the nineteenth century was a sinful period, in which the ordinary tribulations of the soul were increased by the prevalence of false philosophy and misconceptions about the limits of natural science, both of which unsettled religious belief and left even the good man open to the temptations of the prevailing enlightened hedonism.[3] But these temptations do not absolve the individual from personal responsibility for his salvation: to appeal to the sophistry of the age in order to explain the loss of a sense of God's presence and the consciousness of his love "is the foppery of men who want new excuses for old sins. It is still our sins and nothing else that separates us from God."[4] Sin Green identifies in the same context with "some unconquered selfishness" which creates a "darkness of the heart" incompatible with that "perfect openness towards God" which enables him to make us vehicles

---

1. Works, Vol. III, p.xxi.
2. Ibid., Vol. I, p.353.
3. Ibid., Vol. III, p.248.
4. Ibid., Vol. III, p.248.

of his will and to bring about the progress of humanity.

The factors closing off the soul from perfect openness to God vary greatly in character, but one at least seems to be peculiar to the modern age; this is the novel. Novel-reading, Green considered, "aggravates two of the worst maladies of modern times, self-consciousness and want of reverence".[1] It does little to help the politics of the age because many a man, instead of doing some sound piece of work for mankind, spends his time in explaining to himself why it is that he does not do it, and how, after all, he is superior to those who do.[2] But the novel does not affect only the higher beings adversely; the effect of popular culture upon the masses is equally deleterious, for instead of idealising life, the novel sentimentalizes it. The net result is that "no one loses himself in a cause".[3] Green arrives at these conclusions from a more general position, according to which the task of all art is not to copy nature but to idealize it, to introduce harmony and order into the confused multiplicity of sensuous images.[4] The artist reveals to us a glory which belongs to nature, and yet not to nature as the ordinary man sees it, in its material limitations. In degree and mode, however, the idealisation of nature varies infinitely in the various kinds of art; and of these tragedy is the most exalted. But great tragedy can only occur when civilization has not reached the stage of "acquiescence in things as they are, and scepticism as to all beyond them". Green considers that the production of a great tragedy is almost an impossibility in our own time.[5] The mood of the age is better captured in the <u>Spectator</u>, the journal which gave the first expression to the spirit which subsequently manifested itself in the novel. By the <u>Spectator</u> "humanity is taken as reflected in the ordinary life of men...No attempt is made either to suppress the baser elements of man's nature, or to transfigure them by a stronger light than that of the common understanding".[6] So too the novel, in which "man, comfortable and acquiescent, wished to amuse himself by

---

1. <u>Ibid</u>., Vol. III, p.37.
2. <u>Ibid</u>., Vol. III, p.38.
3. <u>Ibid</u>., Vol. III, p.38.
4. <u>Ibid</u>., Vol. III, p.23.
5. <u>Ibid</u>., Vol. III, p.26.
6. <u>Ibid</u>., Vol. III, p.27.

a reflex of the life which he no longer aspired to transcend. He wished to enjoy himself twice over - in act and in fancy..."[1] It offers to his imagination "the full enjoyment of earthly life...unchallenged by yearnings after the divine."[2] The common characteristic of all novels is their conformity to nature as it is commonly seen; Green instances the work, amongst others, of Richardson, Jane Austen, and Fielding (in whom we find "the buoyancy of a generous animalism").[3]

The novelist, then, could fittingly be banned from a new republic.[4] His happy endings are inherently incapable of earning him the citizenship to which his catastrophes entitle the tragedian.[5] Sad endings do not improve his status - they merely leave us sadder but not wiser men.[6] Green is reluctant to settle for less than the annihilation of individuals as the only fitting end to the struggle with destiny. George Eliot, for example, in her book The Mill on the Floss, spoilt things by refusing to end when the heroine and her lover drown in the flood, which would have established that she "had indeed attained the ideal view of life". Instead she gave way to her novelistic instinct and ended the book with the other chief actors standing mournfully over the heroine's grave, thus making the death an occasion of sentiment.[7] It cannot be said that Green mistakes the character of tragedy, identifying it with suffering and pain as such: he is aware that "it is not the suffering but its cause, namely, the action or conflict"[8] which is essential to this art form; but it may be felt that he gives the tragic attitude too exclusive an emphasis not only in relation to other art forms, but also in relation to life itself. It is surely a little hard to upbraid the novel-reader for "thinking his personal joys and sorrows of interest to angels and men".[9]

---

1. Ibid., Vol. III, p.28.
2. Ibid., Vol. III, p.29.
3. Ibid., Vol. III, pp.28-29.
4. Ibid., Vol. III, p.30.
5. Ibid., Vol. III, p.32.
6. Ibid., Vol. III, p.35.
7. Ibid., Vol. III, p.38.
8. A.C.Bradley, Oxford Lectures on Poetry, p.70.
9. Works, Vol. III, p.38.

Angels at least are supposed to have a professional interest in such matters.

But Green is not disposed to find in the novelist an unqualified evil: his work does have a positive side and does not merely sink the soul deeper in the mire of sense. For "though he cannot show the prisoners the way of escape from their earthly confinement, yet by breaking down the partitions between the cells he enables them to combine their strength for a better arrangement of the prison-house".[1]

In order to bring out the social advantages to be derived from the novel, Green has to change his ground a little. He began (we saw) by maintaining that it is only our sins which keep us from God; he now modifies this Christian thesis and moves towards the Enlightenment thesis according to which the origin of evil is ignorance and the deception of the populace by a privileged social group. This ambiguous attitude towards evil, which is sometimes identified with the selfishness (or sin) of individuals and classes, and sometimes with stupidity, runs through the whole of Green's social theory, being reflected in his theory of progress (which must explain the extent of the responsibility of, e.g., the Greek slave-owner) and in his attitude towards the divisive forces in society. He writes that "The most wounding social wrongs more often arise from ignorance than from malice, from acquiescence in the opinion of a class rather than from deliberate selfishness".[2] Elsewhere he finds the origin of social evil in defective organization: the demarcations of family, of territory, or of class, prevent the proper fusion of parts into the whole. Hence the task of the social reformer is to use "the social force" - Green intends this phrase to include agencies such as the novel - to "merge distinctions of privilege and position in the one social organism".[3] We will see at a later stage that his conception of the common good is too abstract to afford a rational criterion for determining the point to which the levelling process (Green notes in this context that "reforming and levelling are indeed more closely allied than we are commonly disposed to

---

1. Ibid., Vol. III, p.42.
2. Ibid., Vol. III, p.42.
3. Ibid., Vol. III, p.41.

admit") must be taken. A completely abstract concept of the common good, of course, would involve the annihilation of the parts to be "fused", and Green does give the impression at times that his concept of the common good is completely abstract. At the moment, however, we will follow a little further the connection between ignorance and social conflict, and will then be able to recognize the valuable part which the novel has to play in realizing a social condition in which a conflict-free common good emerges and the problem of political obligation ceases to exist.

The presence of different groups within society creates estranging barriers between men. Each knows only the "idola" of his own cave. Because the master and servant are unable to enter into each other's feelings, the master cannot understand how any good quality can lead the servant to "forget his station", while the servant regards the spirit of management in the master as mere "driving".[1] This case illustrates on a small scale the general nature of the social problem, which Green states thus: "The relation between the higher and lower classes becomes irritating, and therefore injurious, not from any conscious unfairness on either side, but simply from the want of a common understanding; while at the same time every class suffers within its own limits from the prevalence of habits and ideas, under the authority of class-convention, which could not long maintain themselves if once placed in the light of general opinion."[2]

Green, then, finds the fundamental social requirement to be what would now be called more communication: a dialogue must be created between the classes. Self-criticism, triggered by exposure to general opinion, will remove anachronistic and unpleasant habits within particular classes. Herein lies the significance of the novel. It cannot initiate the dialogue, or give a new birth to the spirit, or initiate the effort to transcend the separations of place and circumstance; but it can facilitate the fusion of opinions and sympathies once the desire for improvement has appeared.[3] It will, for example,

---

1. Ibid., Vol. III, pp.41-2.
2. Ibid., Vol. III, p.42.
3. Ibid., Vol. III, p.44.

facilitate the recognition that crime does not always imply sin, and an appreciation that the feeling which leads one man to an act which he describes as an "indiscretion" leads another to an act which is branded as "game-stealing".[1] The novel, indeed, is "the great reformer and leveller of our time".[2] It is rather odd that, having assigned this radical role to the novel, Green finds amongst its positive contributions to social well-being the fact that it enables the scholar ("the cloistered student") to share in the strife of social forces - in imagination. One would have thought that a spirit of vicarious reforming would be amongst the things to be castigated, as an evasion of reality. As it is, Green writes that "he ((the scholar)) need no longer envy the man of action and adventurer, or sigh for new regions of enterprise. The world is all before him". In like fashion he sees in the novel at least a partial answer to the diminution of human interest which surrounds the duties of one's station in a society where the division of labour, specialization of study and perfection of organization remove adventure, excitement and the demand for individual effort. Social reform, directed to the creation of an order in which such forms of dissatisfaction would not occur, is not urgent, because "((the)) alleviation, if not ((the)) remedy, is to be found in the newspaper and the novel".[3] It was all very optimistic: but no doubt we should remember that the discussion of the political significance of the novel occurs in a youthful essay, written for a competition and probably affected by the need to display ingenuity.[4]

In spite of the difficulties which the human soul has encountered in the past, and still encounters, Green considered the history of mankind to have been one of progress, conceived by him as a movement in which the range of persons by whom a common good is conceived as common gradually increases, until the point is reached at the present day when a duty to man as such is recognized. The moving force in this development is individual conscience. Green's contention appears to be that the recognition of human equality and the inherent worth of personality which is contained in institutions and is the measure

---

1. *Ibid.*, Vol. III, p.42.
2. *Ibid.*, Vol. III, p.41.
3. *Ibid.*, Vol. III, p.40.
4. Memoir, *Works*, Vol. III, pp. xxx - xxxii.

of their adequacy, are constricted by these institutions in the period of settled living which follows upon each advance. This constriction leads the individual conscience to appropriate once more the surroundings in which it is embodied, in a further endeavour to bring them into accord with that ideal of a best life which inspires it.[1]

Progress, however, involves not only an extension of the range of persons between whom the good is conceived to be common. It has a second aspect, which is the further determination of the moral law. Our standards of virtue, while they do not differ in a sense from those to be found at the beginning of the development, are more comprehensive in their demands. Previously unrecognized duties have now been recognized: slavery, for example, is no longer an acceptable institution, and the whole range of social work undertaken today was alien to the spirit of the ancient world.

The main philosophical limitation of Green's theory of progress is its static character: no explanation is given of why individual conscience creates the movement attributed to it. It rests upon an act of faith: selfishness and ignorance – in general the "antagonism of the natural to the spiritual man" – have been overcome, and will continue to be defeated.[2] The witness of the lord shall know no insuperable obstacle to its growth. Green has no equivalent of the Hegelian theory of progress, which was given an internal dynamic by the dialectic of master and slave.

There is a further difficulty. In interpreting the movement of history Green took the Kantian standpoint as absolute. Distortion inevitably followed, with amusing results. In treating of the ethics of the ancient world, Green's main concern appears to be the acquittal of Plato and Aristotle from any taint of Hedonism, "or of Utilitarianism so far as Hedonistic".[3] He insists, for example, that whilst it is unfortunately true that Aristotle's conception of the noble life presupposes slavery, we must set to his credit his refusal to debase that life by introducing any notion of a compensation to be found in the pleasures of another world for present endurance;[4] there is no hint of

---

1. Pro. sect. 215-216.
2. Ibid., sect. 216.
3. Ibid., sect. 253.
4. Ibid., sect. 260.

that appeal to "semi-sensual motives" that has been common in the Christian Church.[1] He does not choose to note that Plato's endeavour to establish the intrinsic satisfaction of the just life eventually gets severely compromised by the recognition that the just man will be happy in this life and the next. Going further, Green elevates Socrates and his followers to the level of honorary Kantians: in their teaching we find the "first clear expression through which (the conviction) manifests itself...that every form of real goodness must rest on a will to be good, which has no object but its own fulfilment".[2] When at a later date Christ observed "Blessed are the pure in heart, for they shall see God", he was only expressing "the same conviction..., not in the form of a philosophy but in the language of religious aspiration", and in a mode which had a more universal appeal.[3] It is noteworthy that Green singles out for particular attention only two of the Greek virtues, andreia and sophrosyne. He considers that taken together they provide the equivalent of our concept of self-denial.[4] Only with reluctance does he acknowledge that Aristotle went a long way before he drew the line at the pleasures incompatible with sophrosyne: this virtue Aristotle considered to be exhibited only in relation to the pleasures of eating, drinking and sexual intercourse, thus accepting a standard which falls short of "that which a conscience, duly responsive to the highest claims, would now require of us".[5] Nonetheless, there is a fundamental identity between the Greek virtue of temperance and the modern virtue of self-denial: both involve keeping the body under control and suppressing "the insolence of overweening lust" in the interest of realizing the good of the community.[6]

Green's endeavour to bring the ancient theory of self-realization under his own Christian-inspired conception of self-denial does considerable violence to pagan ideas. In attributing to Aristotle, and to the Greek consciousness in general, a conviction that the only unconditional good is a good will,[7]

---

1. *Ibid.*, sect. 252.
2. *Ibid.*, sect. 251.
3. *Ibid.*, sect. 251.
4. *Ibid.*, sect. 261.
5. *Ibid.*, sects. 263-265.
6. *Ibid.*, sect. 263.
7. *Ibid.*, sect. 247.

Green seriously misrepresents the ancient notion of virtue. Will never assumed the central position in ancient ethical theory which it acquired in modern; knowledge, and not will, was the main category.[1] It is surprising that Green did not have a firmer grasp of this, because he was acquainted with Sir Alexander Grant's edition of Aristotle's Ethics; in fact, he took it as the point of departure for an essay on Aristotle's philosophy.[2] The first volume of Grant's work contains an essay which brings out very clearly the difference between Aristotle's and Kant's ethical theory.[3] Grant shows in some detail, for example, that the notions of obligation and duty were alien to the ancient world.[4] And in attributing to Aristotle an anti-hedonistic spirit Green is going still further in that process of "naive modernising" justly reprobated by Sidgwick.[5]

Leaving the ancient world behind us we may turn now to consider the place occupied in Green's interpretation of history by the Reformation, an event which many readers of Hegel have agreed to regard as a watershed in the development of the modern consciousness. Green's particular interest was in the history of the English Commonwealth, but he saw this as "the last act in a conflict beginning with the Reformation".[6] The period which intervened in the Western world between the fall of ancient civilization and the Reformation was one in which the spirit was buried beneath a mass of ordinances: the social order was external to the individual conscience in the sense that it had not been subjected to rational criticism and accepted in the light of such criticism. With the advent of Luther, however, reason broke its shell; the spirit once more demanded release from bondage to the flesh, and "again the conscience moved freely in a redeemed world".[7] The social and political problems of Europe in the seventeenth century were a response to the opposition between reason and authority, between the individual and the world of settled right, between the spirit and the flesh, which then emerged.

---

1. Cf. Sidgwick, The Ethics of Green, Spencer and Martineau, MacMillan, London, 1902, p.86.
2. Works, Vol. III, p.46.
3. The Ethics of Aristotle, Vol. I, Essay VII, On the Relation of Aristotle's Ethics to Modern Systems.
4. Ibid., pp.312-313.
5. The Ethics of Green, Spencer and Martineau, op.cit., p.90.
6. Works, Vol. III, p.278.
7. Ibid., Vol.III, p.280.

Green favoured Independency, as the creed which gave fullest scope to the new demand for freedom.[1] In spite of his sympathy for this phase of puritanism, he could not of course share the conceptions of freedom current amongst religious radicals at that time: a freedom founded solely on grace was not his own aspiration. But in the ideas of Sir Henry Vane he found much that was commendable, together with "the best expression of the spirit which struggled into brief and imperfect realization during the Commonwealth".[1]

The "clear spirit" of Vane rejected on the one hand the mischievous attempt to destroy the fixed boundaries of law and morality in pursuit of an immediate enjoyment of the divine fulness, and on the other hand the anti-individualistic policies of the "ancient interests" which would have kept the spirit in bondage to the external social order.[2] His position was founded on a theosophy in which Green could recognize the rudiments of his own metaphysics, and which provided a theory of progress that he could also regard as in essentials the same as his own. Vane conceived of the created world as a reflection of the process by which the Father begets the eternal Son. It involved two elements, "the purely spiritual or angelic, represented by heaven or the light, on the one hand, and the material and animal on the other, represented by the earth. Man, as made of dust in the image of God, includes both..." The history of man is "a gradual progress upwards from a state which would be merely that of the animals but for the fatal gift of rational will, to a life of pure spirituality, which he represented as angelic..."[3] Within this progress Vane distinguished three principal stages, called by him the natural, the legal, and the evangelical conscience. The movement from one stage to the next is very like the "process of reconciliation between will and reason" described elsewhere by Green.[4] The natural conscience guided those who knew not the law; the legal conscience "represents the stage in which the christian clings to rule, letter, and privilege". The evangelical conscience is described by Green, on Vane's behalf, as "the stage in which the human spirit, perfectly conformed to Christ's death and resurrection, crucified to

---

1. Ibid., Vol. III, p.290.
2. Ibid., Vol. III, pp.293-294.
3. Ibid., Vol. III, pp.294-295.
4. Lectures, sect. 24-25.

outward desire and ordinance, holds intercourse 'high, intuitive and comprehensive' ((a quotation from Vane)) with the divine".[1]

Undeterred by the caustic comments of contemporaries[2] and successors upon Vane's writings - Hume found them "absolutely unintelligible" - Green finds in them not only a statement of what Cromwell attempted to put into practice, but "certain practical principles, now of recognized value, which no statesman before him had dreamt of...", and which have retained their potency even when subsequently stated "by the masters of an elegant vocabulary from which God and spirit were excluded".[3] The "universal spiritual force" which found in Vane temporary means of thwarting carnal interests, sank beneath them only to overcome them more thoroughly the next time. And this time Vane's message will be better placed for victory, because "cleared and ripened by a philosophy of which he did not dream".[4] Thus while the same spiritual forces which created the Commonwealth made its endurance an impossibility,[5] the Restoration did not end the new era of progress which began with the Reformation, and the English in particular derived from it a triumph over their animal natures which prepared the way for even greater triumphs. These further triumphs, however, Green considered to have been delayed by the emergence of the empiricist philosophy, which sunk the soul into passive acquiescence in the world of sense. Most insidious of all was empiricism in its ethical phase, as the Utilitarian theory of the good.

The sinner's robe: Utilitarianism

John Stuart Mill was not the only Victorian who felt the age was hanging by a thread, being in danger of a relapse into barbarism. Green considered Vane's evangelical conscience (or Kant's autonomous moral agent) the highest

---

1. *Works*, Vol. III, p.295.
2. Clarendon writes that "he had swallowed some of the fancies and extravagancies of every sect or faction," and that "He was a perfect enthusiast; and, without doubt, did believe himself inspired; which so far corrupted his reason and understanding, (which in all matters without the verge of religion was inferior to that of few men) that he did at some time believe, he was the person deputed over the society upon earth for a thousand years." *History of the Rebellion*, World's Classics ed. pp.150-151.
3. *Ibid.*, Vol. III, pp.295-296.
4. *Ibid*, Vol. III, p.364; the reference is presumably to Hegel.
5. *Ibid.*, Vol. III, p.341.

expression of morality, and welcomed the disappearance of what he considered the sensuous and debasing old Christian morality, with its use of the ideas of heaven and hell in order to keep the masses up to the mark. And yet, if the space he spent in attacking Utilitarianism is any guide, he considered that true morality was a rather precarious thing: he must have suspected that the disappearance of the spectre of eternal torment might lead to a riotous upsurge of self-indulgence. It was an odd idea - in retrospect we can see that the last thing Victorian England was threatened by was an extensive hedonistic outbreak. But in spite of his feeling that the animal nature was lurking only barely hidden in the lives of even the most saintly, waiting to avail itself of the first pleasure-orientated philosophy to spring forth again, he never doubted that the masses were capable of attaining to a self-imposed morality. Perhaps the last statement needs slight qualification: he once indicated that he had overestimated the speed at which the working class could progress, for according to a friend he "dwelt with great disappointment on the use made by the workmen of their half-holiday and their shorter hours". Apparently it was this disappointment which led him to find the origin of the failure of the masses to internalize the moral imperative in drink, and to adopt the cause of temperance.[1]

Concerning that sinfulness by which we exclude from our breasts "that pure self-renouncing spirit which is God's manifestation among men", Green remarks that most of us probably escape the grosser forms - such as that, for example, "which the world lightly calls looseness, and which religious people are apt to call impurity". The mass of mankind are threatened rather by "a more refined self-indulgence, from habits of luxury or indolence, and from nameless desires after all things sweet and pleasant..."[2] But the danger presented by these venial sins should not be underestimated: because they do not issue in overt vice we are apt to call them harmless, but they may eventually obscure God from us almost as effectively as the grosser forms.

Perhaps the greatest danger offered to the soul by the little, easily excused sins is that we come to surround them with "a fence of intellectual

---

1. Memoir, Works, Vol. III, p. cxviii.
2. Ibid., Vol. III, p.249.

self-excusing jugglery, which may in time become impenetrable to the assault of that higher reason which speaks through our own conscience...."[1] Hence a philosophy which puts pleasure at the centre of its scale of acknowledged goods must be particularly dangerous to the soul, since it is eminently suited to intellectual self-excusing jugglery. Green could not countenance Utilitarianism.

A critique of Utilitarianism was made imperative by another consideration. Not only the demands of personal salvation, but the social circumstances of the time require the destruction of hedonism: Green declared that "It is no time to enjoy the pleasures of eye and ear, of search for knowledge, of friendly intercourse, of applauded speech or writing, while the mass of men whom we call our brothers, and whom we declare to be meant with us for eternal destinies, are left without the chance which only the help of others can gain for them, of making themselves in act what in possibility we believe them to be".[2] Personal self-indulgence, then, would be liable to damn not only oneself but also others. Green did not, of course, consider that all the great Utilitarians of the age were defective in their personal lives, nor did he consider that Utilitarianism had simply increased Satan's harvest. On the contrary, Utilitarianism "had the great lesson to teach, that the value of all laws and institutions, the rectitude of all conduct, was to be estimated by reference to the well-being of all men, and that in the estimate of that well-being no nation or class or individual was to count above another".[3] It was only in so far as Utilitarianism went beyond an insistence that it is "the greatest number" whose highest good is to be taken into account, and identified that highest good with the greatest happiness conceived of as a greatest net quantity of pleasure, that it created dangers.

The main danger presented by the Utilitarian identification of the good with pleasure was considered by Green to be the atrophying of the radical

---

1. Ibid., Vol. III, p.249.
2. Pro., sect. 270.
3. Ibid., sect. 351.

spirit. He considered that the speculative hedonist, concerned about his duty in the world, would find no support for his private or public virtue in the doctrines of Bentham, J.S.Mill, Spencer or Sidgwick, and that a weakening of moral initiative would ensue. Why was this?

Green believed that if the logical implications of the Utilitarian conception of the good were rigorously pursued it would become apparent that Utilitarianism cannot answer the question why anyone should trouble himself to alter his own tastes and habits, or those of society in general. Only because the reforming zeal of the great Utilitarians was too strong to allow them to ask this question did they fail to see that their doctrine was more favourable to the status quo than to reform.[1]

The conservative implications of Utilitarianism follow from its deterministic psychology. A man's action in any particular situation cannot be criticized because he is assumed to have acted in accordance with his strongest desire, and that he did so is the proof that his action was the one calculated to yield him the greatest pleasure; whilst that he really did strongly desire the particular pleasure is proved by the fact that he acted.[2] When it is also taken into account that in general the established social order will be capable of removing radical sentiments from the breast of the ordinary individual by deploying the various sanctions it commands, and that even the saintly hedonist will see no indubitable balance of pleasure attending upon social disturbance, it becomes evident that a felicific calculation will not be likely to provide opposition to the established order.[3]

This inability to justify the very radicalism with which it has been associated is not the only shortcoming of Utilitarianism. It is unable, in addition, to explain the phenomenon of obligation. The Utilitarian treatment of obligation must amount in the end to the assertion that "justice is the interest of the stronger", for the assumption that the object of all desire is pleasure makes any "ought" concept unintelligible; so far as Utilitarianism manages to explain ethical language at all, it is only by interpreting it as

1. <u>Ibid.</u>, sect. 351.
2. <u>Ibid.</u>, sect. 340.
3. <u>Ibid.</u>, sect. 338.

referring to one's consciousness of what is expected of one by others, who are "stronger" than oneself in the sense that they have the power to reward or punish one.[1] Only this naturalistic interpretation of ethics makes it possible to claim that there is an identity of individual felicity with the greatest happiness of the greatest number, for that which in the long run seems to the dominant group in society in accordance with its pleasure, is really so, and since this group tends to become the majority, "a man's duty-that which he 'ought to do', or which he feels is expected of him-tends to be that sort of action which conduces to the greatest happiness of the greatest number".[2]

Utilitarianism, then, offers neither a satisfactory account of moral phenomena, nor a justification of radicalism. These deficiencies, which are accentuated when a deterministic psychology is involved, arise as a result of its initial failure to recognize a distinction between the good and bad will: it distinguishes, not between an ultimate good and evil which are constituted by some kind of action, intention or character, but only between kinds of pleasure and pain.[3] Utilitarianism ignores the distinction between the good and bad will because it falls into a simple confusion. Because all action aims at satisfying some desires, and because every satisfaction of desire is pleasurable, it concludes that all action is directed to attaining pleasure, and that the motive in all action, good or bad, is the same. Now while pleasure does accompany the attainment of an end, this does not explain why the end was desired; for to make pleasure the object aimed at is to reify an abstraction, by making pleasure an object lying beyond the concrete end pursued. Hunger, for example, cannot be considered a desire for the pleasure of eating, for there must be a desire to eat before there can be any pleasure in satisfying that desire. Eating is only pleasant because *it* was desired, and not primarily the pleasure.[4]

Green also criticizes the Utilitarian view that the ultimate good is the

---

1. Ibid., sect. 348.
2. Ibid., sect. 349.
3. Ibid., sect. 155.
4. Ibid., sect. 161.

greatest possible sum of pleasures. A sum of pleasures cannot be desired in so far as a desire for pleasure is a desire for a state of feeling, for there can be no such thing as a state of feeling made up of a sum of pleasures. A sum of pleasures, in short is not a pleasure.[1] It follows that the idea of a <u>greatest possible</u> sum of pleasures is not a pleasure, but in this case there is the additional objection that the sum of pleasures admits of indefinite increase, as long as sentient beings exist. Thus, to say that the ultimate good is a greatest possible source of pleasures is to say that it is an end which for ever recedes, and is not only unattainable but can never be more nearly approached. Consequently, the Utilitarian conception of the ultimate good is incapable of serving as a practical criterion, for it provides no indication of what actions bring men nearer to the good.[2]

Utilitarianism encounters its greatest difficulty in dealing with our desire for the good of others. It may achieve consistency by adopting a Hobbesian position, by allowing that all desire whatsoever is for personal pleasure, making the good of others external to each self and dependent upon the will of the sovereign for its maintenance. Or it may allow that we possess a benevolent instinct which enables us to desire pleasure for others as an end in itself, and not merely as a means to our own pleasure. In the latter case the unity of the moral self becomes inexplicable, since the self is divided into a part which pursues personal pleasure and another which disregards pleasure. The only way out of this position for the Utilitarians is through returning to the confusion already noted, according to which benevolent desires would be desires for their own satisfaction.

Green's critique of Utilitarianism clarifies a number of issues in philosophical psychology, but otherwise it establishes relatively little. An intelligent voluptuary might be shown by it to be a bad philosopher, if he really felt that the good lay in a succession of pleasant feelings, or that a desire for pleasure was the source of all action, but it would not follow that he should abandon his way of life. All that would follow would be that his theory was

---

1. <u>Ibid</u>., sect. 221.
2. <u>Ibid</u>., sect. 359.

out of line with his actions, and that he had really been pursuing a conception of personal good.

Green tried to acknowledge that Utilitarianism had possession of an unavoidable truth, the truth that the good cannot be defined as that which is painful to the self. He knew that an ideal of complete self-renunciation was self-contradictory. When comparing modern virtue with ancient he was careful to specify that his preference for the modern life of larger self-denial was not based on the impression that virtue is more virtuous for being painful: modern virtue is superior because it implies a fuller realization of the capacities of the human soul.[1] But this did not prevent him from finding true freedom - complete control over circumstances - in the virtue of the martyr, whose faith is "that highest creative energy which deals with circumstances as it will..."[2] It is perhaps impossible for one who maintained that the emergence of self-consciousness brings with it the conviction that "this world is not our home",[3] to come to terms with pleasure, and the constant tension between egoism and altruism led Green only to a rather grudging acceptance of the inevitable, reminiscent of that displayed by Augustine in the face of the same problem: "This has Thou taught me, that I should set myself to take food and physic. But while I am passing from the discomfort of emptiness to the content of replenishing, in the very passage the snare of concupiscence besets me. For that passing, is pleasure, nor is there nay other way to pass thither, whither we need must pass".[4] Like St. Augustine too Green was able to console himself that the greatest of all pleasures, the beatific vision, lay at the end of the road. He did not use that phrase, but what else could the spectacle be of the realization of all perfection in the ideal self?[4]

Perhaps the most curious feature of Green's criticism of Utilitarianism was his belief that the theory in whose name he attacked it was any less liable to be used to support conservative conclusions. He was aware that a similar

---

1. *Ibid.*, sects. 273, 278.
2. *Ibid.*, Vol. III, p.3.
3. *Confessions*, Chap.10.
4. *Pro.*, sect. 185.

theory had been so used by Hegel, and indeed his own position reflected an optimistic conviction that the major obstacles to progress were well behind. At times he displayed the very self-satisfaction into which he was so concerned that the speculative hedonist might fall.

The sinner's inspiration: Kant

Green considered that the consciousness of sin theorized by St. Paul – "the consciousness of an infinite vacancy only possible to a being capable of infinite fulness"[1] – had been lost during the last part of the seventeenth century, at least in England; he partially exempted "the countrymen of Luther" from this loss, for they continued to recognize in their individuality "the dwelling-place of a spirit that filleth and searcheth all things".[2] He expressed rather graphically his opinion of the consequence of the triumph of individual right upon English intellectual life at the end of the seventeenth century: when there came "the great outburst of personal enjoyment theorizing upon itself, the logic of limitation and exclusion silenced the groanings unutterable of the spirit".[3] The practical and intellectual profligacy of Europe endured for a century, until the rebellion of Rousseau. It was in Germany that there occurred the clearest proof that the modern spirit was being schooled out of its egoism.[4] In the philosophy of Kant the consciousness of sin re-emerged,[5] although Green could also speak of Kant as the philosopher who voiced most clearly the claim of the modern spirit, articulated uncriti-

---

1. <u>Works</u>, Vol. III, p.121.
2. <u>Ibid</u>., Vol. III, p.122.
3. <u>Ibid</u>., Vol. III, p.122.
4. <u>Ibid</u>., Vol. III, p.124.
5. Kant's reflections upon sin were not confined to life on this planet. When he speculated on the character of life on the other planets the same problem worried him. He thought that the inhabitants of Mars were the most likely to be sinful: those of other planets would be too low to be responsible, or too wise to err. (<u>Kant's Theory of Ethics</u>, ed. J. K. Abbott, fourth ed. 1889, Memoir of Kant, p.xxiv).

cally in the popular philosophy, to be free, to enjoy, and to understand.[1] Needless to say, Green found no incompatibility in the two descriptions of Kant - enjoyment and consciousness of sin were intimately connected. This connection is not surprising when it is remembered that Green found "much excellent philosophy" in Rabbi Ben Ezra, in the course of which poem Browning at one point exclaims, "Be our joys three-parts pain!"[2] He would not have hesitated before recognizing in Kant a re-statement of St. Paul's conception of the new life in the Son, if we may judge from the Kantian conceptions he applied to St. Paul, whom he interpreted as referring to the life "in which the self-consciousness recognizes itself as a communication of God practically".[3]

Although he considered that Kant had rightly rejected the Enlightenment view that the real self is the desiring self, to which a categorical imperative is alien, Green was not satisfied with his theory of freedom and the good will. Green believed that Kant had created too many antitheses and divisions within the moral self and within the structure of the moral life. (It is to the resulting abstract character of Kant's theory that we refer in the section heading: Green's own theory was intended to provide not mere inspiration but guidance, by virtue of its concrete character). He was particularly concerned about four of these. In the first place, Kant had insisted that the true principle of morality is independent of experience,[4] thereby giving the impression that the moral law is alien to the self as we ordinarily think of it. This unfortunate view of the moral law is reflected in Kant's manner of analysis: instead of finding its origin "in a principle of consciousness which makes experience what it is,((he treated)) it as an absolutely original datum".[5] Kant's way of putting things leaves us with the impression that in the moral law we have a bit of "a priori furniture" which the

---

1. Ibid., Vol. III, pp.96-97.
2. Cf. Pro., sect. I.
3. Works, Vol. III, p.202.
4. Ibid., Vol. II, p.124.
5. Ibid., Vol. II, p.124.

mind possesses antecedently to experience, instead of making clear the true position, which is that we only have the idea of an absolutely desirable object because a spiritual principle has been at work all the time moulding our desires into the thing we ordinarily refer to as our self, although the spiritual element in this self works unrecognized by us.[1]

In the second place, Kant not only drove a wedge between the law and the empirical self, but went on to divide the self from its acts by refusing to allow that results can contribute to, or detract from, the moral goodness of an act. He thereby left the door open for every manner of hypocrisy, for a man can plead conscience for the worst atrocity.[2]

In the third place, he leaves us with the feeling that the notion of "duty for duty's sake" is self-contradictory, since it appears to be a duty to do nothing.[3] Kant's difficulty in this connection arose from his falling into the error of "supposing that there is no alternative between the determination of desire by anticipation of pleasures and its determination by the conception of a moral law".[4] The difficulty with the idea of obeying the law for its own sake is that a law without an object is nothing at all,[5] and Kant's belief that only actions motivated by pure concern to do one's duty were valuable led him to set aside as valueless the many ordinary, acts of instinctive kindness we do, and to conclude that the moral act was impossible.[6] Kant was led to this belief because he thought that we were made up of two parts, a natural or animal part and a spiritual part; it is as animals or part of nature that we are susceptible to pleasure, on his view.[7] While this view enabled him to show that we were autonomous (free from determination by natural

---

1. Ibid., Vol. II, pp.124-5.
2. Ibid., Vol. II, p.154.
3. Ibid., Vol. II, p.131.
4. Ibid., Vol. II, p.139.
5. Ibid., Vol. II, p.130.
6. Ibid., Vol. II, p.155.
7. Ibid., Vol. II, p.141.

phenomena) in willing the good, it meant that he could not explain how evil is possible, for the self which does evil acts is not really a responsible agent at all - it is merely interacting with other natural phenomena (Kant thought of desires as natural phenomena). He failed to recognize that even our wicked desires are affected by reason; if he had seen this he would not have destroyed the unity of the self and its responsibility for all its acts.[1]

Finally, Kant always conceived of morality as legislation. That perhaps (Green thinks) is one way of drawing attention to the fact that the good is not at the mercy of our passing desires: it emphasises that a conception of the moral law as self-imposed is not a formula for moral anarchy.[2] But we cannot really think of morality as legislation because there is no political superior.[3] There is also the more serious objection, that Kant seems to assume that the law must be <u>consciously</u> self-imposed. This means that the ordinary man, leading his life without thinking about the form of the moral will, is deficient in moral achievement; whereas the truth is that his actions reveal as genuine an experience of the "ought" as do the actions of the reflective man. The moral law is as much self-imposed by the former, who thinks of it as external, as it is by the latter.[4]

Kant, then, had failed to secure virtue by putting it on a completely coherent intellectual foundation. But in essentials he was right and his philosophy needed only modifications, not far-reaching alterations. Green thought that the main modification was that Kant's tendency to look at particular desires in isolation should be abandoned, as too abstract a way of proceeding. Desires - even isolated ones - are really always the detail of a character, and it is from their relation to this character that they derive their significance. Apart from character desires - for pleasure, or for anything else - are neither good nor bad. By "character" is meant "the way in which a man seeks self-satisfaction".[5] An understanding of the idea of char-

---

1. *Ibid.*, Vol. II, p.133.
2. *Ibid.*, Vol. II, p.148.
3. *Ibid.*, Vol. II, p.155.
4. *Ibid.*, Vol. II, p.149.
5. *Ibid.*, Vol. II, p.142.

acter brings another advantage over Kant. Kant had defined moral action as action which aimed at fulfilling the moral law for the sake of the law, and this is impossible. We really always pursue – for we can do no other – concrete objects.[1] The idea of character allows us to both recognize the necessarily "selfish" character of all willing, which always involves the self in presenting to itself a state of itself to be realized, and to concentrate upon distinguishing good character from bad by reference to the nature of the objects willed. Good actions will be those in which a character habituated to pursuing the good seeks its realization in "worthy objects".[2]

Before we ask how worthy objects are to be identified, we must ask whether Kant's divided self has really been unified by this view. How does Green explain the fact that we pursue unworthy objects and are generally regarded as responsible for so doing? The problem is an acute one for him since he accepts Kant's view that to will the good is rational and that to will evil is irrational; this entitles us to restate his problem as the question, How can reason be irrational? Kant, it will be remembered, explained our evil or irrational acts by pointing to their origin in a supposedly animal and natural order lying outside the ego. Green gives a different answer: he argues that the self acts *immorally* when its interests arise from its material part, i.e. the part which stands in the temporal order: this part of the self does not lie outside it (as in Kant's philosophy), because anything which is to influence the self must first have been brought before a self-distinguishing consciousness and so incorporated into the unity of the self-conscious being. The self acts *morally* when it pursues its divine vocation; the motive then arises from its recognition of its identity with the eternal consciousness. But this explanation means only that the problem of obligation is pressed back to the metaphysical level, where Kant's difficulty of explaining how the desiring (or natural) self can belong to the same order of reality as the moral law becomes instead the problem of explaining how the eternal consciousness which reproduces itself in the "spiritual" part of us could also create the "material" part

---

1. Ibid., Vol. II, p.140.
2. Ibid., Vol. II, p.143.

In the absence of an intelligible connection between the two orders and the demonstration of some primacy of the spiritual over the material order, it is impossible to say that one half of the self is more real, and has more of a claim to be obeyed. It is impossible to perceive how the "true" self, which is located outside time, can be responsible for the doings of the "natural" or "animal" self. Consequently the sense in which morality is "self-imposed" remains obscure: what interest the material self might have in taking to itself the trappings of its spiritual companion is not made clear. In Green's language, it is not demonstrated that "...God cannot properly be thought of as standing to us either in the relation of a political superior or in the relation in which desire determined by the conception of an absolute good stands to other desires as a restraining 'imperative'..."[1]

We return now to the problem of "worthy objects". Their nature may be approached by first noticing the difficulty which Green considered Kant had encountered in moving from the recognition of all rational beings as ends in themselves to the specification of goodness as the treatment by each rational being of all others as ends in themselves. Green asks, would not the fact of every man being an absolute end to himself render a common object (conceived by Kant as the enjoyment by all of a rational nature or humanity) impossible?[2] He replies that "the character of the will...though it is always a presentation by the agent of himself as an absolute end, will vary according to the objects determined in thought by relation to himself, which he seeks to attain..."[3] If we can find an order of objects which, when pursued, entitles a man to be considered (a) to be living for an object common to himself with all rational beings and consisting in the perfection of his rational nature; (b) to be living for humanity, and thus (c) to have his will "autonomous", then we will have satisfied all Kant's requirements.[4] Green thinks that he can find such objects, while avoiding (as we have seen) Kant's division of the self by bringing in the concrete idea of character as including both the spiritual and

---

1. Ibid., Vol. II, p.148.
2. Ibid., Vol. II, p.132.
3. Ibid., Vol. II, p.138.
4. Ibid., Vol. II, p.139.

animal sides of the self. These objects are at once worthy objects and common objects.

We discussed the reasons which led Green to assert the universal nature of the self in the section on metaphysics: it is there that we find his ground for assigning to worthy objects a common character. We will leave until the next section a detailed examination of his treatment of the common good. But a few remarks may be made at this point, based upon the text with which we have been primarily concerned in this section.[1] A worthy object is one which others share, in the sense that they are the better for its being pursued by an individual.[2] Pleasure, for example, though not moral or immoral in itself, is essentially immoral when pursued as an <u>object</u>, because its enjoyment is necessarily private to the individual concerned. This, however, does not take us very far. How many people must be able to share in the good pursued? Green thinks that everyone must be the better for it, but what act can ever have this character? He himself has argued that the differing contexts affect the moral nature of the act: what makes one character better makes another worse.[3] And suppose (which is always likely to be the case) that we do not know how many people will be the better for our act? Green considers that we may pursue relatively valuable ends provided that we really do believe that they are absolutely valuable.[4] This, however, seems to open the way to the abuse of conscientiousness which Green thought Kant's theory left open. Finally, who is to judge what acts better everybody? Green could not accept that the opinion of individuals themselves would invariably be a true guide. In practice, he accepted most of the decisions made by the middle class of his time as providing the appropriate guide to conduct likely to better everyone.

Green's endeavour to work with the notion of universally shareable objects created the difficulties just mentioned, and in so doing led Green to abandon (in effect) the pursuit of a "concrete" position concerned with definite ob-

---

1. Viz.,"Lectures on the Philosophy of Kant, II: The Metaphysic of Ethics", <u>Works</u>, Vol. II, p.82 et seq.
2. <u>Works</u>, Vol. II, p.145.
3. <u>Ibid</u>., Vol. II, p.143.
4. <u>Ibid</u>., Vol. II, p.146, Nettleship's summary of <u>Prolegomena</u>.

jects in favour of a "subjective" position in which the only universally valid (and hence true) good is the good will. Thus he was led to replace the abstract Kantian imperative dictating duty for duty's sake with the equally abstract imperative dictating realization of the perfect character. For only this abstraction could satisfy the three conditions (noted on page 155) which Green accepted from Kant as constituting human goodness. But the matters raised in this paragraph are best left until the next section. We will conclude this one by briefly drawing attention to an aspect of Kant's thought which Green never appears to have considered, since to observe what a man drops in his master is often as instructive as to observe what he accepts.

In his shorter essays, dealing with the philosophy of history, Kant had developed an idea which was never brought by him into connection with his moral theory: it was the idea that human antagonism might be the means whereby moral progress is realized, rather than the means of its destruction. In his moral theory Kant had assumed that so far as men do their duty they would never come into conflict with each other: conflict arose only from the pursuit of desire. Green followed him in making this assumption: pursuit of the perfect character brings men into perfect harmony with each other. But in his Idea for a Universal History with Cosmopolitan Intent, Kant laid down as the fourth principle that "The means which nature employs to accomplish the development of all faculties is the antagonism of men in society, since this antagonism becomes, in the end, the cause of a lawful order of this society".[1] He could then proceed to write that thanks are due to nature for man's quarrelsomeness, his environment, competitive vanity, and for his insatiable desire to possess or to rule, all of which things make for human moral development.[2] Kant arrived at this view of conflict by combining a belief in the beneficence of nature with rather unconvincing arguments drawn from analogies with the development of organisms,[3] but the main interest lies in "its close and obvious relation to the Dialectical Materialism which has been adopted

---

1. The Philosophy of Kant, ed. C.J.Friedrich, published by Random House in The Modern Library Series, New York, 1949, p.120.
2. Ibid., p.121.
3. Ibid., p.118.

as the official philosophy of communism".[1] Green, like Kant, believed that there was a force at work in the universe "overruling" bad actions and making for progress, but he could never bring himself at any point to see the positive value in conflict which Kant occasionally recognized, even though such ideas had acquired far wider currency by his time than they had in Kant's day. While the idea of conflict as the mechanism by which a teleological principle develops in the universe is of course problematic, the ability simply to recognise that it may have positive value would perhaps have enabled Green to avoid the retreat which we noticed into a subjective definition of the common good as good character or the will to do good, and might have provoked him instead to delineate a social order in which activity not obviously philanthropic was more securely protected. It might, in short, have made "sin" look less black, and a perfectly harmonious society of pure character less white.[2] But that aspect of the Kantian philosophy which we might call "the sinner's consolation" was not to Green's taste.

The sinner's guide: Green's theory of the common good

Green believed that the ideal of personal good which each man conceives is, when it is a concept of *true* personal good, identical with good for others:

"....however the idea of a true good may vary in the particular aspect which it presents to the individual according to the special nature of his higher interests....it remains true that, in its actuation of the individual, no less than in that ordering of society which at once is affected through that actuation of individuals and in turn conditions it, the idea does not admit of the distinction between good for self and good for others."[3]

Green justified this identification of individual with social good by appealing to the essentially social nature of the self. But it is important to note that the sense which Green gives to the proposition that "the self is social" differs from that given to it by Hegel or Bosanquet. For the latter philosophers the self exists only in and through otherness; recognition by other selves is not merely an external conditioning factor in shaping the development of selfhood, it is *constitutive* of selfhood. Green cannot take

---

1. E.F.Carritt, Morals and Politics, p.103.
2. Cf. Bosanquet on the Chatauqua Lake Assembly Grounds, Value, p.322.
3. Pro., sect. 235.

this view, which makes the self's relations internal to it, because his broader metaphysical position is unable to show how a thing can retain its unity in its relations: it was for this reason that he conceived of the eternal consciousness as a punctum stans, "manifesting" or "reproducing" itself in the finite order, but not actually <u>producing</u> itself in that order. His view that "the infinite spirit is neither fact nor relation"[1] has an implication for his conception of the relation of the self to society, for "If God cannot be described but by negatives, neither can the self within us".[2] Consequently, the view that the self is essentially social is for him not so much a metaphysical principle as a primary doctrine of life.[3] More precisely, in the context of Green's system it becomes a psychological, and not a philosophical thesis: because we must presuppose some sort of community in "any groups of men from which the society that we know can have been developed",[4] we must infer that some men at least were willing a good which was not only a good for each but for others as well; otherwise no social grouping could have come into existence. The sociality of the self is thus a hypothesis tied very closely to Green's account of the character of motivation, which is directed not towards pleasure or towards an abstract law, but towards the realization of desirable objects. It follows from Green's psychological interpretation of the conception of the self as social that the doctrine cannot have the ethical significance which it possesses in the philosophy of Hegel and Bosanquet, where it served to close the gap between self and others which generated the problem of political obligation. Other selves remain ultimately external since they are merely "included in the end for which ((a man)) lives in living for himself".[5] Selves remain essentially independent centres of consciousness, between whose desires there may be a coincidence or similarity (a will of all), but never a substantial identity.

---

1. Quoted by Nettleship in Memoir, <u>Works</u>, Vol. III, p.cxlii.
2. <u>Works</u>, Vol. III, p.87.
3. <u>Pro</u>. sect. 200.
4. <u>Ibid</u>., sect. 202.
5. <u>Ibid</u>., sect. 200.

Green was aware that his identification of personal good with social good created difficulties. Is it not the case that in his conception of the common good the highest kind of life is being sacrificed in the interests of the improvement of the masses, and that it is ridiculous to tell those who are being called upon to make this sacrifice that they are really realizing themselves in the process? More generally, in a world where individuals differ in their interests, does it even begin to look plausible to maintain that true happiness consists in realizing for others the same objects as one realizes for oneself; and that the good man's interest in these objects "carries with it an ascription of a like interest to others..."?[1] In practice, the highest character is that of the saint or reformer, and he cannot "set himself to confer happiness on others without seeking to communicate a character like his own".[2] Hence the problem is, in effect, this: is it mere caprice to refuse to accept the ascription to oneself of the object which interests the saint or reformer, namely, a character like his own?

Green's answer to these objections depends partly on his view of the sociality of the self and the brotherhood of all men as participants in the one eternal consciousness, and would consequently be open to criticisms which have already been made; but it depends also on his conception of the essential content of virtue. He cast the discussion of virtue in the form of a comparison between the Greek and the modern ideal. In Aristotle's specification of the noble life a range of excellence was actualized which went far beyond moral excellence, while Green tended to identify modern excellence with moral goodness. Is this not an impoverishment of the self? Green knew that it was not a full answer to point to the foundation of slavery beneath the ancient conception of virtue, since the richness of the Greek life might still be considered the ideal, if slavery were removed. Though he never denied that moral good does not exhaust the human good, his esteem for the saint or reformer seems to lead him to minimize the importance of values other than moral. The great gain in good which comes from the new spiritual activity of the multitude outweighs all loss to the few: "That this enhanced activity, these

---

1. *Ibid.*, sect. 236.
2. *Ibid.*, sect. 277.

enlarged interests, should involve for the virtuous much voluntary curtailment of the innocent pleasures which, but for such disturbing claims and interests, would be open to them, is, as regards the attainment of moral good, a matter of indifference. For the curtailment in itself they are neither the better nor the worse."[1] Extra-moral excellences appear to be regarded as dispensable trappings, and the moral standpoint is made the absolute reference point in assessing them.

In order to compare ancient with modern virtue Green had first to deprive the idea of virtue of any particular meaning. The Greek gentleman and the modern gentleman see their lives in such different terms, and live those lives in such different circumstances, that all content must be stripped from the notion of virtue before it appears significant to insist that they would agree on one thing at least - that the good is the good will. Green, however, considered that in willing the good will they achieved a fundamental identity of view point.

The origin of Green's willingness to define the good in this circular way was his belief that the true good is a shareable or non-competitive good. Competitiveness, or gain at the expense of another, Green always saw as sin, and the root of all social evil. In a passage which is important for the understanding of his treatment of the state he wrote that:

"Until the object generally sought as good comes to be a state of mind or character of which the attainment, or approach to attainment, by each is itself a contribution to its attainment by every one else, social life must continue to be one of war - a war, indeed, in which the mutual ground is constantly being extended and which is itself constantly yielding new tendencies to peace, but in which at the same time new vistas of hostile interests, with new prospects of failure for the weaker, are as constantly opening".[2]

To define the good as a "state of mind" clearly leaves Green's own conception of the good open to the objection which he brought against the Utilitarian definition of it in terms of feeling: if feelings are enjoyed only by those who possess them and are mutually exclusive of others, states of mind are

---

1. *Ibid.*, sect. 275.
2. *Ibid.*, sect. 245.

equally personal and exclusive. Thus any action done by a person will necessarily be incompatible with the interest of others, if their good is understood as sharing in the state of mind which the act reflects. To will the common good becomes as impossible as to will Kant's universal law. The search for the truly non-exclusive action leaves all action tainted by selfishness.

The indeterminacy which necessarily characterizes such a conception of good means that activities not manifestly involving self-sacrifice become disreputable, for they can only bring social division and propagate conflict. Green's attitude towards economic activity provides an interesting example. Having allowed that a prime interest in attaining the only non-competitive object (the perfecting of man) has never been the only influence at work in maintaining and extending social union, he notes that "trade has played an important part in bringing and keeping men together; and trade is the offspring of other interests than that just described ((i.e. the pure interest in the perfecting of man))".[1] Green immediately proceeds to assign the socializing influence of trade to the work of motives other than the selfish ones displayed in it, for trade as such could only be divisive: "...there must have been another interest at work, applying the immediate results of trade...to other ends than those which the trader...had in view".[2] Such a conception of economic life did not help to make him feel at home in nineteenth century capitalist society, and this is reflected in his somewhat patronizing way of referring to the middle class population of the time as "the children of the counter".

Given Green's attitude towards economic life it is easy to understand why his theory of the state contains no equivalent of Hegel's provision for the sphere of civil society, in which the universal seems to disappear beneath a riot of self-seeking but is in fact deepening its own self-awareness. This section of Hegel's work clearly owes something to Adam Smith's theory of the invisible hand, a theory in which Green would naturally find no inspiration. Commenting on the idea "that desires of which the object on each man's part is his own pleasure, may gradually produce a universal harmony and adjustment

---

1. Ibid., sect. 231.
2. Ibid., sect. 231.

of claims", Green argues that this can never be so because "no two or more persons whose desires were only ((for pleasure)) could really desire anything in common". He recognizes that in existing societies the pursuit of pleasure by one man seems sometimes to contribute to the pleasure of another, as when A buys an article from B; in the market situation A seems to satisfy his desire for pleasure while at the same time providing B with the means of satisfying his own desire for pleasure. The semblance of any invisible hand at work, however, is deceptive. Not only is A's desire directed to an object different from B's, but their desires "if left to their natural course... would lead to conflict". For A certainly desires the object he buys from B, but he does not want to pay for it; for the payment deprives him of the means of satisfying his other desires. Thus "he only pays the price, and so adjusts his desire for pleasure to B's, because under the given social order he can obtain the article in no other way." The analysis of the trading situation, it is to be remembered, is only an illustration of the more general truth, that the desires of different men, "so far as directed to some pleasure, are in themselves tendencies to conflict between man and man". Green notes that the market is only one of many "established means of compromise" between men, created by the action of society in order to control the naturally destructive desire for pleasures. From all this it would seem to follow that force is necessary to hold together any community in which exchange (or indeed any institution which provides pleasure for those who participate in it) has emerged. It is difficult to see how Green accommodates this analysis to his thesis that will, not force, is the basis of the modern community. At a lower level, it is interesting to note that Green had little difficulty in setting the seal of approval on the capitalist economic order, finding nothing essentially divisive in the system of private ownership. We will return to this later.[1]

In discussing Green's concept of the common good, W.D.Lamont distinguishes two possible meanings of the term. The moral consciousness may conceive the society in which it is to operate in terms of a voluntary association with a unitary object for its goal, with all the members agreeing upon this object;

---

1. All refs. are to Pro. sect. 232.

or it may conceive society in terms of a group of persons, who happen to be together irrespective of their wishes and in spite of the fact that their interests are largely discrepant, but who choose to modify their different ends in order to make for equal opportunity to realize their individual goals. As an example of the first type of common good he instances a group of people each of whom is interested in preserving places of historical interest. If they form "a society for the preservation of historical monuments" they will have a common good which is a unitary good, in the sense of being a uniting object of interest to each and all. An example of the second type of common good is the back-yard of a tenement house, where a number of people with different interests are affected - a man reading, a woman washing clothes, a dustman collecting rubbish. The common good in this situation lies in the modification which each makes in his activity to make room for the activity of the others. In Lamont's opinion, Green conceives of the common good as being of the first type, whereas the relevant sense for the study of society is the second.[1]

Lamont appears to have exaggerated the difference between the two kinds of common good. What he calls a unitary good reveals, on closer examination, the same complex structure as the second kind of common good. For the people who form a society for the preservation of historical monuments will be found to have parcelled out the different activities in such a way that if all could be seen engaging in their specific activities at the same time, the situation would not appear to be any less complex than that in the back-yard of the tenement: one man would be pursuing his special interest in the financial affairs of the society, another would be canvassing for new members, and so on. There *is* a difference between the two kinds of society distinguished by Lamont, but it is to be drawn along other lines. What he terms a "unitary good" is strictly a "limited good". The society which exists in the back-yard of the tenement is distinguished from this by its more comprehensive good: in so far as it exists, it aims to realize the interests not only of the man reading, but also of the washerwoman and the dustman.

The most important distinction, however, is between a common good which

---

1. W.D.Lamont, Introduction to Green's Moral Philosophy, MacMillan, London, 1902, pp.216-217.

is common only because it is the negation of all differences, and a common good which not only provides for but actually demands internal differentiation.[1] It is true that there are passages in which Green appears to welcome differentiation; when discussing his contention that social life is the condition of the development of personality, for example, Green writes that "It does not follow from this that all persons must be developed in the same way. The very existence of mankind presupposes the distinction between the sexes... ((and this distinction implies)) a corresponding difference between the modes in which the personality of men and women is developed...Nor does it appear how those reciprocal services which elicit the feeling of mutual dependence, and thus promote the recognition by one man of another as an 'alter ego', would be possible without different limitations of function and ability, which determine the range within which each man's personality developes..."[2] But the principal area in which Green felt there was genuine reason for difference was rather narrowly conceived: he considered that it was permissible to be an "obscure saint" rather than an active social reformer. Because the ultimate good is a state of mind or character and not the amount of desirable social work achieved, the "obscure saint" who leads a life of "unnoticed conscientious goodness" may take a place beside the man who devotes himself to "the redress of wrongs and the purging of social vices".[3] Whatever differences within society Green may have considered legitimate, however, it remains true that his conception of the common good as essentially non-competitive tends to pass into a conception of that good as indeterminate and as negated by the emergence within it of the particular goods of individuals, as when he writes that a man cannot share "any object which is an object to him in virtue of his special temper and tastes".[4] Such an assumption naturally provides no solid foundations for a liberal political order.

Green was aware that his willingness to find a common good only where there are men with pure hearts and wills tends to lead his argument towards

---

1. In this connection, see R.N.Berki on Political Freedom and Hegelian Metaphysics, Political Studies, Vol. XVI, No.3, Oct. 1968.
2. Pro. sect. 191.
3. Ibid., sect. 303.
4. Works, Vol. II, p.149.

the Kantian conclusion according to which it is questionable whether a moral act has ever been done. In the course of maintaining that the state is founded upon a conception of common good he endeavoured to answer the objection that the state has been erected by men whose motives were completely selfish. This difficulty may be related to a broader problem confronting Green. Green believed that his own ethical theory was concrete, avoiding the abstractions of the hedonist position on the one hand and the Kantian position on the other. It offered the sinner - and of course the good man - a determinate and stable condition as an ideal to be realized. His position would only be open to the charge of being an empty conception of virtue (in taking the good as the good will, and the good will as the will that wills the good) "if there had not already taken place such a realization of the soul's faculties as gave meaning, though not its full and final meaning, to the definition of the good".[1] In fact, the spiritual principle has already brought about a realization of the soul's faculties in certain pursuits and achievements before philosophical attempts to define the good commence. Thus "the idea of the good..is an idea... which gradually creates its own filling."[2] It is this doctrine which enables Green to hold that the external social order is not really external, and that freedom is to be found within it in the duties of one's station.[3] But if the social order is the creation of evil wills, how can this be so?

Green's attempts to deal with this difficulty produced a curious result: from defending the notion of man's freedom he moved to a position in which the personal responsibility of even the most potent actors was diminished. More precisely, the individual responsibility which he rescued from its bondage to the natural order he came near to sacrificing to "social influences" which "overrule" selfish action for good.[4]

Green could not content himself with observing that there must (on logical grounds alone) be a preponderance of pure action in the external social order (on the ground that otherwise it would not exist at all); he felt obliged to

1. Pro., sect. 254.
2. Ibid., sect. 241.
3. Ibid., sect. 183.
4. Lectures, sects. 128, 129.

deal with the historical reality, in which the most conspicuous actors on the world's stage are usually found to be wanting in purity of heart. How were the logical hypothesis and the historical facts to be reconciled? Green's problem originated in his conviction that by their works shall men be known. This doctrine would be unproblematic if good motives always produced manifestly good effects, and if bad motives were always followed by bad effects. Green believed that bad motives are indeed always followed by bad effects, but that "our limited vision" makes this difficult to recognize.[1] To us it appears that selfish motives lead an able man to head a movement of political reform which has beneficial consequences.[2] In fact, however, a closer inspection would reveal that "the selfish political leader was himself much more of an instrument than of an originating cause, and that his action was but a trifling element in the sum or series of actions which yielded the political movement". The beneficent results really are beneficent, but their origin is to be found in a source other than the apparent one, i.e. the selfish will of the leader; and the evil motive of the leader does have bad effects in the world, but the limitation which it in fact places on the good brought to society is unperceived by us.[3] Napoleon provides an example of a man whose bad motives seemed to produce good effects. But the more we learn about him the more clear does it become that what was evil in his policy arose from his personal selfishness and that of his contemporaries, while what was good in it was due to "higher and purer influences of which he and they were but the medium".[4]

Green's desire to assess politics from the moral standpoint thus leads him to make Napoleon responsible for evil, whilst responsibility for the good in his act is diffused over suitably virtuous individuals. These turn out to be worthy but faceless members of the mass which lies below the great man. In short, what is overlooked by the person who sees in the social order only the activity of selfish men is the "unnoticed effort on the part of men obscure

---

1. *Pro.*, sect. 295.
2. *Ibid.*, sect. 295.
3. *Ibid.*, sect. 295.
4. *Ibid.*, sect. 298.

because unselfish...((and the)) silent process in the general heart of men".[1] The mass is the least adulterated of the agencies operative in history. The individuals who compose the mass are themselves presumably open to the same selfish interests to which the great political figures succumb, but Green does not explain how their weaknesses are overruled for good. Green admits indeed that neither agents nor patients in the formation of the state have willed the common good from pure disinterestedness, but then proceeds to attribute to the state responsibility for any failure to develop the real but limited sense of common good which is exhibited in the habitual and instinctive conduct of the ordinary man. Specifically, lack of full civic virtue in the ordinary man "is a sign that the state is not a true state; that it is not fulfilling its primary functions of maintaining law equally in the interest of all, but is being administered in the interest of classes". As soon as the corrupting influence of sinister interests is removed from the state, the virtue of the mass will spring forth.

Green finds it much less difficult to explain why good motives may appear to produce bad effects: either the motives were not really good at all, or else the good effects were offset by encounters with evil actions originating in impure wills.[2]

All the difficulties which we have traced in Green's conception of the common good flow from the dualism which his metaphysics never overcame. Personality was divided by him into two halves, and the "animal" half was never quite made respectable by complete integration with the "spiritual" half. The assertion of his particularity by any agent was always tinged with animality or sinfulness. This prevented Green from developing that concrete conception of the good which he desiderated and which would have afforded general guidance on the structure of the good life. The common good and the good will were always defined by him as the negation of determinate, personal good. In a religious idiom, Green's limitation arises from the close relationship he saw between freedom and love: commenting on Galatians v. 13, he observed that St. Paul there brought out the connection between freedom and love in the life of

---

1. Lectures, sect. 130.
2. Pro., sect. 295.

the Son in the maxim "use not liberty for an occasion to the flesh, but by love serve one another".[1] Since St. Paul had not concerned himself with political freedom it is scarcely surprising that such a conception of the new life - a conception which Green never concretized - should appear as an inadequate basis for dealing with the problem of political obligation.

Perhaps the most paradoxical thing about the theory of the common good is that it is "advanced as the key notion in moral philosophy for the first time precisely in the same period in which this concept more and more obviously had no real application in the life of the community".[2] If there really were a number of distinct sections and moralities within the community[3] in the nineteenth century, then it would follow that sociological factors alone would have prevented Green from attaining to a concrete theory of the common good. What we have chosen to emphasize, however, are those limitations in his theory of the common good which flow from his metaphysics.

The instrument of salvation: the state

On the question of whether the human condition was to be permanently marked by sin or selfishness, Green was ambiguous. Sometimes he suggested that the plan of the world assigns a permanent place to a lower nature in the perfecting of the human soul: the tendencies in which that nature consists will never be dominant, but it is only in conflict with them that the higher energies of man can emerge. In that case the perfect condition for man will not be free of pain or the need for sacrifice.[4] At other times he expressed the belief that "There is no contradiction in the supposition of a human life purged of vices and with no wrongs left to set right".[5] Whatever Green's final position on this question, it is the latter belief which is reflected in his treatment of the state; and it is to this belief that some of the chief limitations in his theory of political obligation may be traced.

When Green looked around him he found that the evil remaining in English life was attributable to causes which were not integrally connected with the

---

1. Works, Vol. III, p.202.
2. A. MacIntyre, Secularization and Moral Change, O.U.P., 1967, p.15.
3. Ibid., p.22.
4. Pro. sect. 276.
5. Quoted by Nettleship, Works, Vol. III, p.cxlii.

modern state or social order. These causes were, for the most part, survivals from the feudal age, anachronisms which infected society with their unfortunate consequences, but could be eliminated by determined and well-intentioned men. Most prominent amongst these anachronisms was the surviving English aristocracy. Speaking to the Oxford Reform League in 1867, he said that "We have reached that stage in our history which Lord Macaulay, I think, is said to have prophesied, when the conflict is no longer between the house of commons and the crown or the lords, but between the people and the house of commons...I speak within the mark when I say that four-fifths of the lower house are either great landowners or belong to the families of great landowners..."[1] Evil did not originate, in Green's opinion, in "the people" (by which he meant the bulk of the populace as led by the middle class), but in the landed gentry which still possessed effective political power. It was for this reason that he placed rights in the centre of his political theory, when one might have expected him to have wished to get away from that concept as being too liable to pass over into a vindication of wilfulness and egoism. Rights were needed by the people to achieve that self-realization which the existing social order made difficult or impossible. The great majority of the people - he put the figure at five-sixths - were treated as "political dunces", and the prevailing social policies would have tended by inexorable necessity to create revolution were it not for the statesmanship of John Bright.[2]

Since the people were not the source of political evils no great dangers were to be foreseen from their acquisition of rights. Education would remove any traces of wilfulness in the use made by them of rights; as Green expressed it when discussing the duty of the reforming politicians to the children of the future, "Under God, it is to good books and a knowledge of the laws of nature that we must chiefly trust to make them, when they become their own masters, healthy and wise and virtuous".[3]

Green, then, was more conscious of the evils which lingered from the feudal past than of those which the development of democracy might bring in

---

1. Memoir, Works, Vol. III, p.cx.
2. Memoir, Works, Vol. III, pp. cxi, cxii.
3. Ibid., Vol. III, p.454.

the future. This made him more willing to emphasize the rights of the people, or, as he once put it, to untie the man's legs first, and then to speculate how he would walk.[1] Where Stuart Mill and de Tocqueville fixed their eyes on the future and saw the spectacle of civilization disappearing beneath mass mediocrity, Green looked only to the past and its reflection in the present, and saw a different evil, which was the moral corruption which the aristocratic order created in every rank of society, and not simply in its own: his view was that "Our present system of great estates...gives a false set to society from top to bottom. It causes exaggerated luxury at the top, flunkeyism in the middle, poverty and recklessness at the bottom".[2] The aristocracy produced not only moral corruption: the system of legislation upon which it rested destroyed the very core of the nation, for the system of primogeniture hindered the formation of "that mainstay of social order and contentment, a class of small proprietors tilling their own land", as well as keeping land in the hands of those who have not the money to improve it.[3]

Green did not consider that any extreme measures were required in order to remedy the evils of landlordism and flunkeyism. There was no question of using violence to expropriate the selfish group. This is scarcely surprising when it is remembered that he saw in the novel an important source of social unity. It was in a common education that he found the true social leveller. The central article in his reforming faith was perhaps the belief that

"Men and women who have been at school together, or who have been at schools of the same sort, will always understand each other, will always be at their ease together, will be free from social jealousies and animosities however different their circumstances in life may be."[4]

Green's optimism about the prospects of social harmony through educational reform depended very much on this narrowing down of the most important sphere of self-realization to a very limited conception of the "spiritual" side of life. (viz. to formal education). This enabled him to view with relative

---

1. Memoir, Works, Vol. III, p.cxii.
2. Ibid., p.cxii.
3. Ibid., Vol. III, p.378.
4. Ibid., Vol. III, p.458.

equanimity any differences between classes occurring within the "material" or "animal" spheres, so that he could write immediately after the section just quoted that

"In every nation, perhaps, there must be a certain separation between those who live solely by the labour of their heads or by the profits of capital, between members of the learned professions and those engaged constantly in buying and selling, between those who are earning their money and those who are living on the income of large accumulated capital..."[1]

We have already noted that Green understood the common good to be a non-competitive good, a good which could be gained by each without detriment to the prospects of others. The last two quotations enable us to make clear how Green managed to overcome the apparent impossibility of turning this notion into an operative criterion for his discussion of the best form of social organization. He did it as follows. His conception of the common good required man to do the impossible by willing the purely universal will: but the differences whose elimination he could not desiderate without making the good will as unattainable as Kant had made it are relegated by him to a plane where they are deprived of moral significance. In other words, by denying significance to differences necessarily occurring within the common good Green manages to let in by the back door what would appear to be excluded by his insistence on complete disinterestedness and absolute purity of heart.

What Green objected to in practice, of course, was not a differentiated social order as such - although in his theory he was unable to find a place for differences - but to certain forms of differentiation. Above all he objected to what he considered to be the unnecessary accentuation of social differences by an educational system which placed more emphasis upon class than upon intelligence, and which ran parallel to the social strata instead of intersecting them.[2] Such a system did more than anything else to create conflict in society, for it removed from the community its strongest internal bond, characterized thus by Green:

---

1. Ibid., Vol. III, p.458.
2. Ibid., Vol. III, p.390.

"Parents whose children are taught together have the deepest of all interests in common, and cannot hold very far aloof from each other".[1] However, although he wished to see a ladder of learning which should extend "from the gutter to the universities",[2] his concern was rather with improving the education of those nearest to the gutter than with removing from the great public schools their monopoly of the claim to provide an education for gentlemen.

The term "gentleman", Green felt, had acquired a meaning in England unknown in any other country. It did not refer to lineage, land tenure or moral achievement, but to "a kind of manner and tone of feeling" imparted by the public schools. Thus when Green formulated his vision of English society as it should be, that being a condition "in which all honest citizens will recognize themselves and be recognized by each other as gentlemen,[3] his aspiration was not at first sight very radical: he wanted only a change of spirit in the different orders, and this apparently involved no redistribution of income or extensive legislative programme. In short, his enemies were on the one hand snobbery, or that "unconscious social insolence" which the English mistook for gentlemanliness, and the correlative envy of the lower orders on the other.[4] It is not difficult to see, however, that snobbery often has foundations which extend far beyond the formal machinery of education: Green was extremely optimistic when he saw in the school system the cause, instead of the reflex, of society at large; or if it is more correct to say that the public school system not only reflected but propagated a certain set of values, it is equally correct to say that this instance of Green's concentrating all evil into one centre is typical of his general style of analysis.

It was mentioned in passing that Green was not too disturbed by the exclusion of the working class from the education of a gentleman: the improvement of the lot of those nearest the gutter was not his first concern. No doubt there were good reasons for concentrating upon limited and practicable

---

1. Ibid., Vol. III, p.475.
2. Ibid., Vol. III, p.387.
3. Ibid., Vol. III, p.476.
4. Ibid., Vol. III, p.460.

objectives as Green in fact did, but Green's own rationalization of his limited aims would seem to reveal a little of that self-satisfaction which he enjoined the truly virtuous man to eschew. In his lecture on the Oxford High School for boys, for example, he acknowledged that only the most exceptional of the sons of artisans would be able to gain scholarships to the school, which was candid enough of him, but added that he considered that "the indirect result of their admission will be far-reaching. These boys may grow up to be educational missionaries to the class from which they sprung." Warming to the thought of the vast effects a few scholarships might have in resolving the problems of industrial society, Green was struck by an analogy which seemed particularly appropriate:

"Perhaps not one in a hundred of the soldiers in the French revolutionary armies ever really obtained promotion to the rank of an officer, but the knowledge that the promotion was open to every one gave a spirit unknown before, and a unity higher than mere description can produce, to the body of citizen soldiers. So the knowledge among the citizens of Oxford that at any rate no barrier of social exclusion stood between their sons and the highest university education would, I believe, give them a new feeling of reverence for knowledge and a respect for those who can impart it."[1]

The divorce between spirit and nature which had pervaded Green's metaphysics thus produced dividends when it reappeared in his social thought: if the middle class avoided the conspicuous arrogance of the aristocracy it could retain without serious injustice the enjoyment of the more material advantages society had to offer, whilst claiming in justification that their essence was spiritual and so universal. It does not seem to have occurred to him in this connection that the "missionaries" would be spreading a gospel that offered a balance of advantage in favour of the middle class, although he perceived immediately that the apparent virtue of the English aristocracy in being non-exclusive (because it bestowed baronetcies on the children of the counter) was really a form of bribery; he referred to the conferring of titles as "this corruption ((which)) is eating out the heart of the upper

---

1. *Ibid.*, Vol. III, p.475.

commercial class..."[1] It should in fairness be added that Green concluded the passage in which he drew an analogy between the position of the artisans and the rank and file in the French revolutionary armies with the remark that his might be a student's flight of fancy; although this might only mean that he had little hope that the workers would listen carefully enough to the missionaries amongst them. The subject of armies brings to mind another field in which Green's somewhat formal conception of education led him to an unduly optimistic assessment of the prospects of a smooth democratic evolution. Nettleship records that he had confidence in the future of Prussia, and quotes him as citing in support of this view the fact that "the soldiers can all read, and the artisans...seem to be free from the worse forms of socialism, and under the guidance of Schulze-Delitsch to be developing schemes of co-operation and self-help".[2]

Green's attitude towards the least fortunate section of the community and his view of the appropriate remedies for its condition were determined partly by his willingness to find in feudalism and feudal remnants the source of all ills; partly by his universalistic individualism, which assumed that the material disadvantages of the working-class did not deprive it of the moral and political capacity which he unhesitatingly ascribed to the middle-class; and partly also by what he considered to be the inherent limitations to the scope of state action.

If Green found much that was sinful and socially divisive in the political and social life of the aristocracy, he found surprisingly little egoism to reprimand in the life of the plutocracy. The right to property he derived from the right each individual has to the instruments necessary to lead the free moral life; the power of appropriation only became a right when recognized by society. The life of primitive communities in which the right to private property was limited he found defective because it prevented the development of a full sense of personal responsibility - the individual was given an opportunity to achieve self-discipline in only a few areas, and this in turn meant that he was insensitive to obligations in other fields.[3] He did not pause to

---

1. Memoir, Works, Vol. III, p.cxi.
2. Ibid., p.xlii.
3. Lectures, sect. 219.

consider whether an unlimited development of personality could intelligibly be contemplated but simply moved straight on to make the assumption that the range of appropriation could not be limited without thwarting self-realization. Even if an unlimited development of personality were conceivable it would not follow, of course, that unlimited private property is either desirable or essential to it. One thing Green could not avoid noticing, however, and this was that the emancipation of the individual and the right of unlimited acquisition had been accompanied by the rise throughout Europe of cities thronged with a demoralized proletariat.[1] Surely this meant that under capitalism the pursuit of a legitimate conception of personal good did not in fact coincide with good for others? Green was not prepared to admit that the emerging industrial society involved an essentially competitive form of common good (which for him would not be a common good at all). He argued that there was no causal connection between capitalism and the existence of a proletariat, finding the origin of the latter, instead, in the serf class which conquering landlords had brought into existence in the past: the contemporary proletariat descended from this class and, because they were unable to contract freely for the sale of their labour and were lacking "a sense of family responsibility which might have made them insist on having the chance of saving" they failed to enjoy the opportunity for private ownership which would otherwise have been theirs.[2] Inequality of ownership is traced by Green to the structure of the universe: if the teleological development of the eternal consciousness aims at realizing itself in persons, inequality of property-ownership follows necessarily, both because individuals are variously gifted, and because different amounts of property are required to perform the different social functions which fall to different individuals.[3] Freedom of trade follows from the same principle;[4] and freedom of bequest should not be interfered with because the sense of family responsibility would be weakened.[5] Green considered that the abolition

1. Ibid., sect. 223.
2. Ibid., sect. 229.
3. Ibid., sect. 223.
4. Ibid., sect. 224.
5. Ibid., sect. 225.

of peerages would render less likely unequal endowment of sons by their fathers. Aristocratic landowners should be stripped of the power of settlement.[1] Land, indeed, was the one subject upon which Green did not hesitate before imposing fetters. Land ownership was essentially competitive and so hostile to the public good: "The capital gained by one is not taken from another, but one man cannot acquire more land without others having less..."[2] The evils which Green was prepared to ascribe to unregulated landlords were wide-ranging: they damaged public health by clearing out villages and leaving the people homeless; they left fertile land uncultivated; they built unhealthy houses in unhealthy places, prevented communication and forebade the erection of dissenting chapels.[3] These things aggravated the condition of the proletariat, which the landlords had created, and which was left unschooled, unhoused and with its health injured. The condition in which the irresponsible landlord had left the proletariat explained also its craving for drink and its openness to victimiziation by unscrupulous employers.[4] Thus the middle-class was enabled to retain its moral and political purity.

Green referred to those in trade who were not unduly anxious to keep their workers above the bread line as those "less scrupulous hirers of labour" and as "eager traders".[5] His relatively gentle language in this connection indicates that he was more easily able to take in his stride the misuse of labour by employers than their support for the southern states in the American Civil War. Nettleship confirms this judgment when he writes that "The prevailing judgment of educated English opinion upon the American question remained in his mind as the crying proof of its shallowness".[6]

Slavery was in fact the issue in which Green's emotions were most deeply involved. It trenched most deeply upon the sanctity of individual personality, and consequently commanded his sympathy in a way which no supra-personal

---

1. *Ibid.*, sect. 235.
2. *Ibid.*, sect. 229.
3. *Ibid.*, sect. 229.
4. *Ibid.*, sect. 230.
5. *Works*, Vol. III, pp. 376-377.
6. Memoir, *Works*, Vol. III, p.xliv.

political issue ever could. The issues of Polish independence and the Danish Duchies, for example, and the unification of Italy, never really caught his imagination.[1] This, of course, is fully consistent with the view he expressed in the Prolegomena, that it was "in persons that the spirit operative in man finds its full expression and realisation".[2]

The American war itself Green interpreted in uncomplicated moral terms as "the great struggle between wilfulness and social right across the Atlantic."[3] But even the wilful direction taken by educated opinion on the slavery question did not weaken his faith in the middle-class and in the power of enlightenment; it only suggested the need for further enlightenment. It was not so much to selfish class-interest as to the age's ignorance of true philosophy that he attributed this particular shortcoming: the trouble was that "A philosophy based on feeling was still playing the anarch in its thought."[4] Thus the evils of capitalism, together with the causes of war, could be traced to the past, and the support for slavery could be attributed to ignorance. The people retained its purity.

The tendency to make evil and political conflict unfortunate relics or a passing and incidental malaise in the human condition found theoretical articulation in Green's main thesis in the Lectures on the Principles of Political Obligation, that will, not force, is the basis of the state. He wanted to show that Hobbes and Spinoza had not been able consistently to assert that men are by nature hostile to one another and lack completely any sense of a common good, and to deny also their claim that the state could have rights which were not derived from a moral end to which it was subservient.

It was Hobbes that Green most disliked of the individualist theorists, perhaps because Hobbes made the first determined effort to reduce duty to appetite and self-interest; or perhaps because he never seemed at all unhappy about his endeavour to do this. Certainly for one whose heroes were Vane and Cromwell it was strong language to describe Hobbes' doctrines as "good hearing

---

1. Memoir, Works, Vol. III, p.xlii.
2. Pro., sect. 183.
3. Works, Vol. III, p.117.
4. Ibid., Vol. III, p.117.

for the courtiers of Charles II".[1]

In resisting the endeavour to translate right into might Green found a partial ally in Rousseau, but was dissatisfied by that side of Rousseau's thought which would deny legitimacy to any existing state and indeed would not guarantee that the general will was expressed even in the ideal state. It is interesting (if predictable) to note that Green's critique of Rousseau bears no trace of the objection raised by Burke, Hegel and Bosanquet, that Rousseau errs in insisting that the general will only emerges from the ashes of sub-groups within society.

The difficulties with Green's own doctrine (viz. that will, not force, is the basis of the state) were twofold. In order to overcome Rousseau's potential anarchism he defined the general will so broadly that it could be found practically anywhere: the mere existence of a society was enough to establish its presence. His own treatment of the general will took shape against a critique not only of Rousseau but of Austin also. Austin had the merit of recognizing sovereignty in a determinate person or persons, but made the mistake of deriving obedience from the power of the sovereign. He did not realize that the sovereign only commands obedience because his commands embody the general will. When they cease to do so his power will disappear, although this may take time. Thus Green extends the idea of consent to the point where it exists whenever there is rule.[2] It is this consent which Green refers to as the general will - it is "a sense of possessing common interests, a desire for common objects on the part of the people..,"[3] or the "impalpable congeries of the hopes and fears of a people, bound together by common interests and sympathy."[4] Green endeavours to avoid condoning despotism, not by denying that there is a general will under such government, but by maintaining that there is really no sovereign. More correctly, the real sovereign - the one which embodies the general will - is the customary authorities (priests,

---

1. Ibid., Vol. III, p.98.
2. Lectures, sects. 83-84.
3. Ibid., sect. 85.
4. Ibid., sect. 86.

heads of families, village councils, etc.) of the society, while the despotic sovereign which derives obedience from fear alone is able to maintain its existence only by confining its operations within very narrow limits, e.g. to tax-collecting.[1] It does not exercise sovereignty in the sense of legislative and executive power. Green's analysis has an odd consequence. By holding that the despot is an excrescence on the community he is able to argue that resistance may be justifiable because it will not produce anarchy;[2] but it could also be argued that despotism is not such a bad form of government after all, since it does not touch the lives of the subjects at many points and that therefore the case for resistance is correspondingly weakened.

In the second place, while he recognized the need for sovereignty or coercive power, Green was quite unable to use the concept of the general will for the purpose he intended, viz., to justify the state's possession of coercive power, because he began by making the general will so pure that it could never explain the need for force. Green's attitude towards force, in fact, is only intelligible when the dualism of his metaphysics is once more recalled. Force, for Green, belonged to the external world, the physical world of nature. Hence it operates in a different medium from the good will, and can never bear directly on the moral life. Because sovereignty is a reflection of our animal nature it would seem most consistent for Green to hold that it will naturally disappear as disinterested concern for the common good spreads among the populace. It is interesting to observe Marxist elements of this kind occurring in English idealism: Green must in principle visualize a withering away of the state, while Oakeshott assigns such an important place to economic factors (the distribution of property) in securing and preserving freedom that one is reminded of economic determinism.

It has often been noted that the principle of utility upon which Bentham constructed his position had no necessary connection with the individualism he espoused. A similar observation is true of Green. His endeavour to circumscribe state action by appealing to the intrinsic nature of morality (as something internal and inaccessible) provided a rather precarious foundation for

1. *Ibid.*, sects. 87-88.
2. *Ibid.*, sect. 89.

political liberty, as liable to boomerang as the principle of utility. There is here none of the rugged dislike of interfering fellows which had been part of the classical liberal spirit; his position leaves open the inference that if the internal spirit _should_ prove accessible to force, not being after all in a different medium, then there is in principle no limit to the coercion to which it may be subjected, provided that this makes for an increase in virtue.

Green's contrast between the internal and the external, between spirit and force, created throughout his political theory difficulties with which he wrestled in vain. His treatment of punishment provides a further illustration. Force is required by our animal nature: but the state often punishes acts which do not seem to flow from the animal nature; how can this be just? Green must of course maintain that in punishing the state is fulfilling some moral end, but to do so he has to find a moral failing in every crime: the drunken mother who unintentionally lies on her child and smothers it does so accidentally, but gets drunk intentionally.[1] But if there is to be any point in punishing crime, then the moral failing which produced it must be removed. Green allows this and in so doing contradicts his assertion that the state can only produce external conformity. In terms of his treatment of punishment, this means that Green moved from the initial position, that to use force upon a person is to treat him as an animal or a thing,[2] to the opposite position, that to use force upon a person might well be the means of raising him from animality to a moral or spiritual life: punishment is "morally the best thing that can happen to ((the criminal))" - although Green insisted that it was not supposed to be inflicted for that reason, being only for the maintenance of the general system of rights.[3] But when it is allowed that force may bring about "the moral new birth",[4] it is difficult to see why its application should be confined to those who have broken the law.

It was upon the external nature of force that Green based an even more important step in his argument: from it he derived a principle of limitation upon state action. The part the state could play in human salvation or per-

---

1. _Ibid._, sect. 199.
2. _Ibid._, sect. 176.
3. _Ibid._, sect. 206.
4. _Ibid._, sect. 206.

fection was confined to controlling the range of actions which were external in the sense that they were necessary to the good life and hence to be performed even if done from bad motives. Green retained to the end of his life the conviction that there was an inwardness to goodness which put it beyond the ability of the state to create, but it was difficult for him to be clear about whether he meant that the state simply could not, or whether it ought not, to interfere in the life of the individual. In the last formulation of his position, in <u>Liberal Legislation and Freedom of Contract</u>, he continued to maintain that personal endeavour was the only means of fulfilling the human vocation, but dropped his presumption against state action as such: instead of holding that the presence of a law inevitably tainted the motive to virtue, he allowed that compulsory standards in health, education and land tenure need not at all interfere with the independence and self-reliance of those whom law required to do what they would otherwise do themselves.[1] The law now became "a powerful friend" to the good man. This shift allowed him to extend the sphere of state action, but did not alter his diagnosis of the origin of evil: the landlords, for example, remained responsible for the creation of the proletariat, although the problem could only be solved by state action and not by charity.

We must return to the question of slavery once again, this time in connection with a more general problem it raised for Green in an acute form, which was the nature of rights and of the duty of resistance. Green objected to the natural rights theory, which gave to individuals rights without corresponding duties, but was prepared to accept that there were natural rights in the sense of conditions essential to the development of personality. In his own phrase, those rights may be called natural which are "necessary to the end which it is the vocation of human society to realise."[2] This does not of course indicate which particular rights are natural. In order to strip the theory of rights of its individualistic associations Green advanced a thesis calculated to make rights into a vehicle for collectivism. The thesis by which

---

1. <u>Works</u>, Vol. III, p.375.
2. <u>Lectures</u>, sect. 9.

he hoped to stand individualism on its head was that rights are made by recognition. Until social recognition is given to a man's rights, Green argued, they are merely _powers_. These powers, or potentialities, are most fully actualized when given legal recognition. What the old individualist theorists had called natural rights were in fact only powers, and what they failed to explain was how a power could ever become a right. Just as the appeal to society's vocation did not tell us what rights ought to be secured, so the assertion that rights are made by recognition does not indicate what powers ought to be recognized.

What did Green mean by recognition? He intended the word to mean more than we ordinarily mean when we speak of recognizing a face or motor-car. In this sense we do not think of the recognition as actually bringing the recognized objects into existence; we think of it as a mental act without external consequences - it is what precedes action. Green, however, thought of recognition as actually making rights, and as expressing itself in the world in institutional form; it is not merely a mental act on the part of different individuals. Thus he writes of institutions that "it cannot be said that the most elementary consciousness of right is prior to them, or they to it. They are the expressions in which it becomes real".[1] On the other hand, he constantly tended to fall into ways of speaking which would seem to imply that recognition is a subjective act on the part of individuals. On one occasion, for example, he said that rights are derived from "some idea that men have about each other",[2] without making clear that ideas are anything more than states of mind. On another occasion, when discussing the nature of a man's capacity for good/acts, which is his ability to will the common good or (what is the same thing) to recognize the claims of others to realize the good will, Green distinguished between what was necessary for the provision of rights and for the attainment of true moral goodness. In order to possess rights it is not necessary that interest in a good conceived as common to himself with others should be a man's dominant motive. The posing of the problem in terms of motivation led Green to continue(in a passage which once again interpreted recognition psychologically, as an intermittent mental state of the subject), as follows:

---

1. Ibid., sect. 115.
2. Ibid., sect. 136.

to possess rights, he said,

"It is enough if that which he presents to himself from time to time as his good, and which accordingly determines his action, is so far affected by consideration of the position in which he stands to others - of the way in which this or that possible action of his would affect them, and of what he would have to expect from them in return - as to result habitually, without force or fear of force, in action not incompatible with conditions necessary to the pursuit of a common good on the part of others. In other words, it is the presumption that a man in his general course of conduct will of his own motion have respect to the common good, which entitles him to rights at the hands of the community."[1] This is the sort of analysis which would be appropriate to elucidating what we mean when we say that X is a smoker, even though he is not at present smoking: we are presuming that in certain situations he will smoke. But such analysis will not elucidate that aspect of institutional life which we refer to by words such as "ought" or "right": it does not establish why we ought to preserve anything, let alone that a man is entitled to rights, as Green insists in his last sentences.

Further difficulties with the idea of recognition will emerge shortly. Before proceeding it will be best to state the general problem posed by Green's theory of rights. We have before us two propositions which Green hoped to reconcile. These are that rights are relative to moral ends, and that rights are made by recognition. Unfortunately he was never able to give a satisfactor theoretical answer to a possibility which at once occurs: suppose that some rights necessary to the realization of moral ends are not in fact recognized? And if rights are recognized which are not necessary to moral ends are they really rights? The two propositions never managed to coexist harmoniously in Green's theory.

The most obvious objection to the view that rights are dependent upon capacit to pursue moral ends would be that we do in fact recognize rights in creatures which have no conception of moral ends, such as embryos, lunatics and idiots. Green discusses this objection in connection with the right to life, which he can only explain in such cases by extending the idea of recognition very greatl He suggests that (for example) the lunatic's right to life may be explained

---

1. Ibid., sect. 208.

by ascribing to him a social capacity – an ability to recognize rights in others – which is in abeyance during his temporal existence but will be resumed in a future social life beyond the earthly one.[1] This argument would seem to make the lunatic's fate hinge perilously upon some exquisite reasoning; those who were not convinced by it of the reality of a society beyond the earthly one would have no reason to recognize his right to life. But Green has two further arguments. The lunatic might be the performer of a *passive* social function: he might serve a moral end indirectly, by giving others the opportunity to do good works.[2] This argument seems to prove too much, for those who were able to pursue moral ends but refused to do so might still claim rights on the ground that the opportunity to recognize them unilaterally gave others the chance to display far more virtue than they would in reciprocal recognition. Green's third argument is only a further aspect of the second. We might consider it impossible to determine in practice at what point the capacity for social good was permanently lost, and it would then be safest always to regard it as still present.

Perhaps the most important problem arising from Green's emphasis upon the necessity of recognition to make rights real is that it raised once again that familiar liberal spectre, the danger that the majority was to be left to decide what rights should exist. It was at this point that the issue of slavery came once again into focus, for in the southern states of the U.S.A. Green found "a slave-holding, slave-breeding, and slave-burning oligarchy, on whom the curse of God and humanity rests."[3] Green thought that his own theory had special merits when applied to cases of oppressed minorities such as the southern slaves. The theories which derived political authority from contract would make the right of resistance dependent upon an act of the whole people. Criticising Locke's discussion of the right of resistance, Green noted that the condition laid down by Locke to justify it–viz. an act of the whole people governed – was one which would be impossible to realize except in a Swiss canton.

---

1. *Lectures*, sect. 154.
2. *Ibid.*, sect. 154.
3. Memoir, *Works*, Vol. III, p.xliii.

He allowed that in practice Locke got round this difficulty, but only by assuming that the impossible was possible.[1] Even if Locke's condition could be met, there would still remain the difficulty of ascertaining what was and what was not an act of the people; and no right of resistance lay with any group short of the majority.[2] By deriving political authority from the function of government rather than from contract Green felt that his theory removed the possibility of irrelevance and toleration of injustice which Locke's contained. In principle resistance could be undertaken by a single individual, if he could show that the government was failing to fulfil its moral function.

In theory, then, there appears to be a great difference between Locke's position and Green's. But closer inspection reveals little practical difference. The individual or minority claiming a right to resist must, on Green's view, be able to show that their action is required by the common good, and because Green considered unacceptable any action which would threaten a community with anarchy this meant that the opinion of the majority became once again the determining consideration: "The assertion...by the citizen of any right which the state does not recognize must be founded on a reference to an acknowledged social good".[3] The acknowledgment must be sufficiently general to preclude anarchy, for "a destruction of the state would mean a general loss of freedom, a general substitution of force for mutual good-will in man's dealings with each other, that would outweigh the evil of any slavery under such limitations and regulations as an organized state imposes on it."[4] Thus we get the paradoxical conclusion that the more insensitive is the conscience of the slave-owning majority, and the greater the importance it attaches to the maintenance of slavery, the less justified is the sensitive reformer in contemplating strenuous action. The doctrine that rights are made by recognition and are relative to moral ends turns round upon itself: instead of recalling irresponsible classes and individuals to a sense of their duties, it facilitates the acceptance of an unjust status quo.

---

1. Lectures, sect. 62.
2. Ibid., sect. 61.
3. Ibid., sect. 143.
4. Ibid., sect. 147.

It would be a misrepresentation, however, to give the impression that Green came down unequivocally in favour of non-resistance in all circumstances: in discussing the duty of resistance to a despotic government (the U.S.A. could not of course have qualified for this title) he allowed, although only after cautioning once again that the presumption must generally be that resistance to a government is not for the people's good when made on grounds which the mass of the people cannot appreciate, that in extreme cases constant resistance without public support may be the only way of educating the public conscience. He gave as an example the Mazzinian outbreaks in Italy.[1] This qualification, however, should not obscure the fact that the majority opinion is still in practice the crucial factor. To that extent Locke's position has not been advanced upon.

Green's discussion of resistance led him to introduce a further modification in the concept of recognition, with the result that his theory came to resemble closely the natural rights theory it was designed to supplant. Starting from the view that rights are made by recognition, his awareness that this doctrine would not as it stood serve the cause of social progress led him to maintain that there is a right to be recognized and that this right at least exists independently of recognition. What Green began by referring to as "powers" and "potentialities" were gradually transformed into "claims" and then into "rights implicit", which Green then proceeded to treat as actual rights.[2] When discussing the position of the **slave** Green insisted that the slave's ordinary social relations indicated his ability to share a good with others: he marries and appropriates, and respects the family and appropriation of others, and when this respect is reciprocated rights appear. Thus "he has... rights which the state neither gives nor can take away..."[3] The slave appears

---

1. Ibid., sect. 103. The action of Jan Palach, the Czech student who set fire to himself in Prague in protest against the Soviet occupation, might have commanded Green's sympathy on this ground: The Times, No.57,463; Jan 20, 1969; p.1. Here it would be a question of keeping alive popular liberal sentiment, rather than creating it.
2. Ibid., sects. 144, 145.
3. Ibid., sect. 145.

to enjoy a condition rather like the man in Locke's state of nature: in it he enjoys rights and freedom, yet for some reason this is not enough and it must be replaced by the state.

Green's treatment of the right of resistance illustrates very well the general limitations of his endeavour to advance upon the individualist theory of the state. His discussion of the coercive aspect of sovereignty does not take the problem beyond the point to which Locke had taken it - Green merely wrote "moral ends" where Locke wrote "natural law": the majority remains in the same crucial position. Although Green differed from Locke in assigning a larger area to governmental activity, in acknowledging political and social problems which had not emerged in Locke's day, and in working with philosophical ideas unknown to Locke, he got no further in offering a consistent solution to the problem of political obligation.

Conclusion

In his political theory Green raised some of the problems confronting an industrial society but failed to recognize their full dimension and significance because he saw them through eyes for which the problems of the previous fifty years were still the central ones: thus he criticized those who failed to recognize that contemporary problems resolved themselves into "the same old cause of social good against class interests, for which, under altered names, liberals are fighting now as they were fifty years ago".[1] An unquestioning faith that the old aristocracy was the source of all evils, and that the people were gifted with great moral and political capacity,[2] lay behind this statement. His concern with moral virtue, and his willingness to consider politics only in its effect upon that, tended to blind him to dangers to which even predecessors, such as de Tocqueville, had been alive.

The structure of his political science reflected the structure of his metaphysics: in the latter spirit was put on one side and nature on the other, in the former the good stood in one corner and the wicked in the other. Just

---

1. Works, Vol. III, p.367.
2. E.g., "...we hold fast to the faith that the 'cultivation of the masses', which has for the present superseded the development of the individual, will in its maturity produce some higher type even of individual manhood than any which the old world has known". (Works, Vol. III, p.45.)

as his metaphysics contained no mechanism by which teleological development could be explained, so his political thought reproduced the hostility to conflict and particularity. Activity not motivated by concern for the common good is tainted, at best to be suffered and never to be valued: it did not suit his metaphysics or his temperament to follow his master, Kant, in arguing instead that "nature comes to the aid of this revered, but practically ineffectual general will which is founded in reason. It does this by the selfish propensities themselves, so that it is only necessary to organize the state well (which is indeed within the ability of man), and to direct these forces against each other in such wise that one balances the other in its devastating effect, or even suspends it".[1] What Green lacked in his metaphysics he lacked also in his social theory: a place for mediation. His transition from the individual to the community, made under the banner of the doctrine of the sociality of the self, was too rapid. "Causes" are alright, but men should not be expected literally to lose themselves in them.[2]

Green welcomed the rise of the masses, but in other respects he never came to terms with nineteenth century England. Unlike Oakeshott he did not look back to the civility of eighteenth century England, but found his ideal in another condition of things: a companion who accompanied him on vacations in Switzerland and Germany in 1862 and 1863 was able to recall for Nettleship "the glow with which he greeted Swiss and German peasants, delighting in their homely patriarchal ways", and Green himself once said that he would have lived in Germany in preference to England if he had known the language. He wrote of that country that "the social equality, and the apparent absence of vice and distress relieve one's soul from many burdens, and personally I don't much mind about the stagnation." It is perhaps to his credit that his belief in the moral and social superiority of Germany did not obscure from him one detail, which was the "unquestionable and universal ugliness of the women"; but any suspicion that hedonistic considerations might have determined Green's domicile

---

1. Eternal Peace, reproduced in C.J.Friedrich's edition of The Philosophy of Kant, The Modern Library, p.452.
2. Works, Vol. III, p.38.

should be dispelled by the virtues which Green chose to emphasise as compensation for this ugliness: German women were "more sensible, and more companionable for the men". Green did not ask whether the German men considered the compensation adequate.[1]

---

1. All refs. to Memoir, <u>Works</u>, Vol. III, pp. xli - xlii.

Chapter 8

Bosanquet

The vision

Behind the formal philosophizing contained in the <u>Philosophical Theory of the State</u> there lay a vision. Bosanquet believed that what the age required was "a human or Christian Hellenism; a Hellenism which shall realize the true freedom of every human being ..."[1]

In concrete terms the vision looked like this:

"... we look forward to a society organized in convenient districts, in which men and women, pursuing their different callings, will live together with care for one another, and with in all essentials the same education, the same enjoyments, the same capacities. These men and women will work together in councils and on committees; and while fearlessly employing stringent legal powers in the public interest, yet will be aware, by sympathy and experience, of the extreme flexibility and complication of modern life, which responds so unexpectedly to the most simple interference; they will have a pride in their schools and their libraries, in their streets and their dwellings, in their workshops and their warehouses. In such a society it appears to me a mere question of practical efficiency how far the organisers of labour should be the salaried servants of the State, or, <u>as they are now</u>, its moral trustees. This presents itself to me simply as a question of the amount of line, the degree of initiative, which the community allows to its agents in the performance of their duties."[2]

The vision drew, it is obvious, on a number of sources. It is perhaps best described as a refurbished version of the Greek polis, as idealized by Bosanquet. The refurbishment comprised his attempts to

---

1. <u>Essays</u>, p.52.
2. <u>Ibid</u>, p.45; his emphasis.

integrate into it a Christian humanitarianism, his childhood and youth at the family home in Rock,[1] his admiration for William Morris,[2] together with some provision for the complexities of modern industrial life. This, it might seem, is already to have asked too much of the polis: but overshadowing the whole conception there is, in addition, Bosanquet's connection with the work of the Charity Organization[3] and the Settlement movement. Because Bosanquet's attitude to the problems presented by the growth of industrialisation reflects the spirit of these two phenomena we feel justified in quoting a passage from a paper read by his wife, Helen Dendy, at the first meeting of the Charity Organization Conference, in 1893; the conclusion of the paper captures the spirit well: she writes that

"I like to picture humanity as a great army pressing on towards an invisible goal, and guided by a wisdom not its own. No power can stay its course nor alter its direction, and those who try to turn aside on their own little paths of self-indulgence, or will not keep step with their comrades, or falter with failing strength, are cast down and trampled underfoot. It is with these that we have to deal in our charitable work, and what we must aim at is not to make their fall easy, but to raise them to their feet again, to turn their faces towards the light, to lift up the hands which hang down and the feeble knees. How can we do this unless we ourselves are working with open eyes, unless we understand their mistakes better than they do themselves, and can point out the paths in which they have to tread?"[4]

Drawing all the elements in the vision together, we are brought as near as one can get to what Bosanquet had before his mind's eye when he found the supreme civic virtue in "neighbourly public spirit" and decided that "the true union of social and individual reform lies in the moulding of the individual mind to the public purpose."[5]

---

1. On Rock, See *Bernard Bosanquet*, by Helen Bosanquet; MacMillan, London, 1924, pp. 3-14.
2. *Ibid*, p. 64.
3. *Ibid*, pp. 52-64.
4. *Aspects*, p. 179; for very similar sentiments expressed by Bosanquet see *Civilization*, p. 155.
5. *Essays*, pp. 46-47.

The influence of Bosanquet's metaphysics upon his political vision is already discernible. Although he touched upon the idea of negativity in his metaphysics we saw that the idea was never developed systematically into an ontological conception but remained instead within the moral sphere: we were exhorted to see good in what at first appeared to be painful and morally barren experience. Because Bosanquet concentrated on applying the idea to the moral destiny of the individual finite self, the possibility of permanent social differences and consequent inevitable conflict never took a firm hold upon his mind. As a result, the man who does not quite fit into the society outlined in our first quotation must inevitably appear as deviant, maladjusted, or perverse. He is ignored by Bosanquet, simply disappearing before the might of the male and female egalitarians who fearlessly employ "stringent legal powers in the public interest" - or else seek to mould him to the public purpose, as in a further quotation given above.[1] This unfortunate aspect of Bosanquet's political thought would also seem to be reinforced by his notion that selves can "overlap" one another. When this notion is translated into the terms of Bosanquet's portrait of the ideal society it would at least suggest that the deviants are leading an existence which may well be non-contributory from the standpoint of absolute reality, since their selves are "overlapped" by those who are in a position to steer them back on to the path to virtue. In so far as the quotation from his wife's lecture[2] represents his own views, it supports this interpretation: she insisted that the charity organizers must "understand their mistakes better than they do themselves, and ((be able to)) point out the paths in which they have to tread". And even if their existence is contributory it can be so only in a negative way, viz. by providing opportunities for the exercise of virtue on the part of the majority.

---

1. Above, p.192.
2. Ibid.

Without wishing to impute to Bosanquet any trace of real hostility to values which he would be the first to defend, we think these are genuine difficulties in his position.

There is a further connection between Bosanquet's metaphysics and his political vision. He, like Green, failed to hold the spiritual and the material orders together in one unity, and the cleavage between the two reappears in his political thought (as it did in Green's) in a form which tends to favour the dominant social class of the time. He accepted Green's distinction between "spiritual" goods which are shareable but located in an inner realm necessarily inaccessible to state action, and "material" goods which are not shareable but are accessible to state action; yet he found little difficulty in allowing state activity in the supposedly "internal" world of morality when those delights which he most esteemed were involved: thus "no harm could be done if our municipalities were, for example, to maintain or subsidise first-rate public orchestras under really skilled direction".[1] The state activities which might give those who did not possess them the leisure and material well-being so necessary to develop and pursue such interests were, on the other hand, not always so readily welcomed. This will be illustrated in the following section.

The problem

"Have we not, as a consequence of the great renascence of a hundred years ago," Bosanquet asked, "attained an advance which no one has rightly estimated, at the cost of a retrogression which no one has rightly understood?"[2] What we have attained is the universal right to argue, to have an opinion, to be heard through the speech on the platform, in short, "the recognition that civilized man enjoys as his common birthright the form of articulate human intelligence".[3] But by this very advance we have lost for the time being "the adequacy of the substance of culture to its form".[4] The consequence is that

---

1. Essays, p. 68.
2. Civilization, p. 57.
3. Ibid, p. 57.
4. Ibid, p. 57.

the republic of letters, of which all civilized men are now in theory qualified citizens,[1] is in extreme disorder. Never before in history has there been possible "so wild and immeasurable an ocean of error."[2] The simplest way of stating his meaning, Bosanquet considers, is by insisting that "positive error ... has now taken the place of ignorance. Far from having reached its climax, the movement towards a modern Dark Age has probably but just begun".[3] Bosanquet believed that this state of affairs imposed grave responsibilities upon the more cultured and enlightened members of society. Their duty lies in the direction of an ultimate reanimation of the form of culture by its substance: they have a task, in other words, which resembles that of the advocates of Christianity in the Middle Ages, but which now occurs at a higher level, since intelligence is now articulate, no longer being confined to the form of feeling.[4]

How did Bosanquet consider that this task was to be carried out? Would it involve the use of force, or would the mass of mankind be relied upon to make progress without this? In an essay entitled The Place of Leisure in Life Bosanquet answers this question. What is needed is spiritual leadership, and when this is provided the mass will follow. This simple solution was wrapped up in some remarks relating it to Bosanquet's general theory of the nature of society. The social mind must be thought of as a single spirit pouring itself into different channels. Because it is part of a single spirit, each mind is a microcosm "which lends to, and borrows from, every other mind, or factor of the social spirit." Bosanquet is engaged in an exposition of Aristotle's Ethics, which may explain the examples he gives: he writes that the ruler learns from the workman, the scholar from the soldier, while the workman needs the guidance of his ruler and the soldier can only rightly apply himself to his profession by

---

1. Ibid, p. 59.
2. Ibid, p. 53.
3. Ibid, p.58.
4. Ibid, p. 60.

borrowing the spirit of the scholar. The "organic" theory of the state thus enables Bosanquet to rationalize his optimism about the method by which the progress of the masses is to be secured and thereby to side-step the question of force. It appears to have another consequence. Because the gifts of a minority of individuals can, in the organic theory, be predicated of the society as a whole, it seems that only enough individuals need to attain the relevant excellencies to set what Bosanquet calls "the tone of a society". The tone and worthiness of the lives of even the lowliest are established according as they are or are not, in their degree, conscious of an inspiration and an ideal pervading their society. For example, "The servant who sweeps a minister's study, having respect for his office, shares in his spiritual work, and is the better even for that amount of sharing in it." Bosanquet quickly adds that the minister has also to learn from the servant. It was by pursuing these ideas that Aristotle sought to create states so organized that "the lamp of religion and fine art and high thinking may always be kept burning," and the same ideas (he believed) are just as relevant today.[1]

The same optimism showed itself in another paper, on *Luxury and Refinement*. In this paper another of Bosanquet's fundamental assumptions appears: the separation of spiritual goods from material ones which was found in Green's political thought emerges as the basis for Bosanquet's contention that material discomfort is no barrier to the attainment of spiritual improvement; thus there is no need to take very drastic steps in altering, for example, the distribution of wealth before the masses can progress. Having asserted that "it is not poverty which mainly hinders improvement ...," Bosanquet proceeds to argue that progress is impossible unless those for whom it is easiest will lead the way, and that ".. by the time that they – one-half at least of the community, for I definitely include the well-to-do mechanics – have made a positive advance, the position of those below them, and their capacities, will have been profoundly modified by the

---

1. All refs. are to *Science*, p. 360.

influence of this advance itself."[1] The curious thing is that although he recognizes that moral improvement is easiest for those in comfortable circumstances and consequently assigns to them the task of leadership, he seems to feel that their moral advance will rub off on those less fortunate without any great material alteration in their circumstance. Spirit and its material environment can be held apart because, at bottom, "... the change of mental atmosphere is the most significant of changes."[2] Elsewhere he wrote that the qualities of a man are patience, initiative, co-operation, comprehension and faith.[3] These qualities, apparently, can be cultivated by any man, whatever his social position. Since this is so, Bosanquet is able to follow Green in attributing the major social difficulties of the time to a failure in communication between the different sections of society: if people could be brought to discuss together more, all the basic tensions within society would at least be alleviated, and might well disappear. The following passage displays his optimism very forcefully:

"The barrier between some and others is not really difference in wealth, nor antagonism of industrial interests; it is a lack of subjects to talk about when we meet ... A very great part at least of our class distinctions today have no necessary ground in material differences, and simply rest on oppositions of habits and ideas which a little care and goodwill might remove in the course of a generation."[4] What in particular is needed is more "refinement". Refinement is the opposite of luxury.[5] Luxury Bosanquet associates with self-indulgence or ostentation,[6] and it is of course an exclusive good, intensifying

---

1. Civilization, p. 297.
2. Ibid, p. 298.
3. Ibid, p. 155.
4. Ibid, pp. 275-276.
5. Ibid, p. 277.
6. Ibid, p. 277.

the barriers between men.[1] Refinement he associates with comfort and beauty,[2] and by it "the conquest of nature, with the resources and superfluities implied by such a conquest, has been made subservient to distinctly human ends".[3] What Bosanquet understood by refinement in practice may be gathered in part at least from the interpretation he gave to it in his own life. In 1889, Helen Bosanquet writes, he bought a house in Chelsea (7 Cheyne Gardens), and "he spared no pains in making it beautiful. His Morris wall papers and hangings, and de Morgan tiles were a source of daily pleasure to him, and the few pictures which he allowed on his walls were carefully selected. He took pleasure also in the small and sooty garden behind the house...".[4] She also records that in the last twenty-five years of his life Bosanquet had the satisfaction of detecting "a marked improvement in the manners of the people."[5] Mrs. Bosanquet had in mind the behaviour of "the thousands of holiday-makers who found Oxshott ((where Bosanquet lived from 1899)) a good place for a day's outing."[6] At first they were very rough and noisy and the Bosanquets had to stay in their garden nearly the whole time they were in the vicinity. But as the years passed it eventually "became a real pleasure to walk amongst them and to share their enjoyment."[7]

A striking characteristic of what Bosanquet calls "the qualities of a man" is their vagueness, and it is of course their vagueness which made them so serviceable in bolstering his complacency in face of the more radical social movements of the time. We may dwell for a moment upon the more general significance which may be found in the vagueness of the qualities Bosanquet most admires. A. MacIntyre has

---

1. <u>Ibid</u>, p. 275.
2. <u>Ibid</u>, p. 277.
3. <u>Ibid</u>, p.278.
4. <u>Bernard Bosanquet</u>, op.cit., p. 64.
5. <u>Ibid</u>, p. 90.
6. <u>Ibid</u>, p.90.
7. <u>Ibid</u>. p. 90.

pointed to "the quite new emphasis" from the middle of the nineteenth century onwards in English life upon what he calls "the secondary virtues", and his list of these is fairly close to Bosanquet's own: MacIntyre notes (amongst others) co-operativeness, fair-play, tolerance, a gift for compromise, and fairness. He terms these virtues "secondary" because their existence presupposes another, primary set of virtues which are directly related to the ends men pursue in their lives. The secondary virtues provide no guidance in the selection of these ends but only encourage them to modify their pursuit of them in certain ways: "The secondary virtues concern the way in which we should go about our projects; their cultivation will not assist us in discovering upon which projects we ought to be engaged." He explains the central place which secondary moral concepts have occupied in modern English life by pointing to the fact that the need for economic and social co-operation, a need recognized by the different orders within society, prevented any one order from universalizing or giving cosmic significance to its primary values; the emphasis on secondary values thus expresses an attitude to the world "in which the making of cosmic and universal claims for one's own group, as against other groups, is no longer possible".[1]

MacIntyre's distinction between primary and secondary virtues goes some way towards explaining the rather vague moralizing posture into which Bosanquet often seems to lapse, and also towards explaining why the concrete inquiry into the structure of freedom which he desiderates is not usually pursued very far by him.[2] To give the impression of concreteness Bosanquet tends to give ad hoc examples, either in the text itself or in footnotes. To illustrate what he means by "the possibilities of life among English peasants and machines", for example, he adds a footnote which refers to a small library

---

1. All refs. are to *Secularization and Moral Change*, O.U.P., 1967, pp. 24-25.
2. See, e.g. *Essays*, pp. 102-103.

started and maintained by a knot of London workmen and managed by their own committee, "though with outside assistance and advice."[1] And he then gives a lengthy quotation from a letter describing the low entertainment at a working-class seaside resort - "Miles of awful jugs and cups. 'A present from M.' - of M. rock - a dreadful red and yellow sweet..."[2] - concluding the piece by quoting the passage from Green's address at the opening of the Oxford High School in which Green hoped and prayed for a society in which all honest citizens will recognize themselves and be recognized by each other as gentlemen.[3]

Bosanquet was fond of presenting his diagnosis of the problems confronting the modern world in the form of a contrast between the order of the **polis and** the modern "wilderness of interests", and it will be useful to consider how things appeared to him in this perspective. The ancient city was notable for the absence in it of the divisions and estrangements of modern life. Work did not shut men up within the confines of their own industry or profession: "One would be doing, on the whole, what other did, and their work would bring them into contact mentally and well as physically".[4] The need of civic self-defence ensured that the most fundamental civic duty would constantly be before the mind of every Greek. Extensive participation in government made certain that every individual accepted responsibility for public matters instead of shrugging it off onto the shoulders of elected representatives and gave a sense of direct personal involvement which is absent today. Men were brought together once again by the universal concern with bodily and intellectual distinction.[5] In short, "Nothing stood between you and your fellows in the community."[6] As a result, the meaning of citizenship was plain. Citizenship was visibly each man's whole life, with

---

1. <u>Civilisation</u>, p. 298.
2. <u>Ibid</u>, p. 299.
3. <u>Ibid</u>, p. 303.
4. <u>Aspects</u>, p. 3.
5. <u>Ibid</u>, pp. 3-4.
6. <u>Ibid</u>, p. 4.

common dangers, common responsibilities, common enjoyments, and common ambitions. In the modern world, on the other hand, "it is very much harder to see our way. According to our birth, our education and our profession, we fall into a groove, and some one or two huge incorporated 'interests' fill our horizon".[1] The "negative" freedom we enjoy does not produce character or originality, which emerge only when some plan or value is discernible in our circumstances.[2] Citizenship has been narrowed down to matters related to parliamentary elections, some crisis, or perhaps the municipal elections in a town.[3] Bosanquet's desire is to get us off "the little stages"[4] from which we view things and on which we enact our lives and to create an awareness of citizenship. He insists that this does not mean that every man must devote himself to politics in the narrow sense, nor does it mean that political action must be extended to touch upon every sphere of life. It means rather that we must "understand our whole lives in the light of citizen ideas, in the light of a common good."[5] It is a question of bearing in mind that one's "little life" (Bosanquet is fond of that phrase) only has value as embodying some element in a common good.[6] It will be realized for example, by one who does bear this in mind, that to want nasty, shoddy things, is to condemn somebody to make them, and that to desire cheap things is to condemn somebody to work without proper pay.[7] Citizenship in the modern world may be defined as "the criticism or adjustment or unification of the ... separate 'worlds' through a spirit which takes account of social purpose as a whole".[8]

Like Green, then, Bosanquet fails to assign any positive value to

---

1. *Ibid*, p. 5.
2. *Ibid*, p. 6.
3. *Ibid*, p. 8.
4. *Ibid*, p. 6.
5. *Ibid*, p. 9.
6. *Ibid*, p. 10.
7. *Ibid*, p. 11.
8. *Ibid*, p. 15.

"the wilderness of interests". Unlike Hegel, he is not prepared to assign a specific sphere of life to the unrestricted play of particularity: he cannot overcome the temptation to see selfishness in any activity in which we do not keep before our minds its bearing upon the common good. The "interests" which divide us from the community in the modern-world only become valuable when they are recognized as things which "take us out of ourselves" and move us towards unity with the whole. They are there only to be "criticized" and "adjusted", and never to be for a moment embraced and enjoyed for themselves. There is also the assumptions that well-intentioned men, keeping an eye constantly on the common good and granting bona fides to each other, will not fail to arrive at agreement. The only difficulty will be that of etching in the details of the common good in the process. These problems will return when we consider the general will; before doing this, however, we may observe what happened when Bosanquet tried to indicate how labour and capital might be brought together in a mutually beneficial relationship within the "wilderness of interests".

In a lecture entitled <u>Two Modern Philanthropists</u> Bosanquet compared the careers of "two very respectable tradesmen", both of whose lives covered the first seven decades of the nineteenth century. They were an Englishman, George Moore, and a Frenchman, Jean Leclaire. Moore was a farmer's son who became "the most tremendous commercial traveller that ever was seen".[1] When his fortune was made he embarked upon a philanthropic career and did much good. But in his assumptions and method Bosanquet saw severe limitations. Although Moore was willing to give money and to establish "charitable machinery" on the one hand, and religious instruction by distributing large numbers of books and by financing missionaries on the other, his work did not aim at building up human character.[2] Nor did it ever occur to him that his workmen had something to do with the creation of his fortune.[3] Further,

---

1. <u>Essays</u>, p. 5.
2. <u>Ibid</u>, p. 10.
3. <u>Ibid</u>, p. 10.

although not a dishonourable commercial traveller, he treated trade like war, which revealed that "his ideas were all in patches and scraps. He never thoroughly brought his religion to bear upon his trade."[1] His main failing - which is that of indiscriminate philanthropy in general - Bosanquet finds in his concern for relieving destitution, instead of curing it.[2] In Moore's life, then, no true model of the ideal industrialist is to be found. In the life of Leclaire, however, a truer view is exemplified. He too rose from a lowly position to prosperity, but instead of distributing his fortune indiscriminately he instituted profit-sharing in his business, and eventually made his employees partners and passed the management of the company over to them.[3] In Leclaire Bosanquet found a man who "grasped the true direction of the nineteenth century", and in his life he saw "a thorough and single-hearted religious life, a life good in itself, and good in its effects on others".[4]

Bosanquet did not intend this lecture to be a systematic exploration of industrial problems, and he saw that no realistic schemes for reform could be based on the willingness of an individual rich man to share his profits and hand over his firm to his employees; but his examination of the lives of Moore and Leclaire exemplifies in broad outline what he considered to be the differences between the right and wrong ways of creating a satisfactory industrial order, and also illustrates his sympathy for workers' participation in management.

Bosanquet was prepared to go further than to leave the claim of the workers to the discretion of benevolent capitalists. He considered that production must be more and more self-governing "as its quality becomes higher and its creative effort more intense".[5] The great obstacle standing in the way of a reconciliation of the claim of the producers to self-realization through self-governing productive

---

1. *Ibid*, p. 11.
2. *Ibid*, p. 13.
3. *Ibid*, pp. 15-21.
4. *Ibid*, p. 23.
5. *Ideals*, p. 238.

activity with the claim of the public to efficient production he found
in the divorce of ownership from management. He saw that the more
radical working-class movements of the time were motivated by a demand
for recognition of the creative aspect of production and not for higher
wages,[1] and he sympathized with their underlying idea that "a class, as
determined by its function, is dead if it has not its faith, its gospel
and its pride. It should not live at second-hand, nor copy the manners
and ideas of others whose life is differently determined".[2] But he considered that the divorce between ownership and production had to be
accepted, and the reforms he contemplated occurred within this framework.
It had to be accepted because "the investment market ... is within
certain limits a social necessity as such; that is, as collecting
capital for enterprises, and as enabling individuals to adjust their
resources to a plan of life by exchanging present power of consumption
for future income."[3] In particular the investment market avoids the cut
between consumption and production which modern collectivism creates.
Collectivism emphasises free consumption for all and removes responsibility for production from the producer, passing it to the public
authority: "There is nowhere any check to the suggestion that all
income is for enjoyment alone".[4] The cut between consumption and production which collectivism demands by refusing to allow any individual
to own more property than is necessary for personal needs destroys
private life by taking the creative element out of it: if the public
authorities alone can own the means of production individuals will have
to approach them before their inventions and schemes can gain material
support, and this would choke off all initiative at the outset.[5] The
public interest would therefore suffer, since the morale of the community
would be undermined. Bosanquet does not produce very convincing evidence
to support this argument. He merely writes "imagine William Morris

---

1. Ibid, pp. 230-231.
2. Ibid, p. 231.
3. Ibid, p. 240.
4. Ibid, p. 223.
5. Ibid, pp. 223-4.

laying before a local board the first sketch of the pomegranate paper".[1] But he himself sees the irrelevance of this example for he notes that Morris was rich, and therefore did not have to persuade anyone to support him. The issue turns upon the fate of impoverished inventors. They have to convince banks or individual capitalists of the soundness of their idea, and perhaps it would not greatly alter their prospects of getting the invention carried through if they had to convince officials instead. Perhaps it might even be easier; a public official may be more inclined to spend money which is not his own on developing some invention or scheme than a capitalist would be. Bosanquet may of course be correct, but the consideration to which he attaches so much importance is not conclusive in the form in which he presents it.

Bosanquet proposed to moderate the hardship which the divorce between ownership and production created for the producers by two measures. The absentee owners - the shareholder class - were to be given an inferior rank in the control of production by being reduced to lenders of capital at a settled rate of interest; and management was to be closely bound up with producers' organizations.[2] This latter measure would give more real recognition of working-class interests than public ownership, which is "absentee ownership at its worst".[3] Bosanquet did not examine in detail the possibility of effective workers' control of management: he showed no awareness, for example of the possibility that the representatives of the workers who took part in management would inevitably acquire interests and perspectives which would detach them from the working-class. While he grasped the working-class claim, which he formulated thus: "They want to realize an ethos and a culture of their own; not to live on the ideas of the middle at second-hand, any more than to wear their second-hand clothes",[4] he did not notice that it might be impossible to realize this claim through the ways he envisaged. And he did not foresee that the growth of the producers'

1. Ibid., p. 224.
2. Ibid., pp. 241-2.
3. Ibid., p. 242.
4. Ibid., p. 231.

organizations might present threats to self-realization at least as great as those posed by the shareholders or absentee owners.

Although Bosanquet found some validity in the idea of class-consciousness he considered that the tendency of more radical socialists to make the working-class stand-point absolute ignored the fact that "... every class-mind ... contains in miniature, besides its own, the features which are writ large in others," and that therefore it is reinforced and expanded by contact with them.[1] He himself preferred to draw the essential class distinction along lines other than those according to which control of the means of production is the crucial factor. His own distinction brings us back once more to the difference between spiritual and material goods. The most fundamental and ineradicable tendency of class structure, he considered, "is the distinction between wealth-production and personal service". This distinction coincides with the distinction between the world of business and industry on the one hand and that of politics and the professions on the other.[2] The former class is concerned with "bodily things" - the capacity for the production, acquisition, enjoyment, and control of them - while the professional classes are concerned with "functions which are largely theoretical, and so far as practical involve a large theoretical element." It is a life in "the realm of ideas".[3] Bosanquet referred to Plato in order to illustrate the relationship between the spiritual and material lives: he admitted that there are today what are called "the prizes of the professions", but added that the true view is that which recognizes that the professional classes today possess the function which Plato assigned to the guardians, viz. "that of men who work directly for the community on the basis of removing from it what is necessary for their function and no more."[4] Bosanquet appears to be abusing his author at this point. Plato's conception of the guardians involves at the very least a knowledge on their part of the eternal

---

1. Ibid., p. 233.
2. Ibid., pp. 233-234.
3. Ibid., p. 234.
4. Ibid., p. 234.

order of things; this is altogether too elevated a status to assign to the middle class of the modern world. Further, Plato really did intend material deprivation to be taken seriously; he would not have considered that the "prizes of the professions" could be seen as merely incidental plums. The comparison between the guardians and the contemporary middle class would seem to throw more light on Bosanquet's own opinions than on the social structure and problems of the time. Bosanquet's statement of what he considers to be the essence of the whole matter displays even more forcefully the extent to which he considered that spiritual achievement could be divorced from any specific reference to social structure:

"... the point, I am coming to is this: it is an ineradicable tendency that as wealth and its control and enjoyment go to the productive class, so power and prestige go to the professional and political class. And this ineradicable tendency is also a fundamental principle, for it is essential to a decent society that prestige and ultimate power should not belong to wealth".[1] The trouble is that this ineradicable tendency appears to have been largely eradicated at the time: power, prestige <u>and</u> wealth seem to have been heading in the direction of "the guardians". Bosanquet makes some brief remarks which show a partial awareness of this, but then concludes by writing of the professional and political class that "on the whole, its life is simple and its claims are modest, as is right for a class which is busied directly with the central needs and the most serious interests of mankind".[2] It does rather appear as if "the workman's function of creative production ... whose nature is as yet unrecognized not only by the community as a whole, but by the producers themselves" (as Bosanquet puts it when summarizing the theory of proletarian class-consciousness),[3] has still not quite received the full recognition which Bosanquet feels he has extended to it. For a

---

1. <u>Ibid</u>., pp. 234-235.
2. <u>Ibid</u>., p. 235.
3. <u>Ibid</u>., p. 230.

workman is one doomed to tend the less central needs and less serious interests of mankind. Bosanquet added a note at the end of his Three Lectures on Social Ideals which is of interest in this connection. Having written that "... prestige instinctively rests with the activity which begins to take us beyond material necessities",[1] he adds in this note that in so far as productive activity becomes artistic in character the antithesis between the productive and the professional classes would be progressively diminished in intensity. We may ask at this point, how deep did the aesthetic element in Bosanquet's social theory really go? Was he in earnest?

It is difficult to feel that Bosanquet found a secure place for the beautiful amongst his most cherished social sentiments. Sometimes his aesthetic sense bordered on the trivial, as when he noted that "Some of us need not go far to find a man who cannot raise his hat to a lady when he is riding a bicycle".[2] At other times it tended suddenly to disappear altogether before the immensity of the social problem, as when he insisted that what is wanted is "the habituation of the English citizen to his rights and duties, by training in organization, in administration...", and then held up the traditions of public service in Berlin as a model for London. If Berlin traditions had been adopted, Bosanquet believed, then "we should have (allowing for the difference in size) an army of 7,200 citizens engaged in the administration of poor law relief as unpaid officials, with public authority, and with individual discretion.".[3] Bureaucracy would appear to be in danger of eclipsing beauty.

It would seem that as long as the free market and mass production continue to operate there is no way of bringing the producers up to the level of the "guardians", for the artistic dimension to production is largely sacrificed in the face of their dictates. Bosanquet was of

---

1. Ibid., p.248.
2. Science, p. 295.
3. Essays, p.46.

course mildly hostile to the free market, in so far as it facilitated uncritical consumption and unlovely production. He believed that "if nothing is produced but what is wanted for a genuine 'expression' or a genuine necessity, the healthiness of the economic system is in the main secure",[1] but he did not pursue the question of what was to be done if "genuine" demand was not met. He was content to fall back on a belief that there would be an inevitable rise in standards of taste in mass consumption as education improved. Like Green, he believed that only good things could happen to good men, although he allowed that appearances might obscure this. This optimism brought vagueness into his economic analysis, as when he wrote that "... so far as we join in the social process with a right sense of the values of the principal things in life, we must be contributing an element which will make for betterment in the result. Work thoroughly done with care and sympathy will not be lost; but no-one can tell in what precise form it will survive."[2]

Bosanquet, it will be evident, penetrated more deeply into the problems of industrial society than Green. The divorce of ownership from management, the class-consciousness of the producers, the possibility of trade-union participation in management - these were phenomena which Green had not noticed or examined. But while he acknowledged that there were hardships to be removed, Bosanquet was as convinced as Green that the highest way of life lay outside and beyond productive activity itself. Like Green, again, he did not consider that the modern industrial system inevitably precludes the possibility of self-realisation for some of those within it. While Green had argued that the worst features of capitalism were due to feudal survivals, Bosanquet attributed the evils of the industrial revolution to a different source, but one which was external to the system: he wrote that "perhaps the worst evils of that time arose directly from the intentionally lax or 'socialistic' Poor Law".[3] It was not, in other words, a case of the

---

1. Ibid., p. 247.
2. Ideals, p. 245.
3. Ibid., p.317.

Poor Law merely aggravating tendencies inherent in the system – the relevant tendency in this case being the creation of an impoverished labour-force, owing to the absence of effective labour-organisation or universal benevolence amongst employers. Both Green and Bosanquet, then, failed to integrate into their ethical ideal the way of life which industrialization brought for a large number of the population. For Green those in industry were, at best, the "children of the counter". For Bosanquet, they were the class devoted to material or bodily interests, and as such inevitably inferior to the "guardian" class which did not derive its income from trade – directly at least.

The first look

Bosanquet found the most fundamental expression of the obstacles to the realization of the best life – that life "in which your duties and purposes bind you together with other people ..."[1] – in what he calls "prima facie theories" or "theories of the first look."[2] It is in these theories that he finds the origin of the problem of political obligation. He refers to the first look of the modern man in the street, influenced by scientific or materialist ideas; the man, that is, "to whom the compact self-containedness and self-direction of the swarming human beings before him seems an obvious fact, while the social logic and spiritual history which lie behind the scene fail to impress themselves on his perceptive imagination."[3] The modern onlooker "inevitably proceeds to treat the social whole as composed of units A, B, C etc., who, <u>as they stand, and just as they seem to us when we rub against them in daily intercourse</u>, are taken to be the organs and centres of human life ... To each of us, A, B, or C, all the rest are 'others'. They are 'like' him;   they are 'repetitions' of him, but they are not himself".[4]

The relationship which Bosanquet establishes between theories of the first look and the problem of political obligation is as follows.

---

1. <u>Essays</u>, p. 15.
2. <u>P.T.S.</u>, p. 75.
3. <u>Ibid</u>., p. 75.
4. <u>Ibid</u>., p. 77; his emphasis.

The problem of political obligation is the "paradox of self-government". His formulation of the problem of political obligation may be stated once again:

"The paradox of political obligation starts from what is accepted as authority or social coercion, and asks in what way the term 'self', derived from the 'individual' mind, can be applicable at once to the agent and patient in such coercion, exercised prima facie by some persons over others".[1]

In other words, the paradox of political obligation arises when an absolute distinction is made between self and others, in such a way that obedience to law becomes subjection to the will of others. And this absolute distinction is what characterizes theories of the first look. The main problem of moral philosophy also arises from a commitment to the first look, and is resolved through the same principles as those which govern Bosanquet's treatment of the problem of political obligation. Bosanquet writes that:

"The paradox of Ethical Obligation starts from what is accepted as 'self', and asks how it can exercise authority or coercion over itself; how, in short, a metaphor drawn from the relations of some persons to others can find application within what we take to be the limits of an individual mind".[2] This paradox manifests itself as the conflict in ethical theory between egoism and altruism.

In the first chapter we examined a number of what Bosanquet would term "theories of the first look", but Bosanquet himself concentrates on the theories of Bentham and Mill. Because these see state action as essentially negative they find it impossible to justify the essential role which they eventually assign to the state, for they are not anarchists. In other words, they end with a contradiction: state action is always negative, and it is not always negative. They cannot explain political obligation because state action must always be, for them, the might of the majority triumphing over the one.[3]

---

1. Ibid., p.52.
2. Ibid., p.52.
3. Ibid., p.55 on Bentham; pp.70-71 on Mill.

The curious thing is that after his detailed criticism of the negative conception of liberty, and of the attempt which accompanied it to specify negatively the nature of individuality, Bosanquet appears to accept the fundamentals of that theory himself. This appears most clearly in the form of his attempt to follow Green in replacing Mill's distinction between self-regarding and other-regarding actions with a distinction between internal and external actions, or between actions which promote the common good directly and those which do so indirectly. Bosanquet's claim is that the nature of good is such that it cannot be realized through coercion. The dualism of the spiritual and material enters, as in Green, to provide a means by which state action can be described as not in pari materia with the end, i.e. self-realization. State action is external in the sense that "the state is unable to determine that the action shall be done from the ground or motive which alone would give it immediate value or durable certainty as an element in the best life".[1] The state, that is to say, has as the means at its disposal only the power of reward and of punishment.

The exiguous nature of the distinction between "coercing" and "hindering hindrances" comes into the open when Bosanquet writes of state action that "its negative character cannot restrain it from some degree of positive action. It is only through positive operation that a negative or opposition can find reality in the world".[2] The objection to talk of the state as "hindering hindrances" is that it is a phraseology which can cover any state action, according to one's viewpoint - what will be a legitimate hindering action to one will be a restriction of liberty to another; and because one can bring under it any action at all it appears to be no more than a euphemism which obscures the reality of coercion.

Bosanquet himself recognized the difficulty which he confronts through holding both that state action is negative and that it is to be welcomed as hindering hindrances, but he does not resolve the problem:

1. Ibid., p. 176.
2. Ibid., p. 178.

instead he retreats into the kind of approach which has led some critics to accuse him of positively welcoming impossible positions, for he writes that "this prima facie contradiction is really a proof of the vitality of our principle. It follows from the fact that we accept self-government in the full strength of both its factors and can deal with it on this basis."[1]

What is the origin of Bosanquet's difficulty? Why does he vacillate between negative and positive attitudes towards the state? The answer would seem to be rooted in his metaphysics. We saw that he believed that the separateness of selves is only an appearance, and that he recognized no ultimate significance in such separateness. Just as this made it possible for him to describe one's movement into the absolute as finding oneself when it appeared really to be a case of losing oneself, so it makes it possible for him to describe all contact with the state as the realization of positive liberty, although one knows that particularity asserts itself and makes some state action hostile to liberty. Bosanquet does of course qualify his position, but it remains true that no systematic provision for liberty as it is interpreted by the individual himself is contained in his theory. What is unsatisfactory about Bosanquet's starting-point, viz. his attack on the first look, is, in short, that he fails to recognize that the absolute separation of selves which the first look presents can only be denied at the cost of getting rid of politics altogether, or of making the assumption that there will never be serious differences of opinion and interest amongst individuals.

It is the criminal who really suffers most from Bosanquet's failure to find any theoretical justification for the separateness of selves. While Bosanquet is content to walk a tight-rope between a negative and a positive attitude towards state-action over the main body of his political theory, he drops all restriction upon the positive character of state action when the sinner is involved. (We may note in passing that while Bosanquet does not use the term sin as often as Green, he

---

1. Ibid., p.186.

does not find it at all inappropriate for purposes of social analysis: thus the highest praise he could bestow upon the life of the philanthropist George Moore was that "such a life shows a great awakening in society - a real conviction of sin ..."[1] The difficult position in which Bosanquet's metaphysics place the criminal is made more hazardous by his temperament: he expressed regret, for example, that "It has become a cheap old jest to say, 'To punish you hurts me more than it hurts you'",[2] although he did add immediately that all deep truths are dangerous - which leaves the task of extracting the truth still to be performed. Bosanquet argues that "The end or true self is in the medium of mind and will, and is contradicted and nullified so far as a hostile will is permitted to triumph".[3] The suppression of the criminal will is, then, the upholding of the true self. The analogy by which Bosanquet supports the view that the criminal wills his own punishment is significant. He writes that "We do not indeed will every step that we walk, but we only walk while we will to walk, and so with the whole system of routine automation which is the method and organ of our daily life. At any interruption, any hindrance or failure, consciousness starts up, and the end of the whole routine comes sharply back upon us through our aberration."[4] Punishment, like the interruption of our walking, "brings us to our senses".[5] The inadequacy of the analogy to the argument it is supposed to support lies of course in the fact that it draws upon personal and not upon inter-personal experiences. It is extremely difficult to see what justification there is for assuming that every person (Socrates, for example) who breaks the law is, ipso facto, to be regarded as out of his senses. And the implication that he is either insane or absent-minded - caught off balance, as it were, in his criminal moments - serves to undermine responsibility for the act. Further, even if the analogy is allowed, it breaks down at the point where the interruption in automatic activity no longer calls a

---

1. *Essays*, p. 9.
2. *Suggestions*, p. 122.
3. *P.T.S.*, p. 208.
4. *Ibid.*, p. 209.
5. *Ibid.*, p. 209.

person's attention to his real will, i.e. to the activity in which he is supposed to be engaged. This is important because it may be just to punish a criminal even when the punishment does not "bring him to his senses," and then the analogy offers no help.

Some of the difficulties presented by Bosanquet's criticism of "theories of the first look" have already been touched upon, but the general character of the conception which he opposes to it has not yet been examined. In Bosanquet's view the problem of political obligation created by the first look can only be dealt with if it is possible to find some means of attributing acts of the government to the community as a whole, and this is the task which he sets himself:

"If...we understand 'the self' in 'self-government' to stand for the whole sovereign group or community, which is usually called a 'self-governing,' as opposed to a subject, state, then we have before us the task of showing that this self is a reality in any sense which justifies the acceptance of what is done by the public power as an act of the whole community."[1]

Bosanquet considered that the general will provided the requisite sense of selfhood.

The vision again: the general will

Before we relate the general will to "theories of the first look" it will be useful to say a little about the actual experience out of which the concept of the general will arose. On this matter we have the benefit of Bosanquet's own account of his intellectual biography, and to take account of it will illuminate the paragraphs to follow by placing abstract and general issues in their sociological context.

In an essay entitled Life and Philosophy,[2] Bosanquet recorded with obvious approval a remark made to him by "a friend, a very competent

---

1. P.T.S., p. 71.
2. This was Bosanquet's contribution to the first series of Contemporary British Philosophy, ed. J.H. Muirhead, Allen and Unwin, London, 1924. My references are to a reprint of Bosanquet's contribution in The Idealist Tradition, ed. A.C. Ewing, The Free Press, Glencoe, Illinois, 1957.

philosopher".[1] After visiting Bosanquet's family home at Rock (in Northumberland), his friend told him that this visit had greatly helped him in understanding his social and political theory.[2] Bosanquet relates life at his old home to the concept of the general will as follows:

"It is a place where for several generations there has reigned a practice of business efficiency together with a spirit of cordial co-operation and neighbourly kindness ... It seems to me that a constant habituation, from childhood up, to the feeling of the co-operative will and to what Miss Follett calls 'the art of living together,' is a sound starting-point for social theory. After such a habituation the doctrine of the real social will, for example, comes to one as the recognition of an obvious and solid fact ..."[3] He then adds, as something which is equally obvious, that "the difficulties which are raised on the ground of counter-volitions, tensions, and lacunae in its formation, seem to be nothing but what you expect in speaking of a will at all."[4]

Now while life at Rock was surely calculated to provide a genuine experience of happy and harmonious living, the important thing to notice when judging its adequacy as a basis for political theory is that "... Rock as it exists at present may be said to be the creation of the Bosanquet family,"[5] the fourteen cottages which comprise the village having been re-built by Bosanquet's grandfather. This circumstance in itself would be likely to produce a respectful and co-operative attitude towards the Bosanquet family amongst the cottagers of a small community,[6]

---

1. The Idealist Tradition, p. 154 (see previous footnote).
2. Ibid., p. 154.
3. Ibid., p. 154.
4. Ibid., p. 154.
5. Bernard Bosanquet, by Helen Bosanquet, op.cit., p.4.
6. An entry in his father's (the Rev. R.W. Bosanquet) diary is suggestive: he records that when Bosanquet was baptized on August 6, 1848, "the people had their little present of tea and sugar as usual." Bernard Bosanquet, op.cit., p.7.

but it must also be born in mind that "The inhabitants of the village were all workers on the home farm, or others employed about the Hall ((i.e. Bosanquet's home)): the joiner, the blacksmith, the coachman, and the hinds or labourers."[1] It was no doubt generous of Bosanquet to be "furious at the way people talk of and portray the country labourer as 'Hodge' ..."[2] and to concern himself with the welfare of the villagers, but the altogether untypical nature of the communal relationship which existed in Rock must be stressed. Only in the context of such a semi-feudal relationship does it become plausible to minimize the significance of "counter-volitions" and "tensions" in the community, in the way Bosanquet did in the passage just quoted from Life and Philosophy, and as he does (we shall see) in his philosophical work.

With the sociological origin of the general will clearly fixed we may use it to advance a suggestion which may throw some light on Bosanquet's theoretical discussion of that concept. It is that the influence of Bosanquet's Northumbrian experience of a common good unimpeded by problematic "counter-volitions" combined with his metaphysical hostility to the self as a "dangerous immediate" to produce the chapter of The Philosophical Theory of the State which has perhaps done most to discredit his treatment of the problem of political obligation. This is Chapter VII, in which Bosanquet endeavours to provide a psychological illustration of the idea of a real or general will.

Bosanquet believed that an effective way of weaning his readers from the first look would be to compare the social relationship with the relationship between the elements of mind.[3] In both cases the first look reveals atomistic units, and seeks to characterize any connection which exists between them in terms of association.[4] Bosanquet contrasts the concept of association with a concept which he considers to be more

---

1. Ibid., pp. 4-5.
2. Ibid., p. 5.
3. P.T.S., p. 146.
4. Ibid., p. 147.

suitable for conveying the nature of both mental groupings, or appercipient masses, and social groupings: it is the concept of organization. (It will be clear that we are back with the concrete universal, discussed in Chapter 5, above). This concept is superior because it does not treat relations as external to the units to which they are attached, thereby reducing them to fictions. An army really is an army, and not a mere collection of men, or a crowd.[1] Organisation grasps that intangible something which is not apprehended by sense and yet is constitutive of the reality of personal and mental groupings. That something is the "general scheme"[2] which makes "a crowd" into "an army", and "a fortuitous connection of ideas" into "a valid inference."

What has been said so far has not added anything to what was revealed by the consideration of the doctrine of the concrete universal in Chapter 5 (above). But now Bosanquet gives the concept of organization a new twist, to make it explain the origin of the state's coercive power; and since his argument at this point is suspect, we must follow it with care.

Bosanquet writes that

"... we know by common experience how entirely quiescent is one... factor of the mind while we are absorbed in the activity of another; how utterly, for example, we disregard the botanical character of wild flowers when we are clearing them out of the garden as weeds, and how wholly we neglect the question whether they are 'flowers' or 'weeds' when we are occupied in studying their botanical character."[3]

Just as the botanical character of a flower is disregarded when it is classed as a weed, so a man always regards himself and is regarded from a definite point of view when he acts, and all other points of view tend to be neglected while and in so far as he is acting in that particular capacity.[4] From this arises the need for force, since every

---

1. Ibid., pp. 149-150.
2. Ibid., p. 152.
3. Ibid., p. 155.
4. Ibid., p. 157.

individual life embodies many different points of view, each of which becomes operative in society as a grouping of individuals, and these may be in conflict. A judge, for example, may in his official capacity have to enforce laws of which in his private capacity as a conscientious citizen he disapproves.[1] From this possibility of conflict there arises the state which, "... as the widest grouping whose members are effectively united by a common experience, is necessarily the one community which has absolute power to ensure, by force if need be, at least sufficient adjustment of all other groupings to make life possible."[2]

What is misleading in this argument is that the comparison of organization in mental elements with organization of persons makes no allowance for disagreement upon what is to be the general scheme, plan or idea pursued by a particular social group. It is not too difficult, that is to say, to agree with some of one's fellows to call a plant "Sabbatia" and preserve it for botanical research, instead of calling it "a weed" and exterminating it. But it is much more difficult to agree upon the scheme or plan which is to turn a collection of men from a mere "association" into an effective and durable "organization". The precise point at which Bosanquet's argument ceases to carry conviction is where he attempts to move from the generalization that "... we know from common experience how entirely quiescent is one ... factor of the mind while we are absorbed in the activity of another", to an insight into the nature of social unity founded upon it. That the generalization is true of intra-personal experiences is not denied; what is suggested is that it offers no guidance about experiences of an inter-personal kind. Bosanquet assumes, in short, complete agreement upon the content of the common good; in politics everyone will agree, as it were, to call X "a weed". This might well be an acceptable assumption in the small

---

1. Ibid., p. 157.
2. Ibid., p. 158.

homogeneous community at Rock, but it is not true of larger, more complex, communities. By basing his discussion of the origin of force upon this assumption, Bosanquet fails to recognize that for the political philosopher concerned to deal with political obligation in the modern world the conflict of duties which may trouble an individual is only part of the problem; the conflict which may occur between different individuals is at least as important a part.

Bosanquet's psychological illustration is not only defective in conceiving force purely in terms of intra-personal relationships. He moves on to advance the proposition that "... each individual mind, if we consider it as a whole, is an expression or reflection of society as a whole from a point of view which is distinctive and unique."[1] In other words, "... just as, in any man's idea of London, there is hardly any factor of London life which does not at least colour the background so, in every individual impression of the social whole, there is no social feature that does not, in one way or another, contribute to that total effect".[2] Bosanquet expresses the same thought by a metaphor. If a mind were laid on the dissecting table, a cross-section of it would contain all the elements to be found in society at large, although each of these elements would be perceived from a unique point of view or special angle.[3] Once again one can see the plausibility of such a suggestion when applied to a small community like Rock, with one ancestral hall and fourteen cottages, and with all the cottagers in direct contact with the Bosanquet family; but the denizen of a London yard would scarcely be familiar with life in Cheyne Gardens, and at the level of the national community the suggestion is quite implausible - more so, perhaps, in Bosanquet's own time than today.

But Bosanquet advances yet another idea, not less curious than the one just considered. It is an idea in which the conflict between the two Bosanquets we distinguished in Chapter 5 (above) is clearly observable.

---

1. Ibid., p. 162.
2. Ibid., p. 162.
3. Ibid., p. 163.

It is that

"... the true particularisation of the human universal does not necessarily coincide with the distinction between different persons, and ... the correlation of differences ((of a plurality of individual minds)) and the identity which they constitute remain much the same whether they chance to fall within a single human being or to be dispersed over several".[1]

In other words, Bosanquet is suggesting that if I am my own doctor, the combination of dispositions which occurs in me is not essentially different from the combination of dispositions which occurs within the social relationship arising when doctor and patient are different.[2] He is also suggesting that my full self-realization requires me to do what I am best at, and not what I want to do. Bosanquet's opinion that "The stress seems ... to lie on the attainment of the true particularization which does justice to the maximum of human capacity, rather than on the mere relations which arise between the members of a de facto plurality",[3] has been seized upon by Carritt, who remarks that "if this means anything it must imply a justification of slavery and of almost any degree of exploitation by those who can claim higher abilities".[4] We noticed this ambiguous attitude towards slavery earlier, at the end of Chapter 5 (above), and attributed it to the dominance of the Platonic Bosanquet. Yet over the pages in which the difficulties discussed in the present paragraph occur, statements with a different import are scattered, and in them the other Bosanquet briefly appears (as is recognized by Carritt).[5] There is, for example, the statement that "As in the natural world in space and time, so, in the world of human beings which on one side belongs to it, differentiation implies dispersion into a plurality of centres".[6]

---

1. Ibid., p. 166.
2. Ibid., p. 165.
3. Ibid., p. 151.
4. Morals and Politics, op.cit., pp. 151-152.
5. Morals and Politics, op.cit., p. 152.
6. P.T.S. p. 164.

Again, Bosanquet acknowledges that the presence of human nature in any individual constitutes "a claim that it shall be perfected in him".[1] In the end, however, this view occupies a place in Bosanquet's thought subordinate to that held by the other, of which the best statement is contained in Bosanquet's remark that

"If we consider my unity with myself at different times as the limiting case, we shall find it very hard to establish a difference of principle between the unity of what we call our mind and that of all the 'minds' which enter into a single social experience."[2]

This is the doctrine of overlapping selves, the doctrine which places such a high value upon genius[3] and, in the context of the time, vindicates the hegemony or "guardianship" of the middle-class over the rest of society by appealing to the excellence and range of the experience of its noblest representatives.

Bosanquet's psychological illustration of the general will is not the only point in his political thought where the first appearance gets rough treatment; there is also his distinction between the actual and the real will of the individual. This subject has inevitably been touched upon in the discussion of the psychological illustration, but the difficulties involved may now be made more explicit. No-one would deny that each of us often does things he would *really* prefer not to do (the smoker's plight being the most usual example), but Bosanquet goes beyond this familiar experience when he writes that if each of us tried to clarify the structure of purpose which is his will, then "our will would return to us in a shape in which we should not know it again, although every detail would be a necessary inference from the whole of wishes and resolutions which we actually cherish".[4] When this statement is taken in conjunction with Bosanquet's view that "... it seems plain that one actual human being may cover the ground which, in other instances,

---

1. *Ibid.*, p. 166.
2. *Ibid.*, p. 166.
3. *Ibid.*, p. 165.
4. *Ibid.*, p. 111.

it takes many men to occupy", [1] it does pose in an acute form the question of who is to recognize one's real will for one, for it appears only too likely that one may not be able to recognize one's own will when it has been thoroughly "criticized". In Rock, presumably, there would have been general agreement on who was to determine what was the general will. The day-trippers to Oxshott were more recalcitrant than the hinds of Rock, but the improvement in their manners over the years would doubtless have convinced Bosanquet that they too could overcome their "stupidity" and learn that their real will required them to avoid trespassing.

On one important issue, however, Bosanquet indicated very plainly that he was not prepared to trifle unduly with what people took to be their real will. In June 1893 he wrote to his niece Caroline Bosanquet and explained to her his position on Home Rule for Ireland.[2] He described the demand for Home Rule as "constant and unequivocal", and as "clear and unwavering";[3] and he went on to add the sentence which is most important from our point of view: "Now to say that this demand is unreal and ignorant, and you and I and our friends know better than the Irish electors what is good for them, is to those who think with us quite childish and superstitious. The whole question at issue is which knows best what will express the people's soul and will, and if representative government is to be maintained there can be no doubt of the answer."[4]

To instance particular applications of his theory of the real or general will, however, does not help to answer the theoretical question of where the general will is to be discovered. Bosanquet's handling of this question is very unsatisfactory. He contents himself with three negative specifications. The general will is not to be identified with the will of all; it is not identical with public opinion; and it is not the de facto tendency of all that is done by members of the community.[5]

---

1. Ibid., p. 165.
2. *Bernard Bosanquet*, by Helen Bosanquet, op. cit., p. 99.
3. Ibid., pp. 100-101.
4. Ibid., p. 101.
5. *Science*, pp. 262-266.

The general will does, in fact, have a precise location, although Bosanquet himself is unable to recognize it. It exists as the will of the imaginary community in which all evil has disappeared. It exists, that is, in so far as "the great values" manage to "unite human minds and hearts in a common duty for a universal good".[1] Great values can do this only in so far as stupidity (for Bosanquet identifies evil with stupidity) disappears. By stupidity is meant, in one form or another, selfishness. Stupidity is morally censurable when it is due to "self-absorption, inattention, inappreciativeness of what is important to others".[2] If the general will cannot be found the presumption is that the moral attitude of the individual members of society has encountered "the artificial and transient negation that springs from impotence and unenlightenment".[3]

The nature of the forces which work against the emergence of a general will are most clearly brought out in a passage at the end of Some Suggestions in Ethics in which Bosanquet states the reasons why a universal general will has not yet possessed the world. He writes that:

"Nations are not alert, not sensitive, to the mind and needs of other nations; they do not realise where others want to go and why; nor how their own direction can be modified in harmony with the others', and yet none of their really essential aims be sacrificed. They are not at all clear, perhaps what *are* their own essential aims. Their social arrangements do not permit a distinct vision of them. Their leaders are blinded and biassed by false interests. Still less are they responsive to the needs of others."[4] In short, what Bosanquet calls "the crowning stupidity", i.e. war, is attributed by him to selfishness, in the manifold forms under which it appears as lack of communication, intellectual limitation,

---

1. Suggestions, p. 235.
2. Ibid., p. 216.
3. Ibid., p. 233.
4. Ibid., p. 244, his emphasis.

and bad leadership. The assumption, as in Green, is that a (potentially) morally and politically virgin populace lies beneath the corruption which presents itself to the eyes. In the final paragraph of the book, indeed, Bosanquet places his faith in public opinion, in spite of his rejection of it elsewhere. This paragraph follows immediately upon the one last quoted:

"It is all this stupidity which most emphatically public opinion ought to be hard upon. But, in being so, it might find that first of all it had to be hard upon itself. The only hope for it and for us is that it is a self-criticizing organ; and <u>to be hard upon itself is a function which it is seldom unwilling to adopt</u>".[1]

The concept of the general will, then, is closely tied to Bosanquet's assumptions about the nature of force, war, evil in general, and the purity of the people. It is one phase of what we called his vision. It exists in a world in which the social and metaphysical assumptions behind that vision are allowed to hold good; it disappears to the extent to which they are found untenable.

A heavenly freedom

Freedom, for Bosanquet, meant virtue, and virtue meant religion. This partly explains his esteem for the novels of C. M. Yonge, whose admirers have noticed her conviction that all virtue, all sacrifice, all behaviour of any worth, must be inspired by a genuine religious feeling.[2] A similar conviction was displayed by Bosanquet when he criticized those who wish to claim their actions as their own instead of "offering them to the Absolute".[3]

To gain the true freedom valued by Bosanquet one needed moral education. In the London Ethical Society Bosanquet found one of the most important means of disseminating such education. He was invited to join it in 1887 and welcomed the opportunity, since the Society provided a means of "... organizing the material of noble life, so as to bring

---

1. <u>Ibid</u>., p. 245, emphasis added; see also p. 214.
2. <u>Victorian Best-seller</u>, by Mare and Percival, op. cit., p. 232.
3. <u>Value</u>, p. 20.

it within the reach of all".[1] The secretary of the Society, Mrs. Husband, later wrote to tell Mrs. Bosanquet that "The whole thing is saturated with Mr. Bosanquet, his work, his spirit, his ideals, and his fears at times lest the society should breakaway from his sympathy."[2]

In an address to the Ethical Society entitled How to Read the New Testament,[3] Bosanquet made clear the sort of education a man requires in order to become free. He stated that "... it is our task, and the task of a future moral education, to regain, for ourselves and for our children, some clue to the religion of Jesus and of Paul". He thought he could give such a clue to his listeners and informed them that "There is nothing at all strange in the fact that we now, after seventeen centuries, can see the meaning of the New Testament more truly than it has been seen since it was written".[4] Central to this meaning Bosanquet considered to be, not the ideas of authority, permanence, infallible tradition, or scriptural inspiration, but the idea of "membership in the kingdom of heaven."[5] He did not refer, of course, to anything so coarse as a future life in Paradise, although he was prepared to admit that Jesus himself was perhaps confused about the true meaning of his teaching - he "may have had some ideas which we must pronounce quite unreasonable".[7] He may have believed, for example, that he really would come again to judge the world.[8] What Jesus really meant was that the kingdom of heaven is to consist, on the one hand,

"... in righteousness of heart and life, in genuine human morality, in putting away the selfish will ... And it is to consist, for this very reason, on the other hand, in a purification of human society and the formation of a righteous community not restricted to any nation, rank, or creed".[9]

---

1. Quoted in Bernard Bosanquet, by Helen Bosanquet, op.cit., p. 45.
2. Ibid., p. 46.
3. Reprinted in Essays, op.cit., p. 131.
4. Ibid., p. 161.
5. Ibid., p. 158.
6. Ibid., p. 157.
7. Ibid., p. 142.
8. Ibid., p. 142.
9. Ibid., p. 144.

The kingdom of heaven, as Bosanquet expressed it in another passage, must "be founded on freedom, and be as wide as humanity".[1]

It is difficult to feel that Bosanquet's lecture did much to raise the status of Jesus in the eyes of his audience. Jesus suffered rather badly from a contrast drawn between his teaching and that of Pericles; Jesus, Bosanquet observed, "had something to learn from Pericles".[2] Worse still, Bosanquet could find no indication that Jesus could even claim to be the founder of Christianity - "There were no Christians in Jesus' lifetime".[3] The New Testament also fared badly, for "We can see that neither the disciples nor the Gospel-writers understood Jesus".[4] St. Paul alone survived relatively unscathed, since he is a less elusive figure than Christ and there can be no doubt that "The nature of his doctrine was ... the Gospel of Humanity, ((which)) was implied rather than affirmed in Christ's gospel of the kingdom."[5] It can scarcely have been encouraging, however, to hear that passages in the First and Second Letters to the Corinthians "show-((ed)) that he was subject to trances."[6] Helen Bosanquet records that the lecture led to the formation of a class of working men to study the New Testament under Bosanquet's guidance, but she does not say what doctrines they acquired in the process, or whether they lost their faith altogether.

The freedom which Bosanquet valued was contrasted by him with the "negative" freedom favoured by individualist political philosophers. The concept of "negative" freedom involved theoretical inconsistencies because it implied that an increase in coercion always meant a decrease in liberty, whereas in reality liberty may be increased by coercion.[7] This criticism would be cogent had it been the unqualified doctrine of

---

1. Ibid., p. 145.
2. Ibid., p. 146.
3. Ibid., p. 147.
4. Ibid., p. 147.
5. Ibid., p. 150.
6. Ibid., p. 150.
7. Cf. Civilization, p. 379: "... liberty, in the plainest and simplest sense of the word, does not depend on the absence of legislation, but on the comprehensiveness and reasonableness of life."

the individualist tradition that liberty and coercion are mutually exclusive; but not all thinkers in that tradition approximated this position as closely as (for example) Bentham, whose position Bosanquet singles out for especial attention.[1] Locke explicitly rejects the idea that law and liberty are incompatible, for "law, in its notion, is not so much the limitation as the direction of a free and intelligent agent to his proper interest, and prescribes no further than is for the general good of those under that law."[2] Stuart Mill, again, does not deny Bosanquet's main contention, that government is to be judged by its responsiveness to human control, and its effect upon character. Mill's statement, for example, that "... the most important point of excellence which any form of government can possess is to promote the virtue and intelligence of the people...",[3] hardly displays a conviction that law is inevitably hostile to the "positive" freedom favoured by Bosanquet.

Although Bosanquet somewhat overstated the contrast between his own position and that of the individualist philosophers, there was at least one great difference separating the Lockean tradition from Bosanquet's approach to liberty: philosophers in the Lockean tradition were concerned primarily with political liberty; Bosanquet was not. Consequently Bosanquet did not so much criticize the theorists of negative liberty as just talk past them, for he began by rejecting the "first appearance" within which their problems were located. More precisely, the theorists of "negative" liberty had begun by assuming the separateness of selves and had preoccupied themselves with the problem of inter-personal relationships, while Bosanquet centred his metaphysics and political thought upon a denial of the impermeability of finite selves. He talked instead about the one self of which separate persons are really bodily manifestations. That in itself need not have prevented him from recognizing that the different finite appearances of the absolute might need pro-

---

1. P.T.S. pp. 53 - 56.
2. Second Treatise, sect. 57.
3. Representative Government, Chap. II; p. 193 in the Everyman ed.

tecting from one another, but Bosanquet did not choose to pursue that line of thought. In his chapter on liberty he spoke instead of the separateness of selves as a principle not only of separateness from others but also of "thorough transition into and unity with the life which is at the root of theirs ((i.e. of other selves))"[1] and it was the "thorough transition" which he leaned upon most heavily. The only danger he found in taking literally the usually metaphorical application of the term liberty to a state of the individual mind was that it might lead to a philosophically false emphasis upon freedom as indeterminacy, owing to the "negative" significance of the word in its primary meaning of absence of constraint.

In the course of the movement from "negative" to "positive" liberty, then, all conflict is made internal to each (sensuous) individual. Any social difficulties which arise are a product of stupidity, in its aspect of narrowness and confusion. Bosanquet writes that

"We really know the sensuous individual as such, the will in its impure and uncriticized form, only in our experience, constant as that is, of failure, error and forgetfulness, in adhering to the rational life, which, on the whole, is inherent in the very nature of our rational being, and which we only desert in the same way and to the same extent as we make mistakes in intellectual matters. We go wrong by narrowness and confusion..."[2]

Whenever tension between selves appears, in other words, there has been a lapse from the kingdom of heaven, in which the rational - i.e. the purely unselfish and truly free - life is lived. In the kingdom of heaven (in the immanent sense in which Bosanquet uses the phrase, of course), there would be neither need nor demand for political liberty.

---

1. *P.T.S.*, p. 134.
2. *Ibid.*, p. 137.

Conclusion

Bosanquet was above all an earnest man: morality mattered to him more than anything else. He was fond of repeating that "the basis of life is serious throughout".[1] If his earnestness was softened by his universal courtesy, it was reinforced by his metaphysics, according to which man "is a representative, a trustee for the world, of certain powers and circumstances,"[2] and must live accordingly.

The place of moral earnestness in Bosanquet's life and thought was closely challenged by another quality, which was his optimism about human nature and its potentialities. He was prepared to discuss the advent of the kingdom of heaven, though there was a considerable touch of austerity in the picture he painted of it; the heavenly host would definitely prefer refinement to luxury. His optimism, like his earnestness, found support in his metaphysics. Those who found evil in the world were convicted by him of thinking in narrow juridical terms.

Earnestness and optimism are unobjectionable in themselves, but when they combine to colour the whole of a political theory they inevitably produce in it a certain narrowness. This narrowness was reinforced in Bosanquet's case by the limited nature of his experience of the world. The small community at Rock did not in any sense provide a model upon which a modern political philosopher could hope to build.[3] While he

---

1. Quoted in *Bernard Bosanquet*, by Helen Bosanquet, op. cit., p. 42.
2. *Principle*, p. 21.
3. In connection with Rock we may add that the relevant thing is not so much the proportion of his life that he spent there as the significance which he always attached to his memories of it. Cf. Helen Bosanquet's remark about Rock: "It was a home to which he was deeply attached, and of which the memories formed a permanent background to his whole way of life and thought". *Bernard Bosanquet*, op. cit. p. 7. Elsewhere Mrs. Bosanquet notes that subsequent experience did not fundamentally alter the attitudes Bosanquet acquired in his youth at Rock: after mentioning a note in his father's diary referring to a long walk he had taken his eleven-year-old son in the course of inspecting drains upon the family estate, she writes that "It is a far cry from this long country walk to the days in later life when he was actively interesting himself in the sanitary conditions of the Chelsea slums, but in a life which developed so consistently as his, the connection is obvious." *Ibid.*, p. 6.

lived in London Bosanquet engaged in many activities designed to alleviate the condition of the lower orders, but this experience was perhaps even less likely to expand his range of sympathies than life in Rock; in Rock Bosanquet would encounter the hinds, as the labourers were called, at first hand, but in London "he seldom, if ever, undertook any of the visiting connected with the relief work of the society ((i.e. the Charity Organization Society)) ... personally he found that part of the work uncongenial, and 'did not know what to say'".[1] In Oxshott his main contact with the mass took place while he was preventing them from trespassing in his garden, and when he had to put out the fires started on the Common by holiday-makers from London.[2]

Although Bosanquet's writings ranged over a wide section of social and philosophical problems, the appearance of great wisdom is a little deceptive; all the subjects he considered were viewed from the same standpoint, and the spectacles through which they were seen reflect the limitations of that standpoint. The world as Bosanquet conceived it was very similar to the world inhabited by the characters of Charlotte Mary Yonge; these were characters of "delightful goodness", as an admirer of Miss Yonge's expressed it (see Chapter 5, above).

On the theoretical level Bosanquet's weakness, in his politics as in his metaphysics, lay in his inability to find room for the concrete particularized character of life within the unity he loved so much. Bosanquet seems to have been so struck by the idea that we are not <u>separate</u> that he was inclined to minimize the fact that we are indubitably <u>different</u>. This failure meant that he, like Green, failed to transcend the antithesis of egoism and altruism. It may well be true that "It is not the bare personality or the separate destiny that occupies a healthy mind",[3] but it does not follow that an attitude of sustained hostility to "the bare personality" is a more concrete position to adopt. The failure

---

1. Bernard Bosanquet, op. cit., pp. 53-54.
2. Ibid., p. 91.
3. Principle, p. 21.

also meant that Bosanquet cannot be considered to have found a satisfactory sense in which agent and patient may be said to be united in coercion; and that, after all, was the concern which lay at the heart of his treatment of the problem of political obligation.

===============

Chapter 9.

Oakeshott

We now turn from the optimistic, reforming liberalism of Green and Bosanquet to the pessimistic, conservative liberalism[1] of Oakeshott. The origin of this difference of mood, we have seen, is to be found in the difference in the metaphysical system which underlies Oakeshott's position from those of Green and Bosanquet. In his general philosophy Oakeshott endeavoured to accomplish a dissolution of the internal dynamic of idealism by destroying that "nisus towards the whole" which the universal self had generated in the system of Green and Bosanquet, and which had given their political theory its radical impulse.

The sceptical foundation of Oakeshott's political theory was most clearly exhibited in his treatment of the practical mode of experience. While Oakeshott did not specifically deny that <u>in particular instances</u> of action there was the possibility of realizing the "ought", he preferred to stress that action <u>as such</u> presupposes a gap between "is" and "ought". The rationalist criticized so thoroughly in the political essays is one who fails to recognize the inevitability of this gap, persisting in the foolish attempt to achieve a once-and-for-all unification of the ideal and the actual.

With these recapitulory remarks to remind us of the broader context, we move on to consider the political essays in detail.

<u>Comparison of his treatment of the problem of political obligation with that of Green and Bosanquet</u>.

In Oakeshott's political writings the problems and concepts with which earlier idealists were preoccupied seldom find explicit expression. There is no discussion of the real will and the general will, and little reference to such concepts as negative and positive liberty, or to the abstractions of traditional natural law theory. However, it would be wrong to conclude that these issues have completely disappeared or remain unresolved in his thought.

---

1. Oakeshott himself would not accept this designation since it associates him with thinkers whom he would classify as rationalists. However, his mood and much of his political doctrine make it the most appropriate of those available.

It is rather that Oakeshott feels no inclination to fight the old battles; when the traditional concepts do appear, they occur in a new context, which is the political thought of a philosopher who is primarily concerned to warn his contemporaries of the threat to the libertarian tradition posed by the rationalistic idiom of moral and political conduct.

The old antitheses of "state" and "individual", "self" and "others", "natural" and "social", which lay behind the general form of the problem of political obligation, are now resolved in the concrete idea of a tradition of behaviour. What we are concerned with is not "the individual" and "the state", as mutually exclusive abstractions, but "a way of life" and the conditions of its maintenance. Society is "a common way of life",[1] and politics is "the custody of a manner of living".[2] Reviewing a work by H.C.Simons, Oakeshott commends it precisely because the treatment of liberty in it is concrete, refusing to deal with definitions and to create abstract antitheses: the purpose of Simons' inquiry, he writes, "is not to define a word, but to detect the secret of what we enjoy, to recognize what is hostile to it, and to discuss where and how it may be enjoyed more fully".[3]

In reviewing Quintin Hogg's The Case for Conservatism, Oakeshott makes some brief remarks which make it even clearer that his attitude towards the classical concepts of individuality, nature and freedom is in substantial agreement with that of Green and Bosanquet. Insisting that "we do not begin by being free", he proceeds to add that freedom is to be found embodied within the social order and not outside it: "the structure of our freedom is the rights and duties which, by long and painful effort, have been established in our society. Individuality is not natural; it is a great human achievement".[4]

If Oakeshott agrees with Green and Bosanquet in abandoning some of the abstract conceptions in which the concept of freedom had been entangled in classical political thought, he differs from them in refusing to identify "true liberty" with an ideal of self-sacrifice and service to the community.

---

1. Rationalism, p.73.
2. Cambridge Journal, Vol. 1, 1947-8, p.58.
3. Rationalism, p.40.
4. C.J., Vol. 1, 1947-8, p.468.

We can usefully generalize the fundamental theoretical point at issue here by observing that Green and Bosanquet had erected their moral and political thought upon the assumption that all social problems resulted from "defect in nature." Oakeshott begins from the opposite position, according to which no explanation of reality is satisfactory which attributes the explanandum to defect in nature. When this is noticed it is easy to understand Oakeshott's admiration for Hobbes; Hobbes, like Oakeshott, begins from the view that "The Desires, and other Passions of man, are in themselves no Sin",[1] and that a plurality of selves, each of which is final judge of good and evil acts, is in itself sufficient to create a condition of war.[2] He, like Oakeshott, does not maintain that the extirpation of sin is the goal of individual and social endeavour, and (like Oakeshott) declines to become absorbed in the idea of a positive freedom to be attained by success in that pursuit.

In one respect at least Oakeshott adheres more consistently than Green and Bosanquet to the implications of abandoning the abstract concepts of nature and individuality, for he refuses to engage in a demarcation enterprise, which had (in Green and Bosanquet) stigmatized state action as negative because it is incompatible with genuine self-realization. For Oakeshott "the conditions of individuality are not limitations; there is nothing to limit, and the adjustment of those conditions are not interference (unless they are overhead adjustments); they are the continuation of the achievement".[3] This is not to say, of course, that Oakeshott does not conceive of politics as a limited activity. It is to say that his reasons for so considering it do not rest on what Bosanquet called the "theory of the first look".

It will be remembered that Bosanquet, prior to treating the problem of political obligation, felt compelled to spend a considerable amount of time in distinguishing a philosophical approach to that problem from the sociological, psychological, economic and juridical approaches. There is a very similar line of argument to be found in Oakeshott's writings. The relevant

---

1. Leviathan, chap. 13.
2. Ibid., chap. 13.
3. C.J., Vol. 1, 1947-48, p.488.

piece is his essay on <u>The Concept of a Philosophical Jurisprudence</u>, in which he considers "the meaning and possibility of a philosophy of law and civil society".[1] In his language, however, the issue would be phrased somewhat differently. Where Bosanquet speaks of a philosophical theory of the state, Oakeshott refers to the tradition of philosophical jurisprudence, which is a <u>single</u> tradition "in the sense that it is the universal context of every text in the history of philosophical jurisprudence".[2] And whereas Bosanquet distinguishes philosophical theory from sociological, psychological and economic theory, Oakeshott goes somewhat further, distinguishing a philosophical doctrine of the nature of civil society not only from these but also from an analytical and historical approach. Since we have already discussed Oakeshott's general conception of the nature of political philosophy, and since his discussion of the limitations of sociological, psychological and economic explanation does not differ in substance from that of Bosanquet, we need only add a brief review of his comments on analytical and historical explanation.

Every mode of explanation implies a philosophy of identity; to explain, that is to say, is always to identify a thing on the basis of certain presuppositions. In the case of analytical jurisprudence, the presupposition is that law is a body of interrelated principles.[3] In other words, the analytical approach to jurisprudence seeks to explain law not by relating it to something outside itself but by deducing its nature from a study of what was presupposed to be a legal system.[4] Historical jurisprudence, on the other hand, rejects the view that law is composed of certain essential principles, and finds its essence in its being a product of time. Analytical jurisprudence, or any other form of jurisprudence, may indeed make use of history, but it differs from historical jurisprudence in refusing to recognize history as constituting the essence of law. The differentia of historical jurisprudence lies in its claim that the very meaning of law lies in the history of the civilization to which it belongs.[5] These observations scarcely call for

---

1. <u>Politica</u>, Vol. 3, 1938, p.203.
2. <u>Ibid</u>., p.359.
3. <u>Ibid</u>., p.207.
4. <u>Ibid</u>., p.353.
5. <u>Ibid</u>., p.208.

comment; it is quite clear that the conceptions of the state advanced by analytical and historical jurisprudence could not offer a satisfactory theory of political obligation. Like the other modes of explanation, they fail to afford a stable philosophy of identity; they cannot, that is to say, defend themselves against disciplines which offer rival theories of the state. Neither analytical nor historical jurisprudence affords any answer, for example, to the claim that it is really the economic conditions of social life that cause the appearances which analytical and historical jurisprudence mistake for reality. Nor do they give any guidance when (to complicate matters still further) psychology emerges to maintain against the economic determinist that "not only were ((psychological)) factors already concerned in the establishment of these economic conditions, but, even in obeying these conditions, men can do no more than set their original instinctual impulses in motion".[1]

Oakeshott, then, is as careful as Bosanquet was to avoid the abstractions of the theory of the first look, or of theories which rest upon an arbitrary conception of essence: thus he writes of the concept of tradition that since it "is not susceptible of the distinction between essence and accident, knowledge of it is unavoidably knowledge of its detail: to know only the gist is to know nothing".[2] Setting these to one side, he takes his stand upon the concrete conception of a tradition of behaviour, which, we have seen, is the embodiment of the category of will. What Oakeshott takes to be its place in the concrete totality of experience has already been examined.

What must now be emphasized, however, is the fact already remarked, that Oakeshott's primary concern in developing the concept of tradition is not so much to mobilize it against the abstractions of individualist political thought (to emphasize, that is, its status as a concrete logical principle of practical unity which can both "tolerate and unite an internal variety, not insisting upon conformity to a single character"),[3] as to make it a polemical basis for an attack on the rationalistic style of politics. Because his criticism of rationalist politics necessarily forces Oakeshott to delineate a more acceptable style of politics, the concept of tradition is made to

---

1. S. Freud, New Introductory Lectures on Psycho-Analysis, Hogarth Press, London; 6th impression 1962, pp.228-229; first published, 1933.

2. Rationalism, p.128-9.

3. Leviathan, ed. Oakeshott, p.xii.

afford not only an answer to the problem of political obligation in its general form as the question, Why ought the individual to obey the state?, but also an answer to the question, What set of institutional arrangements will promote a stable and harmonious practical resolution of that problem in the specific context of modern European life? A more detailed examination of this latter aspect of the concept of tradition must be postponed for the moment, but what will subsequently be suggested is that in utilizing the concept of tradition to supply both a philosophy of identity and a basis for conservatism, Oakeshott introduces into that concept a large element of ambiguity. Our immediate concern with the idea of tradition is to show how greatly the style of politics which Oakeshott attaches to it differs from that advocated by Green and Bosanquet, after all the foregoing theoretical similarities have been taken into account.

Green, it will be remembered, complained because the age was lacking in "causes". Bosanquet followed him in advocating self-sacrificing altruism. This concern with virtue gave their politics a telocratic character which is completely rejected by Oakeshott in favour of the nomocratic conception which they had abandoned. Oakeshott distinguished the two styles of politics with some care in an unpublished paper entitled The Idea of "Character" in the Interpretation of Modern Politics.

"Character" is "the recognition of conduct in terms of known and established dispositions", and Oakeshott considers that political conduct in Europe during the last four centuries has acquired sufficient regularity for it to display a character. In the late fifteenth century there emerged ways of thinking about politics differing in important respects from those which had hitherto prevailed. These new ways of thinking only came to prevail gradually, but by the mid-seventeenth century they had established themselves as the boundaries within which all subsequent political activity occurred. Oakeshott refuses to conceive of this character as the realization of a divine vocation, or as in any sense necessary: "...this character is not our 'destiny'....it is neither necessary nor permanent..." It is simply an "historic" character, and is significant "because it is a balance of dispositions in respect of government which, as a matter of fact, has for the time being established itself. It represents, in the manners and enterprises of government, a certain range of movement; among the governed, a certain range of expectations; and for governors and governed alike, a political vocabulary whose words are allowed a certain range of meaning." There is another thing to be noticed about this character, as it appears to Oakeshott. Character is something which emerges and is not made; hence the acceptance of the term is incompatible with the assumptions about the origin of western institutions reflected in (for example) Hayek's reference to "the basic principles on which this civilization was built",[1] and in W. Lippman's assertion, in connection with the natural law doctrine according to which there is a law above the ruler, that "The traditions of civility spring from this principle, which was first worked out by the Stoics".[2] To contemplate character except in terms of gradual growth, or actions except in terms of unintended consequences and ambiguous responses to unforeseen exigencies, is in Oakeshott's eyes already to have donned the mantle of rationalism. Finally, the modern European political character is significant "because there is at present no alternative to it." This is certainly true within Europe, Oakeshott thinks, but may even be true of the world, for European political dispositions have been diffused outside Europe "to such an extent that there is room for doubt whether there is a second political character of any significance to be found in the world."

Thus far the character which might be shared by seventeenth century England, eighteenth century France, nineteenth century Germany and twentieth century Russia has not been outlined by Oakeshott. He now proceeds to remedy this, and advances two propositions. The first is that "the pre-eminent dispositions of the modern European political character are not in respect of the constitution of governments, but in respect of the activities or pursuits of governments." They are thereby distinguished from dispositions in medieval Europe, which were more concerned about how a government was constituted and how it ought to be constituted than about what it did. The explanation for this difference Oakeshott finds in the limited pursuits of

---

1. <u>The Constitution of Liberty</u>, Routledge & Kegan Paul, London, 1960, p.1.
2. <u>The Public Philosophy</u>, Mentor Books, 1956, pp.76-77.

medieval governments. The limited pursuits of those governments he explains thus: "the main circumstance that prevented the activity of governing being, or being thought proper to be, an activity of enterprise was the conspicuous lack of power to be enterprising. For what a government does, what it is expected to do and even what it is thought proper for it to attempt, or to do, are usually conditioned by the resources of power it already commands or plausibly hopes to command." In modern times the power of governments has reached "proportions hitherto unheard of," and it is this fact which has brought about the change in attitudes towards governments.

Oakeshott's first proposition places him in a position to make an interesting observation about the limitations of much modern political thought. A substantial body of writing has progressed on the assumption that the most important political developments in the modern world have been modifications in "our practices and thoughts concerning the constitution and authorization of governments; the tensions that have received most notice are those concerned with the question <u>who</u> shall govern and by what instruments, and the modern political character has often been mistaken for one in which this group of dispositions is pre-eminent." This mistake was reinforced by the belief that the pursuits of governments are intimately related to the constitution of governments. Oakeshott gives as an example Tom Paine's optimism about republican government, grounded on the belief that the pursuits of such a government would inevitably be ones he approved. That mistake was further encouraged by the inherited European political vocabulary, whose words reflected the medieval concern with the constitution and authorization of government. The words "democracy" and "freedom", for example, now stand in part for activities of government, but as late as the eighteenth century their normal meaning related to the constitutions of governments. Montesquieu is perhaps the first to add the peculiarly modern meaning: in Montesquieu's work, indeed, Oakeshott finds the first recognition of the complex or manifold character of the European character, together with an attempt to determine its range.

Oakeshott's second proposition specifies the ideal extremes between which European politics have moved. At one extreme there has been a tendency to regard the proper office of government as engagement in a <u>first order</u> activity, and at the other extreme there has been a tendency to regard it as engagement in a <u>second order</u> activity. In order to clarify the distinction between first and second-order activity Oakeshott refers to the difference between substantive and non-substantive activity. Supposing that the substantive activity is to teach Latin grammar to a class of small boys, then the activity of keeping order in the class is not a substantive activity in relation to it, but is a second order activity, in which Oakeshott detects three characteristics. It (1) may or may not be expressly engaged in, (2) is indifferent to the specific character of the substantive activity, and (3) might be completely successful without in any way advancing the substantive activity. This distinction can scarcely be quarrelled with, but it is not always easy to recognize the point at which a second-order activity ceases to be second-order and becomes substantive: if the state merely lays down regulations for teaching-standards which all schools must meet before they are licenced to teach, it appears to be concerned solely with second-order rules; but the more complex the rules become, the more they infringe upon first-order activities by restricting the type of school which may exist. If it is insisted that in relation to the content of education the rules will always remain second-order, the point may perhaps be allowed, but from a practical standpoint it becomes quite trivial in its significance; for we know that, while the rules certainly contain no references to what should or should not be taught, they equally certainly prevent schools from engaging certain people (assumed for present purposes to be the only available masters of subject X) to teach subject X: thus they cannot be finally separated from first-order activity. The distinction also leaves open the question of what element in any situation is to be regarded as paramount, for what we take to be important determines what we consider to be substantive in any given case. Oakeshott recognizes this when he allows that it is quite possible to treat the keeping of order as the really important thing in the class-room situation, and the Latin as merely the best means of doing this.

In the paper Oakeshott does not try to show that government <u>ought</u> to be confined to second-order activity, but he does give reasons elsewhere for holding such a view, and we will come to them in a minute. What we must now observe is the connection which Oakeshott makes between his second proposition and modern political life. He maintains that on the one hand increased governmental power has brought an increase in first-order political activity; but that on the other hand the multifarious and rapidly changing substantive activities and beliefs of modern subjects lead them to regard second order activity as the proper office of government. The consequence is a tension in our view of the nature of institutions, and in our use of political words. Political institutions will be seen either as means for facilitating the pursuit of first order ends by government, or else as a way of keeping government within the sphere of second order activity; while our political vocabulary displays not *mere* ambiguity, but *specific* ambiguity, being systematically affected by the ambivalence in our attitude towards the appropriate level of government activity.

There is an essay by Oakeshott which illustrates well his conception of the kind of thing which is excluded by second order political activity, and which brings out at the same time the extent of his difference from Green and Bosanquet on political matters. This is the essay The B. B. C.[1] We examined in some detail the role which Green assigned to the novel: we may perhaps infer from that something about his likely attitude towards the mass media. They would have had, in his eyes, the same levelling potentialities, breaking the barriers between classes; and would also have enhanced the danger presented by the novel, notably the direction of public attention to the existing world of sense instead of to the ideal world yet to be realized. He would therefore have favoured the B.B.C. policy of broadcasting "to develop true citizenship and the leading of a full life",[2] and would have been particularly pleased by the ingenious method by which the B.B.C. sought to wean the nation from happy endings to tragic consciousness. Oakeshott quotes the Director-General's account of this method, which involves three programmes:

"It rests on the conception of the community as a broadly based cultural pyramid slowly aspiring upwards. This pyramid is served by three main pro-

---

1. C.J., Vol. 4, 1950-51.
2. Appendix H to the Report of the Broadcasting Committee, 1949: Memoranda submitted to the Committee, Cmd. 8117, H.M.S.O. 1951; quoted by Oakeshott in the C.J., Vol. 4, 1950-51, p.545.

grammes, differentiated but broadly overlapping in levels of interest, each programme leading on to the other, the listener being induced through the years increasingly to discriminate in favour of the things that are more worthwhile. Each programme at any given moment must be ahead of its public, but not so much as to lose their confidence. The listener must be led from good to better by curiosity, liking and a growth of understanding. As the standards of the education and culture of the community rise so should the programme pyramid rise as a whole".[1]

This zealous engagement in substantive activity is severely criticized by Oakeshott, who finds in the B.B.C. "a corporation self-dedicated to the improvement of mankind according to a recipe of its own."[2] The parade of "social purpose" and "public service" is "tiresomely sanctimonious" and "schoolmasterish".[3] Nothing so illiberal exists anywhere else in the world in the field of mass media, for "a similar intensity of control is matched elsewhere by a restriction of the field of interest".[4] He rejects the conclusion of the Report of the Broadcasting Committee, 1949,[5] that the fundamental question for decision is the "issue of monopoly", in favour of "the much larger and more important question – whether broadcasting conducted on a policy such as that pursued by the B.B.C. is desirable at all." The majority of the committee had accepted in advance the propriety of broadcasting with a social purpose, and hence this question was never raised.[6]

Turning to reflect upon the actual consequences of the B.B.C.'s first order enterprise of offering guidance in taste and education, Oakeshott finds them discouraging. The aids to school education only debase it, encouraging "the extensive mind, curious, interested, pseudo-sympathetic, pre-

---

1. Ibid., pp.545-6.
2. Ibid., p.547.
3. Ibid., p.549.
4. Ibid., p.549.
5. Cmd. 8116, H.M.S.O., 1951.
6. C.J., Vol. 4, 1950-51, pp.549-550.

ferring many contacts to few intimacies, preferring fact to thought and crowded with a disordered array of imperfectly realized images – the quiz mentality."[1]

The much-vaunted B.B.C. news service fairs little better. Oakeshott is prepared to take its impartiality for granted, concentrating his criticism in an altogether different direction. What interpretation of social purpose, he asks, requires continuous reports of "the dull and doubtful detail of the serious nonsense that is taking place all over the world?"[2] His conclusion is that its educational effect is "to encourage idle curiosity, listening to the news is becoming a nervous ailment".[3]

Oakeshott, it will now be very clear, is not sympathetic towards philosophies concerned (like those of Green and Bosanquet) to bolster the faith of the social reformer.

We have already examined in detail the metaphysical map of experience in which Oakeshott locates politics, and it will be sufficient at this stage to conclude the consideration of the relationship of Oakeshott's thought to that of Green and Bosanquet by drawing attention to four mutually interdependent themes, which together provide the basis of Oakeshott's political theory and his traditionalism. One of these is Hegelian in character and gives Oakeshott some affinity to Green and Bosanquet; this is his theory of rational will. Another is anti-Hegelian and gives Oakeshott's political writings their distinctively sceptical bias; this is his rejection of the idea of progress. The third theme is Oakeshott's thesis that the British system of common law rights and duties, and of parliamentary government, is "the most civilized and the most effective method ((viz. of securing freedom)) ever invented by mankind".[4] The fourth theme is perhaps not really a theme at all, but something more personal and subjective; it is an aesthetic disposition, and it

---

1. *Ibid.*, p.550.
2. *Ibid.*, p.551.
3. *Ibid.*, p.551.
4. *C.J.*, Vol. 1, 1947-8, p.490.

is this which gives the purely "Oakeshottean" flavour to Oakeshott's treatment of the problem of political obligation.

The four themes further developed

1. The first theme is Oakeshott's conception of rational will. The world of practice or of will, precisely because it is a world, is not a sphere bereft of rationality and requiring the imposition of reason upon it from without. This is not necessarily a conservative theory, but the idealist conception of the external institutional order as the embodiment of reason has often tended to dispose idealists very kindly towards the existing order, and very unkindly towards radical change of it. Marx belaboured Hegel so strenuously for such a tendency, as to make further comment in that direction otiose. In the English idealist tradition, we observe Bradley turning the concrete conception of ethical life offered by "My Station and Its Duties" into a polemic against moral and political reform. At one stage, for example, where he is concerned to refute the claim of conscience to be an infallible guide to right action,[1] he asserts that conscience "presupposes the morality of the community as its basis, and is subject to the approval thereof",[2] and draws from this the implication that "to wish to be better than the world is to be already on the threshold of immorality".[3] Bradley is right to distinguish between the objectivity of the claim of true conscience and the capriciousness of the dictates of false conscience, but when he makes this distinction a basis for inveighing against all social radicalism as such he moves from philosophy to advocacy. This transition has been sharply criticized by M. Cowling,[4] who justly locates its occurrence at the point where Bradley, after allowing that reform within the existing social order and in harmony with its spirit is acceptable, asserts that "it is another thing, starting from oneself, from ideals in one's head, to set oneself and them against the moral world", and forbids us to find morality anywhere but in actual existence.[5] Bosanquet also, although much less readily, was prepared

---

1. Ethical Studies, 1st published 1876; Oxford Paperbooks edition 1962, pp.198-199.
2. Ibid., pp.198-9.
3. Ibid., p.199.
4. Nature and Limits of Political Science, op.cit., p.84.
5. Ethical Studies, op.cit., p.200.

to appeal to the reason in the present, in the hope of circumscribing the more radical criticisms of the existing order. He held up the attitude towards society of Hegel and Bradley as a salutary example to those students of society who "are apt throughout to take up an indifferent, if not a hostile, attitude to their given object. They hardly believe in actual society as a botanist believes in plants, or a biologist in vital processes".[1] And he concluded the preface to the first edition with the assertion "Here or nowhere is your America".[2]

Idealism, then, because of its opposition to any purely "transcendent" conception of reason, might be said to contain a built-in lightning conductor which can be brought into service by a philosopher whose disposition inclines him against radical social reform. This in itself is not a sufficient explanation of Oakeshott's traditionalism, but it does enable us to comprehend more easily his esteem for "negative capability," which is "the power of accepting the mysteries and uncertainties of experience without any irritable search for order and distinctness";[3] for mystery and uncertainty are not disconcerting to one who believes that in the end they fall within reason, being unable to avoid "the despotism of significance". That Oakeshott's belief in the reason in the present is an important element in his attack on rationalism is apparent, again, from his characterization of the rationalist as one for whom "nothing is of value merely because it exists".[4] The first theme, then, unites Oakeshott to the idealist tradition from Hegel onwards, and may be summarized as the determination "to recognize reason as the rose in the cross of the present and thereby to enjoy the present".[5]

2. The second theme is Oakeshott's rejection of the concept of progress. While Green could speak of the vocation of man and Bosanquet write of the gates of the future, Oakeshott is prepared to discuss only the predicament of man. The ultimate ground for the rejection of progress lies in Oakeshott's conception of the general character of experience, which is already known to us. We saw that, unlike Bosanquet, he was unable to assign to practical

---

1. P.T.S., p. x.
2. P.T.S., p. xi.
3. Rationalism, p.2.
4. Rationalism, p.4.
5. Hegel, Philosophy of Right, trans. Knox, p.12.

modality any final necessity or significance. The freedom, or self-recognition, which for Bosanquet constituted the telos of the universe, was consequently confined by him to the world of practice. From this inability to recognize any sovereign purpose or final intelligibility in the scheme of things there springs political scepticism, the rejection of "the illusion that in politics there is anywhere a safe harbour, a destination to be reached or even a detectable strand of progress".[1]

The human predicament, as conceived by Oakeshott, is that of "a race condemned to seek its perfection in the flying moment and always in the one to come, whose highest virtue must be to cultivate a clear-sighted vision of the consequences of its actions, ...whose greatest need (not supplied by nature) is freedom from the distraction of illusion".[2] Oakeshott has related his conception of the human condition as a predicament to one of two traditions which he discerns in political speculation since Plato. (Elsewhere he distinguishes three traditions, but that is not relevant here). The relationship emerges in the course of his Introduction to Hobbes' Leviathan.

After an exposition of Hobbes' argument, Oakeshott proceeds to consider some topics relating to the Leviathan, and the third one he selects is entitled The Predicament of Mankind.[3] He begins by observing that "In the history of political philosophy there have been two opposed conceptions of the source of the predicament of man from which civil society springs as a deliverance: one conceived the predicament to arise out of the nature of man, the other conceived it to arise out of a defect in the nature of man".[4] The first conception is embodied in the tradition of political thought running from Plato through Aristotle to Spinoza and Hegel; the other conception is exemplified above all in the thought of Augustine. Oakeshott notes that Hobbes is often placed in the Augustinian tradition because he portrays man as egoistical. On this interpretation, indeed, Hobbes might even be seen as more consistent than Augustine since he believes in "a genuinely original depravity," for the fall of man is no part of his theory.[5] However, a closer inspection

---

1. Rationalism, p.133.
2. Leviathan, ed. Oakeshott, p. lxvi.
3. Ibid., p. liv.
4. Ibid., p. liv.
5. Ibid., p. liv.

reveals that Hobbes does not conceive man's predicament to arise out of moral egoism: "...what was distinguished as egoism (a moral defect) turns out to be neither moral nor a defect; it is only the individuality of a creature shut up, without hope of immediate release, within the world of his own imagination. Man is, by nature, the victim of solipsism; he is an *individua substantia* distinguished by incommunicability".[1] On a true view, Hobbes' conception of natural man is such that "...a predicament requiring deliverance is created whenever man is in proximity to man..."[2]

The extent of Oakeshott's commitment to the Hobbesian interpretation of the human predicament, according to which man is "an *individua substantia* distinguished by incommunicability," is brought out in his criticisms of a recent book by J.R. Lucas, entitled *The Principles of Politics*.[3] Oakeshott's criticisms are also interesting because there survive in Lucas' argument a number of the assumptions which we found in Green and Bosanquet. At the beginning of his book Lucas lists five "characteristics of human nature": some interaction; some shared values; incomplete un-selfishness; fallible judgement; imperfect information.[4] It is the last three with which Oakeshott finds some difficulty. These are termed by Lucas the "conditions of imperfection," but Oakeshott can see no reason why they should be marks of imperfection.[5] Lucas' concept of "incomplete unselfishness," for example, does not make clear that "...a perpetual and exclusive concern for the interests of others is not a possible condition of a concrete finite personality, and ((is)) therefore not a perfect condition."[6] Similarly, "fallible judgement" is used by Lucas in connection with the idea of reaching "the right decision", and Oakeshott objects to this that

"Mr. Lucas is confident that if men were much more reasonable than they are there would be no disagreements which could not be resolved by discussion

---

1. *Ibid.*, p. liv.
2. *Ibid.*, p. lv.
3. O.U.P., 1966.
4. *Principles of Politics*, p.2.
5. Review of *The Principles of Politics* in *Political Studies*, Vol. XV, No.2, June 1967, p.225.
6. *Ibid.*, p.225.

and argument, and that they would agree in the end on how a question ought to be decided; but in view of the 'dialectical' (non-deductive) character he attributes to political argument, I do not think he is justified in claiming more for even the most reasonable participants than that disagreement about the considerations to be taken into account could with certainty be expected to be resolved."[1]

This criticism would apply equally well to Green's and Bosanquet's faith that more communication between individuals and classes would dissolve all sources of disagreement.

If we wish to know what role politics plays in alleviating the predicament of mankind, Oakeshott's answer is that it has a necessary but subordinate place amongst the available panaceas. The greatest gift which politics has to offer is peace, which is a negative gift, providing a necessary condition for human fulfilment but in no way realizing the full potentialities of the self.[2]

Oakeshott's contention that politics plays a subordinate role in fulfilment, expressed in his confident assertion that "politics, we know, is a second-rate form of human activity, neither an art nor a science, at once corrupting to the soul and fatiguing to the mind, the activity of those who cannot live without the illusion of affairs or those so fearful of being ruled by others that they will pay away their lives to prevent it,"[3] at once presents us with a problem. What reasons can he give for this low opinion of political activity? Certainly it has no necessary connection with his general philosophical position. His overall view of the map of experience would indeed support the contention that reality is not exhausted in practical (and therefore in political) experience. It would, that is to say, provide a basis for distinguishing politics from other experiential forms, but this does not lend support to the low moral valuation of political activity,

---

1. *Ibid.*, p.225.
2. *Leviathan*, ed. Oakeshott, pp. lxv-lxvi.
3. *Ibid.*, p. lxiv.

relative to other activities within the world of practice itself, contained in the sentence just quoted. Oakeshott does not argue the point in the context in which the statement occurs. He contents himself with appealing to the conclusion of previous philosophers. Plato and Aristotle, Augustine, Aquinas, Hobbes and Spinoza all argued that salvation is not to be found in politics. An appeal to authorities, however, does not in itself make clear how Oakeshott would refute the claim of one who considered political activity to be the supremely worthwhile activity. The problem, in other words, is to determine whether Oakeshott is offering anything more than a purely personal valuation of the significance of political activity.

Oakeshott does appear to have reasons which support his position. He has discussed the claim of politics to be considered "the only genuine and adequate expression of a public spirit", and to be "incontestably the most effective expression of a sensibility for the common interests of a society",[1] and has argued that the first claim rests at best upon a perverted social sense, while the second is based upon a false scale of values.[2] If the first claim could be made out, it would follow that the person who devoted his life to entertaining in the music-hall or to philosophy would be failing in his duty. But this is not so, for the claim arbitrarily assumes that life can be divided absolutely into public and private sectors, while the true position is that no such distinction can be maintained. Everything we do has a public dimension; no activity is disconnected from the unity of social life. Hence to criticize a man merely for failing to engage in public activity is to presuppose an "illusory division in the life of a society", and is to display a conceit similar to that of the priest who feels that in virtue of his office alone he is holier than the lay-man.[3] Oakeshott's first point, of course, demonstrates only that there is no universal duty to engage in political activity as such: it does not deny that circumstances may alter the position with regard to an individual case. Churchill, for example, might plausibly

---

1. Scrutiny, 1938-9, Vol. 8, p.147.
2. Ibid., p.146.
3. Ibid., p.147.

have claimed in 1939 that it was his duty to engage in public activity, and (with the benefit of hindsight) we might allow the claim. The first argument, then, establishes that politics as such cannot claim to be a first-rate activity: but the argument applies equally to any other activity, as the reference to professional religiosity makes clear.

Oakeshott's argument against the view that political activity is of superior importance to any other kind is more interesting. It depends upon his assessment of the relative importance of the contributions to civilization of the poet, artist and philosopher on the one hand, and of the politician on the other. The essence of his position is contained in the assertion that "A political system presupposes a civilization; it has a function to perform in regard to that civilization, but it is a function mainly of protection and to a minor degree of merely mechanical interpretation and expression".[1] Politics, then, is a second-order activity, moving for the most part on the surface of the life of a society. It is never a self-contained, or self-explanatory activity: it always points beyond itself and finds its justification in the end which it serves.[2] The real life and the fundamental well-being of a society depend upon the creative activity of the intellectual, embodied in literature, in art and in philosophy; this activity is creative in the sense that it makes a society conscious of its own character, of its values and purpose. In holding up the mirror before a society it protects against "the last corruption that can visit a society", which is corruption of consciousness.[3] And the integrity which the poet, artist and philosopher must sustain if they are to enable a society to recognize itself is incompatible with engagement in political or protective activity, which inevitably produces a corruption of consciousness. If we ask why politics corrupts, Oakeshott's reply is that "Political action involves mental vulgarity, not merely because it entails the concurrence and support of those who are mentally vulgar, but because of the false simplifications of human life implied in even the best of its purposes".[4]

---

1. Ibid., p.143.
2. Ibid., p.143.
3. Ibid., p.150.
4. Ibid., p.148.

Is this argument sufficient to establish that politics is inevitably a second-rate form of activity? Oakeshott allows that the theoretical observation, that political activity always finds its significance in some end beyond itself, does not preclude those who value the "illusion of affairs" from claiming that, for themselves, politics is the highest activity;[1] but he dismisses their claim as having "little more than a personal and psychological importance", since it provides no justification for the view that political activity is a universal duty. The most vulnerable point in the argument occurs when, in order to establish his view that the political is a poor creature compared with (say) the artist, Oakeshott maintains that the artist's contribution to the self-recognition of a society is superior to that of the politician because the artist enables the society to recognize its whole self, while the politician reveals to it only its political self.[2] The assumption is that sound political practice persists only so long as this total self-recognition endures - a society without true artists and intellectual culture will be "a society ignorant of itself and without the power of recreating itself".[3] But this assumption is very difficult to justify. Setting recreation to one side, the historical evidence indicates that a society's greatest achievement in self-recognition occur at the period of its political demise; the owl of Minerva spreads its wings only with the falling of the dusk. Since Oakeshott does not undertake to show that the evidence dictates any other conclusion, it is impossible to feel that he has established that political activity is inferior to intellectual and artistic activities, in virtue of its dependence upon them for its success.

We are left, then, with a knowledge of Oakeshott's personal valuation of political activity - his conception of it as an enterprise in which no salvation is to be sought and no progress to be discerned.

3. The third theme brings us to Oakeshott's traditionalism, in the narrow (political) sense of that term; a consideration of his wider (logical) conception of the traditional character of all practice may be left until later.

---

1. Ibid., p.148.
2. Ibid., p.150.
3. Ibid., p.151.

Since Oakeshott's view of tradition is determined by his reading of the main developments in European moral and political history, we may begin by considering this, proceeding then to discuss the adequacy of the reasons he gives for preferring one strand in our tradition to others present in it.

In his essay on <u>The Moral Life in the Writings of Thomas Hobbes</u>, Oakeshott begins by distinguishing three conceptions of moral conduct which have prevailed in the last thousand years of western civilization. He terms them the morality of communal ties, the morality of individuality, and the morality of the common good.[1] In the first conception, the essential feature is that "all activity whatsoever is understood to be communal activity". A distinction between is and ought does not appear in this idiom of moral conduct because the experience of separate individuality is unknown: the unity of the ethical order remains undivided. In the second conception this understanding of moral activity is reversed: the separate and sovereign individual, rather than the community, is now taken as the basic ethical unity, and moral endeavour is no longer thought of as "the pursuit of a single common enterprise, but (as) an enterprise of give and take...it is the morality of self and other selves". Morality is the art of mutual accommodation, and happiness lies, in large measure, in the exercise of individuality, i.e. in the exercise of individual choice. In the third conception the second standpoint – that of an ethical order which assigns value to individual choice – is preserved, but is considerably modified by the emphasis which is now placed upon "the common good", "the social good", or "the good of all". As Oakeshott expresses it, "approval attaches itself to conduct in which this individuality is suppressed whenever it conflicts, not with the individuality of others, but with the interests of a 'society' understood to be composed of such human beings".[2] This third conception of the moral life unmistakably refers to the ideal held by Green and Bosanquet (amongst others), and it is therefore particularly interesting to note the attitude towards it intimated in Oakeshott's laconic remark that "the lion shall eat straw with the ox."

---

1. <u>Rationalism</u>, p.249.
2. <u>Ibid.</u>, p.250.

This very general picture of the vicissitudes in our moral life in the past ten centuries is important because it provides the background to Oakeshott's interpretation of the traditions of behaviour which manifest themselves at the present time, and it consequently plays a key part in his diagnosis of the contemporary European political predicament. However, it not only colours his notion of tradition, but also has a further implication. Oakeshott's inclination is to favour the second (individualist) conception of the moral life, and this presents him with the task of defending it internally against incautious supporters (for example, Hayek and Quintin Hogg), and externally against the threats presented by the conception of the moral life which is its main rival. His way of defending the individualist tradition is to attack both enemies for their corrupting "rationalism". The term "rationalism", in short, only assumes its full significance when it is realised that the term is being used against the background of the tripartite historical scheme we have just noticed. Our next step must be to develop in more detail Oakeshott's conception of the individualist or libertarian tradition, and of the common good tradition, in order to illuminate his diagnosis of the contemporary malaise of western civilization.

For this purpose, we have only a sketch to go on. It is contained in Oakeshott's essay, <u>The Masses in Representative Democracy</u>.[1] From this we learn that the morality of communal ties was characteristic of the medieval world, and that the period from roughly the thirteenth century to the twentieth century saw its gradual modification, at first in favour of an individualist morality. The latter morality achieved its widest acceptance in the seventeenth and eighteenth centuries, a period when the autonomous individual was invariably the starting-point for ethical reflection.[2] What is particularly important for our present inquiry is the fact that (on Oakeshott's reading of history) the morality of individuality brought with it a new understanding of the office of government. Where the medieval morality of communal ties had found its political reflection in a wide dispersion of power over many different groups, such as family, guild, church and local community, the morality

---

1. This essay is printed in <u>Freedom and Serfdom</u>, ed. A. Hunold, Dordrecht, Holland, 1961.
2. Ibid., pp.154-155

of individuality (which sought to extract the individual from the corporations in which he was buried) required a centralized government recognized as sovereign, and possessing sufficient power to ensure that the individual's desire to choose for himself was not frustrated. The power of the monarchy was checked by another part of the medieval heritage, the estates of the realm which were represented in parliaments and councils in Europe, and which came to exercise a greater influence on policy in the course of time. The mature political expression of the morality of individuality was the parliamentary government which emerged in England and elsewhere in the late eighteenth and early nineteenth centuries.[1] This, it will become clear, is the tradition with which Oakeshott's sympathies lie. It is an aristocratic tradition, but a tradition in which the lawlessness, barbarity and boorishness of the medieval aristocracy have been erased by humanistic sentiments: it is the tradition of the gentleman. The most outstanding of the early exponents of this ethical ideal were the Great Tew circle, whose principal members were Falkland, Hobbes, Clarendon and Sidney Godolphin. They have been compared by Irene Coltman, in her sensitive study of that circle,[2] to Castiglione's courtiers because "they hoped like the friends who talk in The Courtier to reinterpret and refine the heroic code".[3] One in particular of the subjects explored in the conversations of the Great Tew circle is reflected in Oakeshott's own thought: their concern with the implications for the moral and political order of the language of conscience and of appeals to principle. If a further quotation is permissible, we may refer once again to Irene Coltman's study: "Hobbes criticized the scruples of intellectuals because he was forced by his experience of the political consequences of their soul-searching to wonder whether it were not possible to be too afraid of doing wrong and whether this fear did not ultimately spring from a pride more dangerous to society than any aristocrat's".[4] The new pride lay in the aspiration towards a clear conscience - a subject on which we have already given

1. Ibid., p.157.
2. Private Men and Public Causes, Faber & Faber, London, 1962.
3. Ibid., p.143.
4. Ibid., pp.146-147.

Bradley's opinion. Oakeshott too is aware of the incipient ideological element in the tradition he favours, but has been more concerned to point out to those who reject that tradition out of hand their indebtedness to it. Thus, concluding his essay on <u>Rationalism in Politics</u>, he observes that the rationalist takes no account of the fact that the moral ideology he holds is, in fact, "the desiccated relic of what was once the unself-conscious moral tradition of an aristocracy who, ignorant of ideals, had acquired a habit of behaviour in relation to one another and had handed it on in a true moral education".[1]

The modification of the heroic code, then, gave rise to the gentleman, and it is this figure who stands behind the moral and political tradition which Oakeshott defends in his writings. It follows from this, of course, that to the extent to which this character has disappeared from European political life, advocacy of a social order which presupposes him becomes utopian. From the outset the political theory which reflected the gentleman's sentiments had to face the fact that they were not universally shared, and that an adequate account of political obligation must therefore find some other foundation than this character. Hobbes provides an example. For Hobbes, the closest approximation to his ideal was the gentlemanly person of Sir Sidney Godolphin, of whom he wrote that "there is not any vertue that disposeth a man, either to the service of God, or to the service of his Country, to Civill Society, or private Friendship, that did not manifestly appear in his conversation, not as acquired by necessity, or effected upon occasion, but inhaerent, and shining in a generous constitution of his nature".[2] Hobbes, however, based his account of political obligation not on the natural virtue of Godolphin but on the fear of death which is the strongest passion in the majority of men. In short, Hobbes did not take his stand on the tradition of behaviour he personally preferred; he recognized that political inconsequence would be the result, and accordingly modified his theory of political obligation to take account of the sentiments of the ungentlemanly mass. Now

---

1. <u>Rationalism</u>, p.35.
2. <u>Leviathan</u>, Dedication, Everyman ed.; see also A Review and Conclusion, p.386.

this accommodation is precisely what appears to be lacking in Oakeshott's position, vitiating it accordingly as a political analysis. To recognize this we must return to his account of the development of the morality of individuality.

The morality of communal ties did not simply give way before a morality of individuality; this then being superseded by a morality of the common good. The individualist tradition was in fact ambiguous from the outset, for the same circumstances which created the individual in modern Europe, created also what Oakeshott calls the "individual manqué"[1] — a term which refers to those who were not happy about the dissolution of corporate personality and found no satisfaction in making choices for themselves. The "individual manqué" naturally held a conception of the role of government which differed from that of the individualist: he was prepared to assign to it the unwanted task of making choices, and thus there arose the "godly prince" of the Reformation and the "enlightened despot" of the Eighteenth Century.[2] However, the most significant step (from the point of view of understanding contemporary society) in this process of historical change occurred only at a later stage, when the "individual manqué" acquired a more militant attitude towards individuality and eventually recognized that he was in a majority in modern European society.[3] This recognition was accompanied by further development of the conception of government as enlightened despotism: government was now required to provide "leadership" instead of rule, and to impose an undifferentiated equality upon all. And political institutions came to be thought of as a means of converting the system of parliamentary government (through universal suffrage and the theory of the mandate) into a system of popular control. The dilemma of present day society, then, lies in the fact that "modern Europe enjoys two opposed moralities ((that of individuality and that of the "anti-individual"))....two opposed understandings of the office of government, and two corresponding interpretations of the current institutions of government".[4]

---

1. Hunold, *Freedom and Serfdom*, op.cit., p.158.
2. Ibid., p.159.
3. Ibid., p.163.
4. Ibid., p.168.

The most striking feature of this piece of analysis (some, no doubt, would say misrepresentation), is its failure to make any concessions whatsoever to the side of our tradition which Oakeshott describes as "anti-individualist" or hostile to the ideal of self-determination. While many of his strictures (those, for example, levelled at the uncritical conception of government as a centre of leadership, and at plebiscite theory) would command sympathy, it may be asked whether he is not, in the end, narrowing the meaning and implications of the ideal of self-determination in an arbitrary way, with a view to labelling as "anti-individual" those whose desire has been, not for the overthrow of the tradition of individuality, but for an extension to others of the conditions essential for enjoying it. Oakeshott constantly speaks of the "anti-individual" in a way which implies that everyone in the seventeenth century was equally well-placed to enjoy the benefits of individualism, but that some people inexplicably and slavishly chose to turn their backs on such values. In fact, of course, only a relatively small proportion of the community was confronted, in any significant sense, with a choice between individualism and anti-individualism. According to the calculations made by Gregory King from the hearth tax and other data available to him at the time of the Revolution (1688), "over one million persons, nearly a fifth of the whole nation, were in occasional receipt of alms, mostly in the form of public relief paid by the parish.".[1]

In order to maintain that the anti-individualist strain in modern tradition is as negative as he claims, Oakeshott would seem necessarily to commit himself to two propositions, both of which are implausible, and which he himself, in another mood, would qualify. They are that (i) the individualist strain is perfectly satisfactory, containing no internal incoherence. Unless this claim can be sustained, Oakeshott would be open to the charge of misrepresenting the case of what he calls "anti-individualism". Oakeshott does appear to commit himself unequivocally to the view that attempts to extend the individualist strain have been completely superfluous, dismissing nineteenth-century reform movements (for example) as resting on "a great

---

1. G.M.Trevelyan, English Social History, Longmans, London, 1944, p.278.

illusion", because those who wished to enjoy the rights won by individualists failed to realize that they already possessed them, and because, in any case they had no use for them.[1] (ii) In the second place, Oakeshott's desire to rule out of court one half of our tradition commits him to maintaining that all those who have addressed themselves to the plight of the masses have championed the cause of people "moved solely by the opportunity of complete escape from the anxiety of not being an individual".[2] He himself, however, fails in the end completely to sustain the political scepticism arising from this view of the low motivation and political incapacity of the masses. He is compelled to admit that "only in the most favourable circumstances, and then only by segregating him from all alien influences, have his leaders been able to suppress in him ((i.e. mass man)) an unguarded propensity to desert at the call of individuality".[3]

The concession to the masses made in the last paragraph is one of only two passages known to us in which Oakeshott says relatively kind things about the masses and the rationalism which has accompanied their rise. In the other he allows that the politics of "social engineering" have "inspired many great achievements in the suppression of violence by co-operative endeavour in many fields of human activity, and the whole movement for social and educational reform".[4] This latter admission in particular suggests a line of thought which must qualify very greatly the presentation of modern history given in The Masses in Representative Democracy.

For the most part, Oakeshott is content to claim (against the background of his historical conspectus) that rationalist politics and parliamentary government belong to different traditions, and cannot coexist within the same tradition.[5] The difficulty with this view is that it just does not appear to be true. In the same article Oakeshott finds the origin of parliamentary institutions in "the least rationalistic period of our politics...((i.e.)) the Middle Ages..."[6] That may be so, but the end of the Middle Ages brought the

---

1. Hunold, *Freedom and Serfdom*, op.cit., p.264.
2. *Ibid.*, p.160.
3. *Ibid.*, p.169.
4. C.J., Vol. 1, 1947-8, p.350.
5. C.J., Vol. 1, 1947-8, p.357.
6. C.J., Vol. 1, 1947-8, p.357.

growth of rationalism, and so we have now had several centuries of rationalistic parliamentary tradition. Even Burke gave his sanction to a rationalistic element when he advocated parties founded upon principle. Thus there is no reason to suppose that rationalistic politics and parliamentary government cannot coexist, unless we ignore the past two and a half centuries.

We have yet to indicate the greatest difficulty presented by Oakeshott's analysis of history. This is the unsatisfactoriness of his central concept, "the mass". This concept is one of the keystones in the political theory of conservative-liberals in general. Ortega y Gassett, for example, is very close to Oakeshott in his attitude towards the mass. Ortega believed that as one gets older "one realises more and more that the majority of men - and of women - are incapable of any other effort than that strictly imposed on them as a reaction to external compulsion".[1] What the mass-man lacks, he thought, is the sporting outlook special to the intellectual man - the sporting outlook being identified by him with a capacity for wonder at the universe, and not with attendance at football matches.[2] This style of analysis reveals the same vagueness that we find in Oakeshott: precisely what "the mass" is is very hard to find out - the concept is so overwhelmingly pejorative in the hands of its exponents that an objective criterion is not readily available. And even if we can get a clear notion of the reality referred to, it would seem that the concept of the mass is far too simple to do justice to contemporary society at least: nothing as amorphous as the name suggests presents itself to the student of society or of politics.

It would appear, then, that Oakeshott leaves himself open to the charge of failing to meet the criterion by which he himself judges the work of a political theorist, which is by the success with which he translates "current sentiments into the idiom of general ideas and universalizes a local version of human character by finding for it some rational ground".[3] No rational ground has emerged so far to support Oakeshott's view that the strain of

---

1. *Revolt of the Masses*, first published in Spain 1930; published in London by Unwin Books, 1961, p.49.
2. *Ibid.*, p.10.
3. *Rationalism*, p.251.

"anti-individualism" in our tradition is in fact invariably negative and parasitic in character; and there is even some doubt about the usefulness of the concept of mass-man for political analysis.

It has been argued,[1] however, that (in effect) Oakeshott's espousal of only one side of our tradition has a ground altogether different from any that has so far been examined. This is his aesthetic sense. We may consider this in connection with our fourth theme.

4. It is hardly to be denied that Oakeshott finds a higher aesthetic content in the tradition of the gentleman than in the tradition of the anti-individual. Blumler is on safe ground when he writes that, in Oakeshott's view, "philistinism is the capital sin of rationalism, and traditionalism is the only political style that should appeal to a cultured person". His aesthetic appreciation of conduct, his dislike of all vulgarity, is frequently evident. He hastens to defend Hobbes from the charge of hedonism; felicity is not "an undignified scramble for suburban pleasures".[2] There is, again, the splendid observation with which he commences a review of the work of one rationalistically inclined author: "After forty, one naturally prefers a holocaust to the ignominy of being buried alive under the indiscriminating volcanic ash of 'social reconstruction'".[3] The aesthetic emphasis, however, is apt to be misunderstood. In Blumler's argument, for example, it seems to be implied that the aesthetic dimension to Oakeshott's thought is a superfluous ornamentation, inessential to an adequate moral ideal, for he describes it as a piece of "extra-rational armour", a mere device to escape "the force of arguments which might appeal to....conscience".[4] The criticism is not plausible. Bosanquet, who would strongly sympathize with Oakeshott, remarks that on first reading Aristotle's Ethics one may be surprised to find prominence given to the "excellences of social intercourse", such as equableness, true modesty, and wit or the power of saying the right thing; he sets against this initial reaction the true position, in which morality passes into aesthetic, to "the degree in which intelligence and good-will have found express-

---

1. By J.G. Blumler in an essay entitled Politics, Poetry and Practice, Political Studies, Vol. 12, 1964.
2. Leviathan, ed. Oakeshott, p. lxv.
3. C.J., Vol. 1, p.326.
4. Blumler, Political Studies, Vol. 12, 1964, p.361.

ion in the detailed behaviour of body and of mind".[1] In other words, other things being equal, the gentleman is more of a man than is a mere man; humanity is in him achieved more thoroughly: "something is perfected in ((him)) which is present, but not perfected, in the others".[2] Pursuing this line of thought, we may suggest that when Oakeshott writes that in moral goodness there is "a release from the deadliness of doing and a possibility of perfection, which intimates poetry",[3] it would be rash to conclude that his reference to a "release" implies that the poetic dimension to morality is escapist and superfluous: it is, rather, the full revelation of the possibilities contained in the moral life. And there is nothing in this view which might justify the contention that the poetic character of moral goodness involves a transition to an "extra-rational" position. The argument of Experience and Its Modes identified the extra-rational with mere nothingness, and in the essay in which the poetic aspect of moral goodness is mentioned Oakeshott explains that the poetic standpoint is more rational, in the sense of less abstract, than the purely practical standpoint, for to regard a thing poetically is to take it in its individuality.[4]

The aesthetic foundation for Oakeshott's traditionalism is most prominent in his essay On Being Conservative. To enjoy the present, and to cherish it because of its familiarity, are the springs of the conservative disposition.[5] This disposition does not imply the exclusion of change, although it does not regard it favourably: for all change is a threat to the identity of the self.[6] It therefore naturally opposes change which is liable to exceed expectations, and consequently resists radical plans for change.[7] The delight in the present, on which Oakeshott takes his stand, is evidently coloured to some extent by an aesthetic sense. Rational prudence is indeed an important part of his position,[8] but in so far as the present enjoyed is constituted by

---

1. Science, p.301.
2. Ibid., p.301.
3. Rationalism, p.245.
4. Ibid., p.220.
5. Ibid., p.168.
6. Ibid., p.170.
7. Ibid., pp.170-172.
8. Ibid., p.173.

activities engaged in for their own sake, the aesthetic element begins to appear. Friendship and love are the outstanding examples of relationships which, while finally inseparable from the world of practice, come closest to constituting a connection between "the voices of poetry and practice".[1] The whole concept of "familiarity", in fact, appears to be tinged with a poetic character, a blurring of the distinction between "fact" and "not-fact" which goes some way towards constituting the delight in a mere, and merely present, image which is aesthetic experience.[2] And to the extent that the poetic dimension appears in activity, Oakeshott argues that the conservative disposition is not only appropriate but necessary.[3] To change one's butcher if his meat is bad is perfectly appropriate, for the relationship is governed by one's wants and desires and does not (for the most part) transcend them, but to discard friends because they fail to subordinate themselves to one's desires and wants is to mistake the character of friendship. And what is true of private relationships shades over, to some extent, into public ones: patriotism is an example. As Oakeshott summarizes it, "The relationship of friend to friend is dramatic, not utilitarian; the tie is one of familiarity, not usefulness...And what is true of friendship is not less true of other experiences - of patriotism, for example, and of conversation - each of which demands a conservative disposition as a condition of its enjoyment".[4] In general - and this is the crucial (and dubious) step in the argument - the disposition to be conservative in politics requires not only a delight (on balance) in our existing way of life, but also a belief that governing is "a specific and limited activity, namely, the provision and custody of rules of conduct", when these rules are understood as providing a framework for that way of life and not the content of life itself.[5]

The question is whether we have now found in the aesthetic theme an adequate basis for Oakeshott's selection of the individualist and libertarian side of our tradition, and consequently for his hostility to what he termed the "anti-individualist" side. It would scarcely seem so, since the aesthetic

---

1. Ibid., p.244.
2. Ibid., pp.216-217.
3. Ibid., pp.175-176.
4. Ibid., p.127.
5. Ibid., p.184.

disposition, as such, has no connection with any moral or political doctrine at all. Any action may be assessed from the aesthetic standpoint, but such assessment tells us nothing about the appropriateness of the action to the political context. There is a further difficulty. Oakeshott wishes to establish that a certain kind of disposition (one tinged with aesthetic appreciation) is a necessary presupposition of engagement in certain forms of activity. This may be so, but the difficulty would still remain that engagement in those activities also presupposes the occupancy of a concrete situation in the world. If we allow, for example, that the enjoyment of the style of politics preferred by Oakeshott presupposes a delight in things present and familiar, it is equally true that it presupposes (inter alia) a certain level of material prosperity. When the subjective concept of a disposition is not brought into relation with all the objective conditions it presupposes, the political analysis which flows from it is correspondingly incomplete. At the most general level, we may say that the relevance to our present situation of the politics which Oakeshott attaches to the aesthetic disposition presupposes the homogeneity and general acceptance of the libertarian side of our tradition, as that side is interpreted by Oakeshott. Consequently, as one writer puts it, the doctrine "loses in relevancy where history and tradition are ambiguous, where there are conflicting traditions to which men think it proper to appeal".[1] Oakeshott himself admits, we have seen, that our tradition has been ambiguous from the beginning.

A similar difficulty occurs in connection with Oakeshott's essay, <u>The Political Economy of Freedom</u>. The way of life which Oakeshott presupposes in defining his view of the nature of freedom and the scope of government action, is not sufficiently widely shared to make it a plausible solution to the problem of political obligation. The disposition which lies behind it is of course intelligible, and even noble: but in the end it constitutes only one element in our political situation, something which must be taken account of, but which is not itself a solution to the problem of political obligation. Even if it were true that Oakeshott's political theory is "essentially, and not unintentionally, parochial",[2] this would still be a relevant criticism,

---

1. H.S.Kariel, <u>In Search of Authority</u>, The Free Press, Glencoe, 1964, p.87.
2. Ibid., p.87.

for even if Oakeshott's parochialism leads him to concentrate on the British circumstance, it remains true that on his own reading of that circumstance the gentleman is a rapidly disappearing phenomenon. He himself writes that "The problem today is not 'how to translate the ideal of the cultivated gentleman into democratic terms and combine an intensive and relentless pursuit of excellence with a new sensitiveness to the demands of social justice: in the past a rising class was aware of something valuable enjoyed by others which it wished to share; but this is not so today. The leaders of the rising class are consumed with a contempt for everything which does not spring from their own desires, they are convinced in advance that they have nothing to learn and everything to teach, and consequently their aim is to loot..."[1]. This passage reveals a more pessimistic diagnosis of our present predicament than Oakeshott was disposed to make in his later essay on The Masses in Representative Democracy, when he said that there was still an inclination to respond to the call of individuality, but the fundamental incoherence which he perceives in our tradition is thereby only qualified, and is in no way resolved by the form of social order which he desiderates.

The objections to this libertarian social order considered by Oakeshott come from rationalist quarters; he remarks that the libertarian will have to listen, for example, "to the complaint that he has neglected to consider the efficacy with which his economic system produces the goods".[2] But there is a larger difficulty in Oakeshott's defence of liberty, one which is obscured by his concentration on the rationalist's false gods of efficiency and productivity, with their implications of planning and centralization. In After Utopia Judith Shklar drew attention to the abstract either/or approach to social ideas and deeds found in the political thought of all conservative-liberals, noting that in the realm of economics they find *any* state interference incompatible with the price mechanism, and believe that *any* attempt to regulate employment must at all times and in every place lead by an iron chain of causes and effects to the establishment of totalitarian rule.[3] She related

---

1. The Universities, in C.J., Vol. 2, 1948-9, p.538.

2. Rationalism, p.47.

3. After Utopia, Princeton University Press, 1957, p.238. C.J.Friedrich also remarks the either/or approach in The Political Thought of Neo-Liberalism, Am.Pol. Sc. Review, XXXIX (1945), pp.575-579.

the fatalism of conservative liberalism directly to this either/or approach: "What is disturbing...is that no attention at all is given to the actual course of events. The inner urge to fatalism has obliterated all those distinctions among actual forms of government, and the real sequence of events ceases to matter".[1] Now we appear to find the either/or approach not only in Hayek, Roepke and Von Mises (with whom Shklar is mainly concerned), but also in Oakeshott, who begins his discussion of "collectivism" (a term he uses to cover communism, national socialism, socialism, economic democracy and central planning) by stating that "...collectivism and freedom are real alternatives- if we choose one we cannot have the other" and then proceeds to discuss "...the defects...inherent in the system".[2] It is fair to ask, which system? yet what we find discussed is a model, an abstraction. As Shklar notes (in another connection), "the question of what types of planning are dangerous and of whose freedom suffers under a fully or partially planned economy can thus be disregarded".[3] She recognizes that planning does bring a growth of bureaucracy which presents a real threat to liberty, but puts her finger on what we consider to be the most problematic aspect of Oakeshott's treatment of liberty when she questions the justification for tying liberty closely to the free market, and tyranny to the planned economy:

"...it cannot be shown that totalitarianism in Italy or Germany had its origins in 'planning' or that this was ever a vital characteristic of these regimes. Even in Russia the terror clearly began as a means of eliminating political opposition rather than as an adjunct to the planned economy. The polemic against planning cannot, therefore, be regarded as a serious analysis of current history. It is rather a matter of warning, of predicting."[4]

Setting aside Oakeshott's more fanciful sallies against collectivism (e.g. "...the real spring of collectivism is not a love of liberty, but war.")[5] it is worth noticing that he does not find in it the greatest threat to

---

1. Ibid., pp.246-247.
2. Rationalism, pp.50-51.
3. After Utopia, op.cit., p.247.
4. Ibid., p.252.
5. Rationalism, p.52.

liberty. Obsession with communism and fascism, he considers, threatens to distract attention from the real antithesis of a free manner of living, which is syndicalism. Syndicalism rejects not only liberty but order, converting society into the scene of a perpetual civil war between militant interest groups.[1] It is labour monopolies which Oakeshott considers the most dangerous of these groups. Unlike monopolistic business corporations, growth does not bring diseconomies for them, and popular opinion sympathizes with even their most scandalous activities.[2] These monopolies are to be destroyed by legislation designed to maintain effective competition.[3]

On another occasion Oakeshott has attempted to indicate the form which an intellectual defence of liberty might appropriately take. He would find a serious defect in the body of literature from Milton to J.S.Mill devoted to providing a theoretical basis for liberty. These classical authorities always sought to establish a connection between free speech and the idea of truth. Maurice Cowling has drawn attention to the way in what Mill's use of the idea of truth means that "without straining words unduly, ((he)) may be accused of more than a touch of something resembling moral totalitarianism".[4] That Oakeshott would sympathize with this criticism may be inferred from his review of a work by Walter Lippman, in which he indicates why liberal thinkers of Mill's kind would necessarily be open to a charge like Cowling's. Oakeshott writes that "'truth' seekers in politics are potential enemies of free speech because they are unprotected against the belief that they have reached their goal.".[5] A sound defence of free speech, and of the government's right to limit it, must abandon "the belief that every utterance is a bona fide participation in a search for some one 'truth'",[6] and must begin by accepting that politics is an enterprise where mutual accommodation is the only end.

---

1. Ibid., p.53.
2. Ibid., p.53.
3. Ibid., p.56.
4. Mill and Liberalism, C.U.P., 1963, p.xii.
5. The Customer is Never Wrong, Listener, Aug. 25, 1955, p.302.
6. Ibid., p.302.

For in liberal democracy utterance is largely free because it is recognized not as argument but conversation".[1] The real reason why we value freedom of speech is not because we have complex theories about truth, or indeed because we have theories of any kind: it is "because we have become people with a variety of opinions about all sorts of matters and we do not see why we should not utter them." If we want instruction about the theory of liberal-democratic freedom of speech, Oakeshott refers us, not to Milton or to Mill, but to Montaigne and Hume.[2]

These remarks upon the theory of liberty are interesting for a number of reasons. They display the hostility towards intellectualism shared by most of the conservative-liberals; and they involve the same paradox, that they are themselves written from a deeply intellectualist standpoint. For although Oakeshott's attack on rationalism presupposes that the concrete flow of action is the really important thing, with theorizations of it being a poor and relatively impotent abridgment, Shklar's comment upon Hayek and Roepke seems to apply also to him: systematic philosophy, she writes, "is given an exaggerated importance as an agent of social change, (and) the inner validity of a thing is never separated from its presumed social effects...".[3] Thus, although Oakeshott rejects the politics of Mill and insists that "what holds a man back from being a demagogue is not a complicated intellectual doctrine about the nature of government, but some simple moral qualities; courage, or perhaps pride, or indifference, or even mere laziness",[4] he proceeds immediately to replace one intellectual doctrine by another when he asserts that liberal-democratic politics are sceptical politics. More generally, there is the importance which Oakeshott evidently attaches to (for example) the work of Bacon and Descartes, for he spends a considerable number of pages in criticising them directly, or in criticising variations on their theories of mind. Why bother, if ideas only reflect the traditional "substructure"?

Whether we find the foundation of Oakeshott's libertarianism in the poetic delight in the present, then, or in rational prudence, or in scepticism,

---

1. Ibid., p.302.
2. Ibid., p.302.
3. After Utopia, op.cit., p.240.
4. The Customer is Never Wrong, Listener, Aug 25, 1955, p.302.

it presupposes too much that is questionable for it to be completely satisfactory. The consideration of liberty took us beyond the aesthetic theme, but we may conclude this section by returning to that theme and adding that the aesthetic defence of conservatism is most noticeably successful in those areas of life - friendship, love, religion - which lie outside the political arena. Thus it may well be that in the end the man of conservative disposition is last seen swimming against the tide, and that we might wish for his victory should not obscure from us the sheer magnitude of the waves confronting him, nor exclude from our minds the reflection that if his craft had been more solidly constructed his present plight might (perhaps) have been less desperate.

There remains, however, one further ground for Oakeshott's traditionalism, and this is his contention that all activity is traditional in character, because it can take no other form.[1] This thesis rests on a logical distinction between technical knowledge and practical (or traditional) knowledge, and it must now be considered.

The logical foundation of traditionalism

The rise of a new social class to power in European civilization was accompanied by the growth of what Oakeshott terms "rationalism". The two phenomena are closely related, for "the politics of Rationalism are the politics of the politically inexperienced, and...the outstanding characteristic of European politics in the last four centuries is that they have suffered the incursion of at least three types of political inexperience - that of the new ruler, of the new ruling class, and of the new political society..."[2] To the politically inexperienced, the natural tendency is to seek a substitute for genuine knowledge in a crib, a technique; rationalist politics, in short, are the politics of the book.[3] The rationalist understanding of politics, and the style of political activity which accompanies it, should not be confused with the love of modern democracies for "generic terms or abstract expressions"

---

1. Rationalism, pp.123-4.
2. Rationalism, p.23.
3. Ibid., pp.23-24.

noted by de Tocqueville, who compared the abstract expressions to boxes with false bottoms: into each box "you may put in what ideas you please, and take them out again without being observed".[1] This undoubtedly is one aspect of the rationalist style of politics, but it is not an aspect which Oakeshott has in mind. Again, the criticism of rationalism should not be mistaken for an attack on rationality, or on all reflection whatsoever upon practical conduct; Oakeshott has insisted that "a morality in which reflection has no part is defective."[2] What Oakeshott understands by rationalism is the doctrine that the only conduct which can claim to be rational is conduct "in which an independently premeditated end is presumed and which is determined solely by that end".[3] Elsewhere he describes rationalistic conduct as activity determined by "the reflective application of a moral criterion," and detects two common varieties: it appears as "the self-conscious pursuit of moral ideals, and as the reflective observance of moral rules".[4]

The generation of rationalism in politics, in Oakeshott's opinion, is "by sovereign power out of romanticism",[5] and romanticism involves a theory of mind which is completely antithetic to the view of mind which is maintained by the theory of rational will. The general inclination of the romantic spirit is to stress the inwardness of mind, finding freedom outside the social order or concrete tradition of behaviour of a society and within the self. Oakeshott summarizes its main features as follows: "Beliefs, ideas, knowledge, the contents of the mind, and above all the activities of man in the world, are not regarded as themselves mind, or as entering into the composition of mind, but as adventitious, posterior acquisitions of the mind, the results of mental activity which the mind might or might not have possessed or undertaken. The mind may acquire knowledge or cause bodily activity, but it is something that may exist destitute of all knowledge, and in the absence of any activity..."[6]

---

1. de Tocqueville, <u>Democracy in America</u>, World's Classics ed. pp.339-340.
2. <u>Rationalism</u>, p.73.
3. Ibid., p.83.
4. Ibid., p.66.
5. Ibid., p.6.
6. Ibid., p.86.

The theory of mind which Oakeshott attributes to rationalism took shape, however, prior to the emergence of romanticism in the second half of the eighteenth century. The seventeenth century search for a method which would guarantee progress in the acquisition of certain knowledge, exemplified in the writings of Bacon and Descartes, contributed to the rationalist position by holding that "genuine knowledge must begin with a purge of the mind, because it must begin as well as end in certainty and must be complete in itself".[1] The social order was undermined by this view because it set on one side everything traditional as mere opinion: only what was produced by the infallible method or technique was recognized as knowledge. In one sense, indeed, the origins of rationalism go even further back. The self-conscious pursuit of moral ideals became the form of European civilization upon the collapse of the habitual morality enjoyed by the Greco-Roman world.[2] Oakeshott refers to Epictetus, for whom it was a virtue merely to have self-conscious ideals.[3] And Christianity, which originally enjoyed a customary morality, soon found that circumstances forced upon it the necessity of a self-conscious morality.[4] Does it follow, then, that Oakeshott's criticism of rationalism is a criticism of western morality from its earliest beginnings? To some extent this is so. But he distinguishes modern rationalism from its earlier forms, and the body of his writing is devoted to exhibiting the logical error which lies behind the most recent variety. The distinction he draws between ancient, medieval and modern rationalism is that "Plato is a rationalist, but the dialectic is not a technique, and the method of Scholasticism always had before it a limited aim".[5]

The "false ideal of freedom of mind"[6] upon which rationalism rests may well have profoundly revolutionary consequences, although this is not necessarily so: while destruction comes naturally to the rationalist,[7] his understanding of freedom would not be incompatible with quietism. But in either

---

1. Ibid., p.15.
2. Ibid., p.76.
3. Ibid., p.76.
4. Ibid., pp.76-78.
5. Ibid., p.16.
6. Ibid., p.92.
7. Ibid., p.4.

case, the temperament of the rationalist contains "a deep distrust of time, an impatient hunger for eternity".[1] He is one who has failed to come to terms with life, looking (if he turns to politics) always for a universally valid solution to every difficulty: not content to remedy a limited and specific evil, his must be a war to end all wars, a classless society, universal socialism, complete commercial interdependence among nations.[2] And because of his contempt for the tradition which lies behind him and around him, he naturally locates every problem he encounters in the narrowest of contexts — he is conscious of the immediate situation only, and feels that his only source of salvation is the application to the situation of his techniques. In short, he assimilates politics to engineering, and recognizes only the felt need.[3]

Oakeshott's critique of rationalist politics rests on the contention that, in the end, it is impossible to formulate in terms of rules, principles or ideals the governing factors in behaviour. The rationalist commits the sin of abridging a tradition of behaviour and then assigning to the abridgment a task which it cannot possibly fulfil, viz., the specification of appropriate behaviour in any given set of circumstances. It is possible to distinguish within any piece of praxis two kinds of knowledge, technical knowledge and practical (or traditional) knowledge, and it is from this possibility that the plausibility of rationalism derives. What the rationalist fails to realize is that this is only a distinction, and that neither kind of knowledge can exist independently of the other. Technical knowledge alone is taken by him to provide a full specification of the character of any praxis. Technical knowledge is that element in the praxis which is knowledge, capable of being stated or formulated.

The different kinds of knowledge imply different kinds of education, since they differ in respect of the manner of their communication. Since practical knowledge "exists only in use"[4] and is incapable of being formulated,

---

1. Ibid., p.3.
2. C.J., Vol. 1, 1947-8, p.352.
3. Rationalism, pp.4-5.
4. Ibid., p.8.

it can be acquired only through imitation. Technical knowledge, on the other hand, can be imparted verbally or in book form. This difference should not, of course, obscure the fact that neither type of knowledge occurs without the other.

The full significance of Oakeshott's distinction between the two kinds of knowledge will not be appreciated unless it is remembered that what is involved goes beyond a logical cavil; this may be seen by relating it to his conception of rational will, for it then becomes clear that the two kinds of knowledge, taken in their concrete unity, yield not merely concrete practical knowledge, but a concrete conception of the self, for "the self appears as activity. It is not a 'thing' or a 'substance' capable of being active; it is activity".[1] This is true even if we appear to be concerned only with the analysis of an isolated piece of praxis, for in fact an activity occurs always within an already organized whole; and the important thing to grasp is that this organization or pattern in activity is not superimposed, but is inherent in the activity.[2] On this foundation Oakeshott erects his conception of the nature of the desiring self, of institutions, of tradition, and of the relationship of practical political and moral thought to political and moral action:

"Elements of this pattern occasionally stand out with a relatively firm outline; and we call these elements, customs, traditions, institutions, laws etc. They are not, properly speaking, *expressions* of the coherence of activity, or expressions of approval or disapproval, or of our knowledge of how to behave - they *are* the coherence, they are the substance of our knowledge of how to behave. We do not first decide that certain behaviour is right or desirable and then express our approval of it in an institution; our knowledge of how to behave well is, at this point, the institution".[3]

This quotation makes it clear that Oakeshott's objection to the abridgment of a tradition of activity into a body of technical knowledge is not that this is invariably a valueless enterprise, but that the understanding of activity which it embodies is untenable. The view that all knowledge is reducible to

---

1. Ibid., p.204.
2. Ibid., p.105.
3. Ibid., p.105; his emphasis.

technical knowledge implies that moral activity consists in the translation of an idea of what ought to be into a practical reality,[1] and hence assigns to self-consciousness a task that it cannot fulfil: it asks it to be creative.[2] In fact, reflection or self-consciousness cannot create; the truth is that "the projects we entertain are the creatures of our tradition".[3] The cook (or any other practitioner) owes his ability to carry out his particular project not to his knowledge of certain rules or principles, but to his skill; and his skill is "his participation in the concrete activity in relation to which his particular engagement is an abstraction".[4] His rules, or technical knowledge, do not precede the making of the pie: they are derived from the activity. That is to say, to formulate rules about an activity, or to know how to engage in it, involves being *already* within the activity.[5] In short, no means-ends analysis can do justice to activity, for both categories are abstractions from the concrete whole of the activity itself. As abstractions, they result in the false isolation of a project from its whole context and implications, rendering it unintelligible.

Perhaps the best example, because the one most carefully worked out by Oakeshott, of the deficiencies of the rationalist's concept of rational practice is that of the Victorian dress designers who considered that the appropriate dress for young ladies to cycle in could be arrived at by reflecting on the structure of the human body and the design of the bicycle alone. Clearing their minds of all preconceptions, they concluded that the "rational" dress was "bloomers". That, at least, was their view of why that garment was suitable. Oakeshott has no difficulty in exposing the fallacy. Only "prejudice" explains why the designers did not conclude that shorts, rather than "bloomers", were "rational". Without their realizing it, their project had been condititioned by the concrete tradition of behaviour in which they conceived it and carried it out. To understand why they chose bloomers, we have

---

1. *Ibid.*, p.72.
2. *Ibid.*, p.75.
3. *Ibid.*, p.129.
4. *Ibid.*, p.99.
5. *Ibid.*, p.99.

only to recognize that the question to which they addressed themselves was not really (and could not be) the question, What garment is best adapted to the activity of propelling a bicycle of a certain design? but the question, What garment combines within itself the qualities of being well adapted to the activity of propelling a bicycle and of being suitable, all things considered, for an English girl to be seen in when riding a bicycle in 1880?[1] And what is true of the Victorian designers is true of political ideologists: they cannot escape the tradition of behaviour in which they formulate their schemes, no matter how desperate the measures they take to attain "pure rationality".

This, then, is Oakeshott's account of rationalism and its errors. It is not, we may note, an entirely new departure in the idealist tradition: in a lecture entitled *The Communication of moral ideas as a function of an Ethical Society*, Bosanquet distinguished between "ideas about morality" and "moral ideas", maintaining that "ideas about morality" are "the abstract or scientific renderings of moral ideas"[2] which can offer no substitute for ideas worked out in life. What he refers to as "the carcass theory of knowledge - the theory that ideas are stowed away in a sort of bank and it is stingy not to distribute them",[3] comes very close to the view of ideas (attributed by Oakeshott to the rationalist) as things existing apart from and prior to all activity. But the important thing to determine is what Oakeshott's criticism of rationalism establishes.

In the first place, there appears to be no difficulty in admitting that Oakeshott demonstrates beyond doubt that all activity is necessarily traditional in character. But to admit this is to admit that Oakeshott is unable to use his argument to defend his own preferred moral and political style, viz. his "traditionalism". We may agree that practical activity is more correctly understood as the "pursuit of intimations" than as the pursuit of independently premeditated ends, and we may allow also that it is nonsense

---

1. *Ibid.*, p.95.
2. *Civilization*, p.180.
3. *Ibid.*, p.186.

to suggest that intimations are blind hunches,[1] or irrational intuitions,[2] and yet we may still insist that all that follows is that a purely rationalistic explanation, or style, of politics is impossible. As Oakeshott himself expresses it at one point, we can only conclude from an analysis of the activity and reasoning of rationalists in any given instance that "there were elements in the situation which might lead us to doubt whether what they thought they were doing....properly coincided with what they were in fact doing".[3] Since nearly all critics of Oakeshott have made this point, we will not labour it any further.

In the second place, it might be argued that while Oakeshott's logical criticism of rationalism does not in itself imply any specific style of political activity, he is to be taken rather as claiming that it is *in fact* true that a rationalistic way of life, in so far as it can be realized, tends to destroy moral sensibility and to produce paralysis of the will (both in the individual and in society) because of the uncertainty which it creates about how to act on any particular occasion.[4] This may indeed be so, but all we can say is "perhaps". There is no overwhelming case to be made in favour of the view that the politics of those who do not delude themselves in their theories and arguments about what they are doing will be more successful than ideological politics. This seems to agree with Oakeshott's own opinion, expressed in the light of subsequent criticisms of his inaugural lecture.[5] He wrote that it may "perhaps" be an advantage to think, speak and argue in a manner consonant with what we are really doing, but added that this was a proposition which "I do not think to be very important."

Finally, we may note that the nature of Oakeshott's attack on rationalism precludes a solution to the problem of political obligation through education. This contrasts strongly with the view of another political theorist within the idealist school, viz. R.G.Collingwood. Collingwood wrote in the New Leviathan that "The future of the world lies with peoples among whom there are no

---

1. See J.H.Franklin, Review of Rationalism in Politics, in The Journal of Philosophy 60, (1963), pp.811-20.
2. Benn and Peters, Social Principles and the Democratic State, op.cit.,p.317.
3. Rationalism, p.95.
4. Ibid., pp.68-69.
5. Ibid., p.134.

professional educators and every man educates his own children".[1] But even removing education from the professional would not help matters, in Oakeshott's opinion. His conception of the scope of moral and political education is naturally conditioned by his general theory of the relationship between thought and action: since a concrete tradition of behaviour can only be acquired in direct contact with those who possess a practical knowledge of its operation, it follows that political salvation is not to be found in knowledge acquired at second-hand through books. At one point it does appear as if Oakeshott would be prepared to allow a greater part in overcoming rationalism to reflection conducted independently of practice, for he writes that the disruptive character of rationalism "may be held in check by more profound reflection, by an intellectual grasp of the whole system which gives place and proportion to each moral ideal", but he adds immediately that "such a grasp is rarely achieved".[2] On another occasion he makes the tentative suggestion that a study of history might prevent "the misunderstanding in which institutions and procedures appear as pieces of machinery designed to achieve a purpose settled in advance, instead of as manners of behaviour which are meaningless when separated from their context ((in a tradition of behaviour))".[3] It is not clear whether Oakeshott hopes that this conclusion would merely make the student more conversant with the logical relationship between thought and action, or would make him (in consequence) more likely to engage in a traditionalist style of political activity; if the former, then there can be no ground for disagreement, but the latter hope is scarcely well-founded. To know that institutions are not machinery does not, in itself, commit one to preferring any particular kind of institution. The study of one's own history may be deepened by studying other traditions as well, but Oakeshott emphasises that the purpose in this case is purely heuristic: the only **gain** is the possible illumination of passages in our own tradition which might otherwise have passed unnoticed.[4] Political philosophy, likewise, leads only to the

---

1. New Leviathan, op.cit., p.313.
2. Rationalism, p.69.
3. Ibid., p.130.
4. Ibid., p.132.

clarification of concepts, offering no practical guidance.[1]

Political reasoning

The logical defence of traditionalism involved a theory of practical knowledge in general. Oakeshott did not have to distinguish political reasoning from other forms of practical reasoning in order to show that the ideologist was committed to an untenable theory of the relationship between thought and action. It was as appropriate to discuss the production of bloomers or the art of cooking in order to make the point which Oakeshott wished to apply to political activity. But in one essay Oakeshott has advanced a view of the nature of political reasoning in particular, and his position is interesting, if only because it reveals the immense depth of his scepticism.

In Political Laws and Captive Audiences,[2] Oakeshott defines thinking and talking about politics as "activities which are concerned with things that have to be done, and things which have to be done in political situations."[3] The situation may be narrow or wide: as an example of a narrow situation Oakeshott instances the discovery of long-range missiles in Cuba; as an example of the widest level there is "a sketch of an ideal society, such as appeared in Campanella's City of the Sun, or Bacon's New Atlantis." The example which really interests him, however, is Marx's attempt to diagnose the total contemporary situation. Before we consider his opinion of that, however, we must notice what he has to say about the logic of political reasoning.

A political thinker, Oakeshott maintains, always confronts an audience, and his thought is always an endeavour to persuade it that what he is saying is the correct diagnosis, and that what he is doing is the right thing. Persuasion, in short, "is the purpose of political argument: persuasion to act, or persuasion that what has been done has been correctly or appropriately done".[4] From this Oakeshott draws an important conclusion. Utterance which is designed to persuade is a peculiar sort of utterance or argument "because it is governed by the nature of the audience even more than by the nature of

---

1. Ibid., pp.132-133.
2. Printed in Talking to Eastern Europe, Eyre & Spottiswoode, London, ed. G.R.Urban.
3. Talking to Eastern Europe, p.291.
4. Ibid., p.292.

the theme".[1] This has two unfortunate consequences. The argument advanced by a thinker will tend to contain the reasons which he considers will affect his audience, rather than those by which he himself has been led to his conclusion; and (secondly) the argument may become even more debased if it is recognized that it is the support of the audience which counts in the last resort, and if the inference is drawn that _any_ reasons will do, provided they produce this.[2]

Against this sketch of the logic of political reasoning Oakeshott turns to examine two styles of political argument. He refers to the acceptance in the seventeenth and eighteenth centuries of the model of geometric proof as the ideal to which political reasoning should approximate; the "axioms" were either absolute moral values, or natural or human rights, or a natural law. But this rhetorical style, he finds, was eventually discovered to be incapable of addressing itself to any actual circumstance, and was replaced by "a new manner in which persuasion might be achieved - persuasion by purporting to prove."[3] The new rhetoric dropped "geometrical" in favour of "scientific" argument: the fashion was now to see political situations as governed by "laws" of human nature or of social development, and the aim was to exhibit political actions as dictated by such "laws". Marx, above all, wished to present the ends he favoured as so dictated.[4] Oakeshott's view is that really there are no such laws, but what he chooses to emphasize in the present context is that, even if there do appear to be, it is only the fact that an audience _thinks_ there are that gives this style of rhetoric any plausibility. And of Marx he writes that his chief claim to fame "is his part in manufacturing world-wide audiences susceptible to this particular rhetoric".[5] It is a peculiarly insidious rhetoric because it enables political leaders completely to escape responsibility for their actions, which can be referred to some "law" which is held to dictate the actions.

---

1. Ibid., p.292.
2. Ibid., pp.293-294.
3. Ibid., pp.295-6.
4. Ibid., p.297.
5. Ibid., p.298.

What is most striking about Oakeshott's theory of political reasoning is that in developing it to provide yet more ammunition against the rationalist he comes very close to overturning the foundations of his own philosophy. He emphasises the "persuasive" side of political reasoning so strongly that he appears to end by driving a wedge between thought and reality (the reality of political action, in this case). He speaks of "the world outside" the imaginary world of political rhetoric,[1] but it would seem that any attempt to speak about the world outside must necessarily appear (like all political thought) as a piece of practical thinking and so as itself an attempt to persuade some audience. His view of practical reasoning seems in fact to come very near to that taken by C.L.Stevenson in Ethics and Language, a work in which Stevenson suggested that moral concepts lack any rationality at all, being designed only to produce favourable or unfavourable responses in those who hear them. To adopt such a view would, however, contradict the view of practice maintained in Experience and Its Modes, where Oakeshott argued that practice was as much a "world of ideas" as any other form of experience. Oakeshott manages (formally at least) to avoid this step, but cannot of course avoid the boomerang contained in the nature of his argument, that he too is governed by his audience and not by the theme. The charge lies all the more strongly as the essay was in fact a broadcast on Radio Free Europe.

There are one or two other unsatisfactory elements in his account of political reasoning. Oakeshott might have mentioned the importance of factors contributing to integrity, or the lack of it, in different societies: the degree of scepticism which might appropriately be entertained about political utterances would obviously vary as between this country and, say, Red China. To talk about "political reasoning" as such, or in the abstract, is to misrepresent the facts in some cases at least. He might also have mentioned that a piece of political reasoning can be assessed as a more or less acute diagnosis of political reality *in spite of* its persuasive dimension. Oakeshott would wish audiences to become sceptical,[2] but they would be fools if they

---

1. Ibid., p.299.
2. Ibid., p.301.

looked at every utterance addressed to them only as an attempt to persuade; each utterance will of course be that, but it will also be good or bad advice, and Oakeshott seems to permit his suspicion of the practical aspect (as such) almost to eliminate this aspect.

Conclusion

The real problem presented by Oakeshott's politics is, How much of his analysis is produced by fatalism, and how much of it by penetration into political reality?

There is a strongly fatalistic vein in Oakeshott's thought, although his is a serene fatalism (Kariel seems to misjudge his mood when he writes of "stoic resignation to worldly experience").[1] It is this fatalism which perhaps explains his failure to bring his political thought into harmony with the argument of Experience and Its Modes. While the "is" and the "ought" cannot be reconciled once and for all, it does not follow that all particular projects for reconciling them and making our situation a little more responsive to rational control, must be rejected as foolish "rationalism". This Oakeshott allowed in Experience and its Modes. In his political essays, on the other hand, he gives the impression that any attempt whatsoever to bring some thought to bear on political affairs will lead to planning, despotism and vulgarity: thus of "social engineering" he can write that

"The purposes pursued and the enterprises embarked upon under the inspiration of this faith are *bound*, by their abstraction, generality, and claim to absolute and permanent validity, to be rigid and to be (or to become in the course of time) out of touch with concrete, specific realities of *any* political occasion."[2]

In so far as Oakeshott assumes that the ideal and the actual have been brought together in one particular case at least, viz. in the libertarian tradition, his view is open to the objections which emerged in the course of this chapter. These were that the libertarian tradition is less free from rationalism than Oakeshott sometimes implies; that the mass-man who is supposed to lie outside that tradition is perhaps not so completely detached from

---

1. In Search of Authority, p.81.
2. C.J., Vol. 1, 1947-8, p.352; emphasis added.

it, and hostile to it, as Oakeshott supposes; that an appeal to the aesthetic character of that tradition is not politically relevant; that to show that all activity is necessarily traditional in character is to prove too much, for there always are ways of doing anything other than the traditional ones, and it is not plausible to suggest that the non-traditional ways will necessarily produce anything but a <u>different</u> way of doing things. Putting this last point in other words, we may say that to have convicted an age of pursuing "the politics of the book" is not ipso facto to have made a compelling criticism.

We have noticed one manifestation of Oakeshott's fatalism. Two further aspects of it may now be briefly mentioned, in the light of the ground we have covered.

There is, first of all, Oakeshott's method or style of analysis. He is fond of detecting two antitheses or ideal extremes, neither of which corresponds closely to anything in the world, and then building an equally abstract and general model which undoubtedly avoids the defects of the ideal extremes but still fails to correspond closely to any concrete historical situation. This method, of course, inevitably commits him to that very abridgement of traditions which he criticizes so strongly.[1] That the method is in some sense "dialectical"[2] is not in itself a recommendation, if the dialectic does not follow the movement of the real but takes place within thought alone. Oakeshott's method, in short, does nothing to arrest the distorting influence of his fatalism: if anything, it serves as an admirable vehicle for it. (More was said about this in the body of the chapter, in connection with the either/or approach).

Turning now from method to content, a number of examples emerged of Oakeshott's willingness to go through the bottom of the barrel in order to find ammunition against the rationalist, but we may add one or two more. At times one feels that his hostility to the rationalist has led Oakeshott to abandon Green's conspiracy theory only to assume another. In the absence of "open tyrants" whose existence may be attributed to rationalism, Oakeshott is

---

1. Specimens of this method may be found in <u>The Tower of Babel</u>, <u>Rational Conduct</u>, <u>Political Education</u>, <u>The Political Economy of Freedom</u>, and in other essays.
2. Cf. Greenleaf, <u>Oakeshott's Philosophical Politics</u>, op.cit., pp.14-15.

determined to find "hidden enemies" of freedom, although he thinks that "their cunning is only circuitous folly and will find them out".[1] He goes further, finding hidden enemies even in the most ardent libertarians (such as Hayek). Tyrants, in fact, begin to loom up everywhere: "The propensity of all modern leaders (politicians included) is to become demagogues."[2] Our favourite example occurs in the course of Oakeshott's review of Labour Marches, by John Parkes: he writes that

"Suspecting a tyranny, we look for a Strafford and find only a Cripps, we look for a Cromwell and find only a Clem Attlee – and we are reassured".[3] What Oakeshott fails to take seriously is the possibility that perhaps it is, after all, only old Clem Attlee. His treatment of the B.B.C., already considered, provides a further instance of lack of perspective. The Director-General's policy might indeed have been obnoxious – but who else besides that officer has ever taken the B.B.C. seriously? What worried Oakeshott in this particular case was neither the monopoly aspect nor the three-tier system of programmes as such (he would probably favour it in fact, as a contribution to variety of entertainment), but only the pompous verbiage behind it. If every remnant of Victorian liberalism in high office were made into a real threat to liberty we would surely cease to sleep immediately. We do not, of course, intend blindly to ignore the truth in Oakeshott's conviction, that "if the experience of our time has any unmistakable message for us, it is that tyranny can spring from mediocrity and despotism from inferiority",[4] but wish only to notice that his pessimism does seem to lead him to forget that mediocrity is often just mediocrity and not invariably the source of tyranny.

The chapter revealed the impact of Oakeshott's pessimism on some of the structural concepts of his political science. Examples were, most notably, his concepts of the "individual manqué" and of "the mass"; and his concepts of "planning" and "collectivism," terms which were almost synonyms for a host of political evils. Behind many of our political ills Oakeshott also sees

---

1. Rationalism, p.39.
2. The Listener, Aug.25, 1955, p.302.
3. C.J., Vol. 1, 1947-8, p.485.
4. Ibid., p.485.

another phenomenon, which he therefore gives an important place in his political theory. This is "intellectualism": Bacon, Descartes, Milton, and Mill all come in for criticism. All these concepts and phenomena are very clearly "value-laden": Oakeshott's pessimism gives them a pejorative significance, and they are of course defined from the standpoint of one who takes the libertarian tradition as an absolute reference-point.

Between the mass on the one hand and the intellectuals on the other there stood the figure idealized by Oakeshott, the gentleman, half-aristocrat, half-bourgeois (and so, of course, half-rationalist). Oakeshott's treatment of the problem of political obligation is hinged upon him: but Oakeshott does not really foresee any future for the gentleman, who appeared about to disappear beneath the deluge of rationalism. We end, then, with a partial return to the politics of Locke and Hume, although their "empirical" politics have come to rest upon the philosophic remnant of that very school which did most to overturn the foundations they had provided for those politics.

===============

Chapter 10

Conclusion

We began by formulating the problem of political obligation and then attempted to unravel the philosophical doctrines which had reinforced the gap between fact and value, or between the "is" and the "ought", reflected in the word "obligation". (Chaps. 1 and 2). We then examined the different philosophical systems by which the idealist philosophers sought to overcome that gap. (Chaps. 3 - 6). In each case it emerged that the concrete universal was not so concrete after all.

Green, and Bosanquet to a lesser extent, worked with the concept of the absolute as a self of which everything else in the universe was a phase or manifestation. Green's endeavour to provide a unified account of experience never really got off the ground: he was too closely tied to Platonism and Kantianism to be able to explain why there should be a temporal order. This order always appeared as a defect, a limitation upon the spiritual self which lies behind all things. Bosanquet, in the course of developing his own metaphysical theory of individuality, put his finger on the origin of Green's difficulties when he said that in the end he did not cease to take personality (or finite individuality) in its "given" or "immediate" form. It was this, together with Green's belief that the eternal self is already perfect and complete, that left the impression that each of us has no essential connection with it and so has no fundamental identity with other finite selves.

Bosanquet appeared at one stage to be advancing beyond Green's dualism. He took over from Hegel the idea of negativity, of conflict as the mechanism of teleological development. But he did not move on to make a systematic use of the idea, and left us with a non-relational concept of the absolute. Dissatisfied with Green's emphasis upon the bare form of experience, he proceeded to emphasize its content, but in so doing appeared to be negating personality and moving towards a pantheistic position. In the end, Bosanquet too failed to make clear the relationship between the temporal order and the eternal. This meant that while he argued with greater plausibility than Green that the community has greater reality than the individual self, he left the unity of the self in question. Consequently, the problem of my obedience to the state was simply pressed back to the problem of why I should obey myself.

Oakeshott was notable mainly for his endeavour to preserve the unity and intelligibility of experience without the absolute self and its dialectical movement. In his view we do indeed have a common experience, but our enjoyment of it is not to be mistaken for participation in an absolute self. Nor can any inferences about our obligation to our fellows be drawn from it. The difficulty which we found in his view was that his "critical" conception of philosophy was far from being concrete: philosophy seemed to end up as vacuous as Bosanquet's absolute, so that while abandoning the absolute self might be said to have got rid of some excess baggage it could not be held to have brought forth any new clue to the mysteries of determinate being. Oakeshott did however achieve something of particular importance. In his treatment of the practical mode he managed to hold the "is" and the "ought" together, without making them identical.

Because the concrete universal was less concrete than we had hoped, we seem to have moved in a circle, though not quite: one problem was eliminated. The problem of political obligation, in the form in which it is generated by the pure individualism which would conceive the self as an indeterminate point apart from all social life, was shown to be a product of abstraction - although Green perhaps sustained this position less effectively than Bosanquet and Oakeshott. Otherwise, however, we find old philosophical problems appearing in new forms and old politics emerging on a new foundation. The early idealists sought to find meaning and purpose underlying the mechanical view of the universe, by incorporating it into a teleological theory. But the imperfections in their endeavour meant that the epistemological problem, How do we know anything? merely gave way to the question, Can we know the absolute?, while the ethical problem, What is the relationship between "is" and "ought"? merely gave way to the question, Why should one (the natural) part of the self obey another (the spiritual) part?

The return of old politics followed upon the abandonment of teleology by Oakeshott: with teleology there went telocratic politics, and with its replacement by philosophy conceived of as one voice in the conversation of mankind there reappeared the sceptical nomocratic position of Hume and Montaigne.

APPENDICES

Appendix A

A brief comparison of Oakeshott and Bosanquet, in the light of Chapters 5 and 6.

We touched on the salient differences between Oakeshott and Bosanquet at the end of Chapter 5. At the risk of some repetition we will pursue the matter a little further. Since we consider that Bosanquet preserves what is worthwhile in Green's philosophy, while taking the argument considerably further, we will try to keep the issues simple by referring only to Bosanquet.

The main difference of opinion between Bosanquet and Oakeshott centres upon the nature of determinacy and is reflected in Bosanquet's belief that "The general formula of the Absolute, ((viz.)) the transmutation and rearrangement of particular experiences, and also of the contents of particular finite minds, by inclusion in a completer whole of experience, is a matter of everyday verification".[1] While the "completer whole of experience" eclipses, for Oakeshott, finite experience (without, however, destroying that experience or becoming a substitute for it), for Bosanquet the complete individual includes in itself the finite aspects, which "carry out its character and intensify its value".[2] In other words, while Oakeshott is content to note that absolute reality is present implicitly in its appearances or modifications, without holding that they are essential to that reality, Bosanquet wishes to claim that absolute reality would

---

1. *Principle*, p 373
2. Appearances and the Absolute, in *Philosophical Review*, 1920, p 573

be nothing without its appearances. This is his belief in cosmic progress, according to which the absolute is enriched by each new form it assumes.[1]

This difference of opinion has an important consequence for the solution to the problem of political obligation. If the question, Ought I to obey the state? is part of a more general puzzlement and scepticism which demands to know the significance and value of the world of will as a whole, Oakeshott can offer no answer. Practice is a mode of experience which is not severed from the concrete whole of experience, but its raison d'être is not established by reflection on concrete experience. Bosanquet, however, although he refuses to ascribe moral value to the universe,[2] is able to argue that man is a trustee for the universe:

"The man is a representative, a trustee for the world, of certain powers and circumstances. And this cannot fail to be so. For suffering and privation are also opportunities. The question for him is how much he can make of them. This is the simple and primary point of view, and also, in the main, the true and fundamental one. It is not the bare personality or the separate destiny that occupies a healthy mind. It is the thing to be done, known and felt; in a word, the completeness of experience, his contribution to it, and his participation in it." [3]

Thus Bosanquet's metaphysic, like that of Plato and Hegel, aims at achieving an ultimate "ought", although it is not strictly a moral "ought". It is an "ought" which arises through the recognition that one has a

---

1. For the charge that Bosanquet, like Bradley, separates appearance from reality and ends with an absolute which is the night in which all cows are black, see R. A. Tsanoff's review of the Principle of Individuality and Value in Phil. Review, Jan. 1920, and Bosanquet's reply in the same volume. (Vol. XXIX).

2. Principle, p 310.

3. Ibid., p 21.

necessary place in the scheme of things, a role to discharge in the cosmic nisus towards perfection. The existence of the state is not merely to be accepted as a form assumed by an arrested experience of reality, an experience to be rejected if concrete reality is to be attained. It is, rather, a form of experience "in which individuality ((i.e. the absolute)) strongly anticipates the character of its perfection." [1]

For Oakeshott the problem of political obligation was heavily laden with the concerns of the practical world: so long as it remained a problem for a thinker, it is evident that (for Oakeshott) he was a man for whom the incoherencies of practical life had become too acute to be born. The need to determine where his allegiance lay (to which government perhaps, or to his conscience, or to God), was the motive behind his inquiry, and the practical concern remained predominant so long as he adhered to its initial formulation. At some stage in the inquiry, however, the man who initially concerned himself only with settling to his own satisfaction the practical difficulties confronting him, might well stumble upon questions which led him some way beyond practice, into an incipient critique of the very presuppositions of the practical world itself. He might, for example, cease to concern himself with the particular course of action which was best for him in relation to a particular political situation and ask questions about the nature of the state as such. He would be led in this way to draw universally valid distinctions, such as that made by Hobbes between a natural and an artificial person. He would then have entered the field of political philosophy and embarked upon an indeterminate arrest in experience, "indeterminate" because he is still trying to keep a foot in two camps. By continuing to concern himself with the state he is accepting a practical identity; and in so doing he makes clear that he has not freed himself entirely from the presuppositions of the practical

---

1. Ibid., p 316.

world. Yet by posing the question he has in some degree become a
philosopher, for he has relaxed his commitment (qua practical man)
to consider only such problems as bear on his immediate difficulties
in life. His position will thus be as ambiguous as that of the
moral philosopher who comes to the problem of goodness in general
by wondering what things in particular he ought himself to consider
good. In Oakeshott's view, the significance of the terms "moral"
and "political" when predicated of philosophy is only to indicate
the point of departure, the specific area in which the philosopher
began his inquiry. Within philosophy itself no areas can be demarcated - the terms "moral" and "political" are extraneous to it. Philosophy is always the whole, the concrete world of reality, and to take
it as less than that is, inevitably, to accept incoherence and abstraction in experience. The ambiguity of the political philosopher's
position has one (intellectually) dangerous consequence: he may
think that he can carry his philosophic laurels back into the world
of practice, but (for Oakeshott) this is a mistake, a failure to
realize that "what is farthest from our needs is that kings should be
philosophers....philosophical thought can make no relevant contribution
to the coherence of ((the practical)) world of experience."[1] Or the
political philosopher may fall into the opposite trap, by trying to
carry the (uncriticized) entities of the world of practice into
philosophy with him. In the former case he will, in all likelihood,
make a mess of practice by (perhaps) becoming an ideologist and
complaining because philosophers are not kings. In the latter case
he will (certainly) make a hash of philosophy, by failing to go far
enough towards meeting the full obligations of experience, with its
requirement of absolute coherence. We saw, furthermore, that the
political philosopher who moved from the problem of political obligation in its practical form to an examination of the general character
of the experience which is implied in it, had disappointment in store

---

1. *Experience*, p 321

for him at the end of his journey. If he hoped to console himself, in the midst of his practical difficulties, with at least the philosophical recognition of the necessity of the state, then he expected too much. For Oakeshott, no mode could claim a necessary place in concrete experience.

For Bosanquet, matters were otherwise. Concern with the problem of political obligation (or the "paradox of self-government") did not involve devotion to two ultimately incompatible mistresses, philosophy and practice. He would agree with Oakeshott that the problem of political obligation might provoke only polemical reflection and literature, and that it might equally well rise to reflection on the nature of the state and of individuality. But if it did rise to this level there would be some prospect of perceiving, in the end, the necessity of the state in the scheme of things, and certainly the political philosopher could claim at least that he had the absolute (and not merely some remaining presuppositions of the abstract world of practice) between his hands. Whereas for Oakeshott the concept of individuality was merely a presupposition of the practical mode, to be avoided by the philosopher, for Bosanquet it provided an insight into the nature of the absolute itself.

The implications of the difference between Bosanquet and Oakeshott on the nature of the concrete for the problem of political obligation may be summed up as follows. For Oakeshott the question "Why ought I to obey the state?" (as also the question, "Why be moral?") can be answered only when the presuppositions of the practical world are granted and the question is seen to fall within that world. If the questioner refuses to accept those presuppositions his question becomes absurd, or meaningless. For Bosanquet, however, a further answer is possible, even when the questioner is challenging the presuppositions of the practical world. The answer will not, of course, be ethical, for it is not meaningful to predicate value of the whole. It will take the form of a demonstration of the logical (not moral) necessity of the world of will, and the person posing the problem of political obligation will, in the light of this demonstration, be given intellectual satisfaction through the recognition that mind (i.e. his own nature) entails the existence of a place for will and all the determinations implicit in that term.

We may now venture an opinion as to the merits of the respective positions of Oakeshott and Bosanquet. Oakeshott's dialectic was, in the last resort, negative in character. Certainly the modes were not mere appearance, in that sense of "mere" which would imply their absolute detachment from reality, and to that extent Oakeshott avoids the complete negativity of the Bradleian dialectic. But nonetheless the modes are ultimately set aside as completely non-contributory to concrete experience, thereby leaving their own significance (on the one hand) totally unintelligible, and philosophy itself (on the other hand) without any content to fill out the bare, empty, critical form in terms of which Oakeshott conceives it. Whatever we may say about Bosanquet's position, such pure virginity was far from his aspirations. Although his position presents its own difficulties, they do not include an _explicit_ attempt to remove all content from absolute experience. Bosanquet's position also avoids some of the difficulties involved in Oakeshott's conception of the relationship between the modes; it is more fluid and dialectical, since it implies a recognition that the complete specification of the differentia of a mode will necessarily carry one beyond that mode into another, while preserving the truth upon which Oakeshott insists, that it is not possible to conclude directly from one world of experience to another.

Appendix B

A note on Dr. Milne's discussion of the concrete universal [1]

We may take advantage of the ground which has been covered in order to protest against the unduly narrow significance apparently attached to the concept of the concrete universal by Dr. Milne, in his work <u>The Social Philosophy of English Idealism</u>. We have outlined the philosophical issues involved in the idealist concept of universality - the problem of the relationship of experience to thought, truth and reality - and they are so broad that it is difficult to see Dr. Milne's justification for confining the concept of the concrete universal to the explanation of the nature of rational activity. He completely disregards the first-order philosophical difficulties to which, in the opinion of the idealists, the doctrine of the concrete universal provides the solution. For example, at the outset he simply <u>assumes</u> the unqualified reality of something called "the individual", without making any attempt to specify the criterion of individuation upon which that entity is constituted. He then distinguishes degrees of reality, or "levels of rationality", and identifies the highest level (self-realization) with the truly concrete. What makes it more real or concrete (as opposed to more logically complex) than the other levels is not explained. Putting the same point otherwise, we may say that what is called self-realization by Dr. Milne does not establish its claim to that title: his argument leaves it open to us to argue that this highest level of rationality is certainly one form of activity known to the self, but that there is nothing to indicate that in it the

---

1. In chap. 1 of <u>The Social Philosophy of English Idealism</u>, Allen and Unwin, London, 1962.

self has come closest to realizing its true nature, for no independent ground is developed by which we can recognize that nature. Relating this to the problem of political obligation, we can say that Milne's position is inadequate to establish that the community is a higher reality than the individual; and it was this, after all, that Bosanquet and Green were anxious to show, deducing it from their critique of the abstract principle of logical identity (viz. A is A) upon which they felt that previous moral and political philosophy had rested. Because of his uncritical acceptance of the individualistic starting-point, Milne can never show that there would be any absurdity in a person's refusing to accept the conception of concentric circles by which he seeks to elucidate the relationship between the self and the community; the outer circles correspond to progressively higher levels of rationality and are also more real than the inner ones. But how, for example, could a person who wished to maintain that he found his highest level of self-realization in the sphere of employment and not (for example) in leisure or citizenship, be shown to be irrational, without a petitio principii (i.e. by merely defining rationality in such a way that this inevitably followed)? In short, it is difficult to accept Milne's contention that "my view is in fact the one to which the English Idealists were committing themselves in their social philosophy". They did not divorce their social philosophy from their general philosophy to anything like the extent to which Milne implies they did, by circumscribing his conception of the concrete universal in the way in which he does.

BIBLIOGRAPHY

Bibliography[1]

A: Primary sources, chronologically.

T. H. Green — *Prolegomena to Ethics*; Oxford, 1883.

Works of T. H. Green; 3 vols., ed. by R. L. Nettleship. Longmans, Green & Co., London, 1888.

Lectures on the Principles of Political Obligation; reprinted from Green's *Works*, Vol. II, and published by Longmans in 1941.

B. Bosanquet — *Logic*; first edition, Oxford, 1888; second edition (revised) 1911.

Essays and Addresses; Swan Sonnenschein, London, 1889.

The Civilization of Christendom and Other Studies; Swann Sonnenschein, London, 1893.

The Essentials of Logic; MacMillan, London, 1895.

Aspects of the Social Problem; MacMillan, London, 1895.

The Philosophical Theory of the State; MacMillan, London, 1899; fourth ed., 1923.

The Principle of Individuality and Value (The Gifford Lectures); MacMillan, London, 1912.

The Value and Destiny of the Individual (The Gifford Lectures); MacMillan, London, 1913.

---

[1]. With the exception of two works mentioned in Section C, the bibliography details only works mentioned in the thesis.
A short but useful bibliography on T. H. Green is to be found in W. D. Lamont's *Introduction to Green's Moral Philosophy*.
A comprehensive bibliography of Bosanquet's writing and of related works and criticisms is to be found in F. Houang's *Le Néo-Hegelianisme en Angleterre*.
A comprehensive bibliography of Oakeshott's writings has been compiled by W. H. Greenleaf and is to be found in *Politics and Experience*, ed. P. King and B. C. Parekh, C. U. P., 1968.

B. Bosanquet (cont.)	*Social and International Ideals*; MacMillan, London, 1917.
	Some Suggestions in Ethics; MacMillan, London, 1918.
	The Meeting of Extremes in Contemporary Philosophy; MacMillan, London, 1921.
	"Life and Philosophy" in *Contemporary British Philosophy*; ed. by J. H. Muirhead; 1st series, Allen & Unwin, London, 1924; reprinted in *The Idealist Tradition*, ed. A. C. Ewing (which see, below).
	Science and Philosophy, ed. by J. H. Muirhead and R. C. Bosanquet; published posthumously by Allen & Unwin, London, 1927.
M. Oakeshott	*Experience and Its Modes*; C. U. P., 1933.
	"The concept of a philosophical jurisprudence" in *Politica*, Vol III, 1938.
	"The claims of politics" in *Scrutiny*, Vol. VIII, 1939-40.
	Hobbes' *Leviathan* (edited with an introduction: Oxford, Blackwell, 1946).
	"The 'collective dream of civilization'", *The Listener*, Vol XXXVII, 1947.
	"Scientific politics", *C.J.*, Vol. I, 1947-48
	"Contemporary British politics", *C.J.*, Vol. I, 1947-8.
	"Science and society", *C.J.*, Vol. I, 1947-8.
	"The universities", *C.J.*, Vol. II, 1948-9.
	"The B. B. C.", *C.J.*, Vol. IV, 1950-1.
	"The idea of 'character' in the interpretation of modern politics", an unpublished paper presented to the Political Studies Association Conference at Cambridge, 1954.
	"The customer is never wrong", *The Listener*, Vol. LIV, 1955.
	"The masses in representative democracy", in A. Hunold (ed.), *Freedom and Serfdom: An Anthology of Western Thought*; Dordrecht, Holland, Reidel, 1961.

M. Oakeshott (cont.)	*Rationalism in Politics and Other Essays*; Methuen, London, 1962.
	"Political laws and captive audiences", in G. R. Urban (ed.), *Talking to Eastern Europe*; Eyre and Spottiswoode, London, 1964.
	Review of J. R. Lucas' *The Principles of Politics*, in *Political Studies*, Vol. XV, No. 2, Jan. 1967.

B: Secondary sources, alphabetically.

R. I. Aaron	*John Locke*: O.U.P.; first ed. 1937; second ed. 1955.
J. K. Abbott, ed.	*Kant's Theory of Ethics*; fourth ed., Longmans, London, 1899.
Aristotle	*Nicomachean Ethics*; Loeb classical library series; trans. H. Rackham, Heinemann, London.
Augustine	*Confessions*; Pocket Books Ltd., New York, 1957.
G. Battiscombe	*Charlotte Mary Yonge: the Story of an Uneventful Life*; Constable & Co., London, 1943.
G. Battiscombe and M. Laski, eds.	*A Chaplet for Charlotte Yonge*; The Cresset Press, London, 1965.
S. I. Benn and R. S. Peters	*Social Principles and the Democratic State*; Allen & Unwin, London, 1959.
R. N. Berki	"Political freedom and Hegelian metaphysics", in *Political Studies*, Vol. XVI, No. 3, Oct. 1968.
J. G. Blumler	"Politics, Poetry and Practice", in *Political Studies*, Vol. XII, 1964.
H. Bosanquet	*Bernard Bosanquet*; MacMillan, London, 1924.
A. C. Bradley	*Oxford Lectures on Poetry*; MacMillan, London, 1965 (first ed., 1909).
F. H. Bradley	*Ethical Studies*; O.U.P., 1962 (first ed., 1876).
	The Principles of Logic; O.U.P., 1963 (2 vols.), first ed. 1883; second ed., in 2 vols., 1922.
	Appearance and Reality; O.U.P., 1962 (first ed., 1893).
	Essays on Truth and Reality; O.U.P., 1962 (first ed. 1914).

E. F. Carritt	Morals and Politics; O.U.P., 1935.
R. W. Church	Bradley's Dialectic; Allen & Unwin, London, 1942.
A. Cobban	Edmund Burke; Allen & Unwin, London, 1929.
R. G. Collingwood	Autobiography; O.U.P. ed., 1967; first ed. 1939.
	The New Leviathan; O.U.P., 1942.
I. Coltman	Private Men and Public Causes; Faber & Faber, London, 1962.
M. Cowling	The Nature and Limits of Political Science; C.U.P., 1963.
	Mill and Liberalism; C.U.P., 1963.
M. Cranston	John Locke, A Biography; Longmans, London, 1957.
G. W. Cunningham	The Idealistic Argument in Recent British and American Philosophy; The Century Co., New York and London, 1933.
A. Donagan	The Later Philosophy of R. G. Collingwood, O.U.P., 1962.
A. C. Ewing, ed.	The Idealist Tradition; The Free Press, Glencoe, Illinois, 1957.
W. H. Fairbrother	The Philosophy of T. H. Green; Methuen, London, 1896.
J. H. Franklin	Review of M. Oakeshott's Rationalism in Politics, in The Journal of Philosophy, Vol. 60, 1963.
S. Freud	New Introductory Lectures on Psychoanalysis; first ed. 1933; published by the Hogarth Press (6th impression) in London, 1962.
C. J. Friedrich	"The Political Thought of Neo-liberalism", in American Political Science Review, Vol. XXXIX, 1945.
C. J. Friedrich, ed.	The Philosophy of Kant; Random House, New York, 1949.
Ortega Y Gasset	The Revolt of the Masses; first published in Spain in 1930; published in London by Unwin Books in 1961.

Sir. A. Grant	Aristotle's Ethics; 2 vols.; second ed. (revised and completed), Longmans, London, 1866.
W. H. Greenleaf	Oakeshott's Philosophical Politics; Longmans, London, 1966.
H. Haldar	Neo-Hegelianism; London, 1927.
F. Hayek	The Constitution of Liberty; Routledge & Kegan Paul, London, 1960.
G. W. F. Hegel	The Philosophy of Right; trans. J. M. Knox, O.U.P., 1958.
	The Logic of Hegel; trans. by W. Wallace; O.U.P., second ed. 1892 (reprinted 1963).
T. Hobbes	Leviathan; Dent (Everyman ed.), London, 1962; with an introduction by A. D. Lindsay.
	English Works; ed. by Sir William Molesworth; 11 vols., Bohm, London, 1839-45.
L. T. Hobhouse	The Metaphysical Theory of the State; Allen & Unwin, London, 1960; first published 1918.
Q. Hogg	The Case for Conservatism; Penguin Books, Harmondsworth, 1947.
F. Houang	Le Néo-Hégélianisme en Angleterre: la Philosophie de Bernard Bosanquet; Paris, 1954.
G. Huehns, ed.	Selections from Clarendon; O.U.P. (World's classics ed.), London, 1955.
D. Hume	A Treatise of Human Nature; Dent (Everyman ed., 2 vols), London, 1920; with an introduction by A. D. Lindsay.
	"The Sceptic", in Essays, O.U.P., 1963
Sir. H. Jones and J. H. Muirhead	The Life and Philosophy of Edward Caird; Maclehose, Jackson & Co., 1921.
I. Kant	"Idea for a universal history with cosmopolitan intent", in The Philosophy of Kant (which see), ed. C. J. Friedrich.
	"Eternal Peace", in the same volume.
H. S. Kariel	In Search of Authority; The Free Press, Glencoe, 1964.
W. D. Lamont	Introduction to Green's Moral Philosophy; Allen & Unwin, London, 1934.
P. Laslett, ed.	Two Treatises of Government; see under J. Locke.
P. Laslett, ed.	Philosophy, Politics and Society, first series; Blackwell, Oxford, 1956.

W. Lippman	*The Public Philosophy*; Mentor Books, 1956.
J. Locke	*Two Treatises on Government*; ed. with an introduction by P. Laslett, C.U.P., 1960.
	An Essay Concerning Human Understanding; Dent (Everyman ed., 2 vols), London, 1965; ed. with an introduction by John W. Yolton.
W. F. Lofthouse	*F. H. Bradley*; the Epworth Press, London, 1949.
J. R. Lucas	*The Principles of Politics*; O.U.P., 1966.
A. MacIntyre	*Secularization and Moral Change*; O.U.P., 1967.
T. McPherson	*Political Obligation*; Routledge & Kegan Paul, London, 1967.
M. Mare and A. C. Percival	*Victorian Best-seller: The World of Charlotte M. Yonge*; Harrap & Co., London, 1947.
J. S. Mill	*Representative Government*; Dent, (Everyman ed., which also contains Utilitarianism and Liberty), London, 1910.
A. J. Milne	*The Social Philosophy of English Idealism*; Allen & Unwin, London, 1962.
Abbé Paul Montagné	*Un Radical Religieux: T. H. Green*; Toulouse, 1927
J. H. Muirhead	*The Platonic Tradition in Anglo-Saxon Philosophy*; Allen & Unwin, London, 1931.
J. H. Muirhead, ed.	*Contemporary British Philosophy*, first series; Allen & Unwin, London, 1924.
J. H. Muirhead, ed.	*Bernard Bosanquet and His Friends: Letters illustrating the sources and the development of his philosophical opinions*; Allen & Unwin, London, 1935.
P. H. Nowell-Smith	*Ethics*; Penguin ed., 1961; first ed. 1954.
J. Parker	*Labour Marches On*; Penguin Books, Harmondsworth, 1947.
B. Pfannenstill	*Bernard Bosanquet's Philosophy of the State*; H. Ohlsson, Lund, 1936.
Plato	*Republic*; trans. P. Shorey; Heinemann (Loeb Library ed., 2 vols.), London.
M. Postan	"Revulsion from Thought", in *C.J.*, Vol I, 1947-8.
A. Prichard	*Moral Obligation*, and *Duty and Interest*; first issued together by O.U.P., 1968.

J. Pucelle	L'Idealisme en Angleterre; Neuchatel, 1955.
A. Quinton	"On Punishment", in Philosophy, Politics and Society, first series, ed. P. Laslett (which see).
M. Richter	The Politics of Conscience: T. H. Green and His Age; Weidenfeld and Nicolson, London, 1964.
J.-J. Rousseau	Social Contract; Oxford (World's classics ed.) 1947; with an introduction by E. Barker.
B. Russell	Philosophical Essays; London, 1910.
	The Problems of Philosophy; Thornton Butterworth (H.U.L. series), London, 1912.
T. T. Segerstedt	Value and Reality in Bradley's Philosophy; Lund, 1934.
A. Seth	Hegelianism and Personality; Blackwood, London, 1893 (second ed.).
J. Shklar	After Utopia; Princeton University Press, 1957.
H. Sidgwick	"Green's Ethics", in Mind, Vol. IX, 1884.
	The Ethics of Green, Spencer and Martineau; MacMillan, London, 1902.
W. T. Stace	The Philosophy of Hegel; Dover ed., U.S.A., 1955.
G. C. L. Stevenson	Ethics and Language; Yale University Press, 1945.
A. E. Taylor	Elements of Metaphysics; first published 1903; seventh edition, Methuen, London, 1964.
	"Francis Herbert Bradley", in Proceedings of the British Academy, Vol XI, 1924-5.
A. de Tocqueville	Democracy in America; trans. by Henry Reeve, with an introduction by H. S. Commager; O.U.P. (World's classics ed.), London, 1952.
G. M. Trevelyan	English Social History; Longmans, London, 1944.
R. A. Tsanoff	"Bosanquet's theory of the destiny of the self", in Philosophical Review, 1920.
T. D. Weldon	States and Morals; published by J. Murray, London, 1946.
S. G. Wolin	Politics and Vision; Allen & Unwin, London, 1961.
R. Wollheim	F. H. Bradley; Penguin Books, Harmondsworth, 1959.
C. M. Yonge	Daisy Chain; MacMillan, London, 1901.
E. Zola	Nana; Collier-MacMillan Ltd., London, 1968; with an introduction by Henri Peyre.

C: Supplementary reading

Two works seem to me to be of particular value for the study of idealism in general and, by implication, for appreciating the differences between Hegel's doctrine and those developed by the English idealists (although neither deals directly with English idealism). They are:

R. N. Berki — *From Hegel to Marx: a Dialectical Critique of Marx's Concept of Man*; an unpublished thesis, submitted to Cambridge University, 1967.

A. Kojeve — *Introduction à la Lecture de Hegel*; Gallimard, 1947.